LIVING LANGUAGES

LIVING LANGUAGES
Multilingualism across the Lifespan

Tracey Tokuhama-Espinosa

Westport, Connecticut
London

KH

Library of Congress Cataloging-in-Publication Data

Tokuhama-Espinosa, Tracey, 1963–
  Living languages : multilingualism across the lifespan / Tracey Tokuhama-
Espinosa.
      p. cm.
  Includes bibliographical references and index.
  ISBN 978–0–275–99912–4 (alk. paper)
  1. Multilingualism. 2. Bilingualism. 3. Language and education. 4. Language
and languages—Study and teaching. I. Title.
  P115.T65 2008
  404'.2—dc22   2007036497

British Library Cataloguing in Publication Data is available.

Library of Congress Catalog Card Number: 2007036497
ISBN: 978–0–275–99912–4

First published in 2008

Praeger Publishers, 88 Post Road West, Westport, CT 06881
An imprint of Greenwood Publishing Group, Inc.
www.praeger.com

Printed in the United States of America

The paper used in this book complies with the
Permanent Paper Standard issued by the National
Information Standards Organization (Z39.48–1984).

10 9 8 7 6 5 4 3 2 1

9/3/09

To my encouraging husband and inspirational children.
For my linguist mother and teacher father.
In loving memory of the amazing lives of my grandparents,
Hazel Hawk and Howard McBride, and
Gladys Kimie Zakahi and Edwin Mako Tokuhama,
lovers of languages all.

Whoever is not acquainted with foreign languages
knows nothing of his own.

—Johann Wolfgang von Goethe, 1749–1832

Contents

Introduction

Living Languages is a play on words. Are the languages being lived by the people, or are the languages themselves alive? I hope that by the end of this book you agree that both are true. This book is about multilingualism across the human lifespan: how languages are learned at different developmental stages, why this is so, and how to take advantage of this knowledge to more efficiently integrate languages into our lives. This book is also about the brain and languages and how studies in cognitive neuroscience explain (or reject) theories from linguists, psychologists, and bilingual educators. Different periods in human development lend themselves to different language learning processes for social, neurological, and psychological reasons.

There is no one-size-fits-all recommendation for parents and teachers related to foreign language acquisition. This book argues that a person's learning potential can be nurtured and maximized through the application of best practice strategies and methodologies. Finally, this book is about you and all the key players in your multilingual life. When an individual and his family choose a life with many languages, each person in that unit has a role to fulfill. Are the home, school, and community all sending the child a unified message about the benefits of multilingualism? Or does one or more of these players devalue the experience? Does the school curriculum lend itself to cultivating languages, or does it impede such growth? Do community leaders recognize the value of multilingual and multicultural contributions, or are they ethnocentric in their views? This book explores the many combinations of the realities that are possible in today's world, placing special emphasis on the roles of families and schools in enhancing the foreign language learning experience.

Chapter 1 begins by reviewing the ten key factors in raising multilingual children (aptitude, timing, motivation, strategy, consistency, opportunity, the linguistic relationship between the languages, siblings, gender and hand-use as a reflection of cerebral dominance), which are detailed in my first book, *Raising Multilingual Children*. Each of these factors and its importance, even in its absence, is explained. When an individual can determine his own "recipe," or combination of factors, then his unique mix points to how he can best manage languages in his life.

Chapter 2 celebrates how lucky we are to be living at this particular point in history. Today languages are highly valued around the world by a myriad of professions, something that marks a turning point in human linguistic endeavors. Never before in the history of the world have so many people been literate in multiple languages. Never before has the demand for people who speak other languages and have a window into other cultures been so high. Never before has there been so great a need to improve communication between different countries, businesses, and individuals as there is today.

Chapters 3 delves into languages across the human lifespan and defines seven different life stages from birth to adulthood: (1) bilingualism from birth; (2) early childhood; (3) the elementary school years; (4) the middle school years; (5) the high school years; (6) the university years; and (7) adulthood. This book acknowledges the differences between child and adult foreign language education and offers recommendations for how to maximize language learning at each stage.

Chapter 4 focuses on the distinction of language for school versus language for play, or academic versus social language skills. This is followed by the developmental steps of language acquisition, from comprehension to speaking to reading and finally writing. The chapter details the difference between learning to read and write in first, second, and third languages as well as the importance of the mother tongue, or native language, as it relates to learning subsequent languages.

Chapter 5 explains how third languages differ from second languages in terms of how they are learned. The discussion covers seven key elements that influence the success of trilingualism: (1) first language proficiency; (2) linguistic awareness and metacognition; (3) time on task; (4) education level of the learner; (5) parent involvement; (6) teacher qualifications; and (7) learner self-esteem. This section shows how undertaking more than two languages is distinct from, yet complementary to, bilingualism.

Chapter 6 is dedicated to explaining how the brain works when it takes on more than one language. This chapter explains what is known to date about the location of language in the brains of monolinguals versus multilinguals, including how age of acquisition, language combinations, and the level of formal or informal instruction can be influential. Knowing how the brain works when it takes on more than one language helps readers understand what normal complications can arise and how to respond in order to become more efficient in the learning process. We then conclude with one of the least tangible aspects of language learning but one of the most important, in my opinion, the role of emotions in language learning. Because no two brains are alike, generalizing about the localization of skills would be irresponsible, but so would ignoring data that can aid emerging multilinguals. This section supplies a cautious, descriptive analysis of the multilingual brain.

Chapter 7 focuses on the impact different key players in a person's life have on language learning—including families, schools, and society—and what these players can do to encourage the best possible learning environments. It begins by looking at realistic spheres of influence, or feasible things the individual and his family have control over and can actually do to help language flourish in the home. This section then considers what parents should expect from the school, as well as which curriculum structures appear to be most conducive to foreign language acquisition. Finally, this chapter gives examples of what successful multilingual schools look like in practice.

Chapter 8 offers a personal reflection and recounts our family story covering five countries, four languages, three kids, two nationalities, and one home. This section shares several real-life examples in keeping with *Raising Multilingual Children*'s documentation of the development of multilingual skills in my own three children and others we have the privilege of knowing. In keeping with recorded accounts in my first two books, this book tracks our family's continued language development and demonstrates how we daily turn theory into practice.

Throughout these chapters this book asks the reader to philosophize as to whether languages are being lived by the people, or whether the languages themselves are alive. From an individual's view, *Living Languages* is how we sense the emotion of words differently when we speak in distinct tongues. It is also about the cultural insight that diverse vocabularies bring us, and the introspection that words from different countries inspire in us. Most importantly, *Living Languages* describes the distinct conceptual organization of the mind when using different languages. On the other hand, languages themselves are alive. From a linguistic perspective, *Living Languages* explains how each individual language is bathed in different connotations of significance, how an object is open to interpretation based on its placement in a sentence, and judgment about the hierarchy of meanings based on distinct grammatical forms. The structure of each language influences how we interpret our world when we use it. Combined, the individual and linguistic perspectives of *Living Languages* confirm our identity as multilinguals using various lenses to see the world. We'll begin by looking at the factors that influence successful multilingualism.

1
Raising Multilingual Children: The Ingredients, the Recipes, and Your Personal Banquet (Why This Book Is for You)

RAISING AND TEACHING MULTILINGUAL CHILDREN

When I wrote *Raising Multilingual Children*, my first book about children and foreign languages, I wanted families and practitioners to understand that there are various ways that children can combine ten key factors influencing successful language acquisition, and that each combination is unique to the individual. This means that no one can tell you, "Do X and you are sure to raise a balanced bilingual," or, "Avoid Y and you can be sure your students will leave your class biliterate." The ten key factors in raising multilingual children are aptitude, timing, motivation, strategy, consistency, opportunity, the linguistic relationship between the languages, siblings, gender, and hand use as it reflects cerebral dominance. Each one of these ten factors is important in every child's success with foreign languages. Awareness of these factors can help teachers in their vital role of facilitating the language-learning process. These factors are briefly described here.

Aptitude

Each person is born with a certain aptitude for different life skills. People with a high aptitude for foreign languages learn languages easily; people with low language-learning aptitude learn languages with difficulty. You cannot influence how much aptitude a person has, but you can make the most of what exists. The aptitude for foreign languages runs on par with aptitudes in other fields—such as a gift for physics, ballet, math, or painting. Roughly ten percent of the population has high aptitude for learning foreign languages. Is aptitude inherited? Some acknowledge that high aptitude for foreign languages runs in families, but this could be due to family lifestyles rather than to genes. It may some day be argued that the gene for language (FOXP2) is what lends itself to aptitude, though that has not yet been confirmed. John Carroll and Stanley Sapon's *Modern Language Aptitude Test* (1959) and the *Pimsleur Language Aptitude Battery* (1966) have three things in common: auditory capacity, sound-symbol relations (written codes), and grammatical sensitivity. Individuals with language-learning aptitude enjoy these three abilities. Aptitude is a gift that a few lucky people enjoy, but other factors can work in your favor with equal efficiency. If you were not born with aptitude, you have probably received other gifts in life.

Timing

Timing represents the window of opportunity when certain skills can best be learned. There are three windows of opportunity for foreign language acquisition: from roughly birth to nine months, between four and eight years old, and from nine years on. The first window (0–9 months) is due to neurology: the brain treats languages learned during this time period as "first" languages. If the two languages are learned as first languages, the learner has no foreign accent, develops distinct yet complementary vocabularies, and "moves" with ease within the two worlds that the languages represent. Bilingualism from birth has many advantages, which are discussed in further detail in Chapter 3. Depending on whether or not the languages receive equal opportunity for use and are spurred on by equal levels of motivation, they can be managed with equal fluency. The second window is typically between four and eight years old, but it can sometimes extend into adulthood, depending on the personality of the individual. This window relies primarily on an individual's level of self-assurance, and it is rooted in basic psychology. The self-confidence with which a three- or four-year-old tackles a foreign language is distinct from the approach of individuals who begin to let their egos get the best of them. One of the greatest gifts a person can maintain is the ability to approach new challenges (as in a new language) with joy, curiosity, amusement, and excitement.

If we could all do that, we would maintain a great deal of the edge that children have for learning languages compared to adults. This third window is approximately from nine years old through adulthood, grounded in sociology and neurology. The human brain stops growing in absolute size at more or less nine years old. The primary differences between nine-year-olds, adolescents, and adults are the number of neuroconnections made in the brain. Every experience creates new connections, and the brain changes every day. Social pressures change drastically between a nine-year-old brain, an adolescent brain, and that of an adult, meaning that while, neurologically, the brain of a nine-year-old and that of an adult uptake languages similarly, the experiences are distinct.

Motivation

Motivation includes positive versus negative, and internal versus external factors. Falling in love is a fantastic, positive, motivating force, just as hatred is a strong, negative, motivating force. Additionally, one can feel impelled to do something from the inside (intrinsic motivation), or be forced to do something from the outside (extrinsic motivation). As we will see in Chapter 6, emotions have an impact on learning, both in a positive and in a negative sense. Emotions trigger different neurotransmitters, which send chemical messages throughout the brain. Some of these messages facilitate memory and learning, but others block the learning process. The combination of internal and positive motivations is the best way to learn anything, including languages. The combination of negative and external motivations is the worst way to learn anything, because it is not sustainable. For long-term learning, as parents, teachers, and caregivers, we should be concerned with finding ways to get the children in our lives to pursue new languages because *they* want to, not because *we* say so. Helping children develop their own love for languages by understanding their use and function in their lives can help them cultivate their own internal drive and desire to learn.

Strategy

Strategy means making a conscious decision to approach language development in a certain way, with different players accepting the assignment of specific language roles. *Raising Multilingual Children* discusses seven of the most studied strategies in the world, including strategies based on person, place, or time. The popular one-person, one-language strategy, in which each parent speaks a different language to the child, the use of time or place as a marker for language differentiation, and acquiring one language in the home and another in the community are examples of each of these. The main point related to strategy is that it is only as successful as the strategy's consistency rates. Families should ask themselves which strategy they are best able to maintain consistently before they choose one. Not every family is successful or has the option of using one-person, one-language; some families will find using physical space markers (such as home, school, grandma's house, church, or soccer practice) or time markers (dinner time, story time, or weekends) to be best suited to their life style. Whatever strategy one chooses, consistency is the key to its success.

Consistency

Consistency is the ability to stay true to the agreed upon strategy. When a family decides to embark on a multilingual adventure, all of the players need to agree on a family language strategy and then be consistent in fulfilling their language relationships with each other. For example, if a family decides to go one-person, one-language, but Dad often forgets and uses the community language with his son instead of his designated native language, there is no consistency in the strategy (e.g., David's mom agrees to speak English to him, David's dad agrees to speak to him in German, but they live in an English environment, and David's dad often forgets to use his native German with him and often lapses into English).

Other challenges with consistency come from the children. For example, some families decide that the home will be the place for one language, for example, Mandarin Chinese, and that the community language will be another, say English. However, during the course of their lifetimes, the children decide they don't want to be "different" from the community. As a consequence the children begin to respond to their parents in English instead of in the agreed-upon Mandarin Chinese. A common occurrence is that parents worry that they are not communicating well with their children because the kids are responding in English. The truth of the matter is that children are exerting what I call the *Law of Minimal Effort*; that is, kids think to themselves, "Why bother? I know my parents understand me, so why should I stretch myself; they'll get it if I just use English." As a result, the parents slowly give up the Mandarin, and everyone ends up speaking English. When the parents let the children drive the language strategy, they often sacrifice the possibility of preserving a home culture and developing multilingualism. Parents have more language success when they maintain a consistent strategy and stay loyal to their language choice.

Opportunity

Opportunity is the daily use of the language(s) in meaningful situations. One of the most challenging aspects of foreign language, whether in school settings or in family situations, is often the lack of application. Students frequently complain that they will never use their classroom vocabulary, and kids think no one but Grandma speaks Hebrew (or Spanish or Chinese). Teachers often note how accelerated student language skills become when they are placed in contexts in which the student can use the language in real life situations. Memorizing long lists of verb conjugations in French is not how language is really used, is it? Being able to converse, read a newspaper, and decipher communication messages is the goal of language. Unless studied for purely academic and linguistically analytical purposes, languages are meant to be living elements in people's lives, which offer insights into the people who use them and the cultures they represent. Opportunity for use means placing language in its true context.

The Linguistic Relationship between Languages (Typology)

Language typology is a very important factor that denotes how similar grammatical structures or languages that share historical roots are easier to learn than those that do not have these commonalities. Does the child's native language share roots with the second language? If so, the second language is easier to learn because of the similarity of grammar, vocabulary, and sound systems. For example, French and Portuguese are extremely similar languages, both with Latin roots, which share not only grammatical structure, but the base roots of many verbs, making them mutually intelligible in both spoken and written contexts. Similarly, Spanish and Italian (also with Latin roots) are mutually intelligible. It should come as no surprise to note that when languages share the same typology, one learns them faster. Grammatically speaking, this implies that if a person who speaks Arabic, which is a Semitic, verb-subject-object structured language, attempts to learn Korean, an Altaic or isolate language with a subject-object-verb language structure, and then attempts to learn Hebrew (a Semitic, verb-subject-object language), she will find Hebrew far easier than Korean because of the typologies.

Siblings

Siblings can have a positive as well as a negative effect on learning a new language. In the positive sense, siblings learn a great deal from one another because having siblings in the home increases the number of verbal exchanges and conversations a child has in a day, increasing the total amount of opportunity for practice, experimentation, and use. However, in the negative case, one child may dominate the language exchange and stunt the other's development. Two main problems occur with siblings. First, an older or more dominant sibling often runs the show and dictates to others in which language they should communicate. That is, a dominant sister can decide that she and her brothers will speak English together, effectively reducing the time in the family's other languages. Second, some siblings do not allow others to use as much language as they normally would. For example, when a helpful sibling decides to translate all the needs of her (usually younger) siblings, that reduces those siblings' need to speak or use language on their own. The best way to make the sibling factor a positive one is through good parental management of language exchanges, ensuring equal time for all children.

Gender

Sexist as it may at first sound, we now have the technology to understand how boys and girls approach language from different parts of the brain. These differences are influential in first, second, and subsequent languages. Boys and girls continue to approach language differently throughout the adolescent years. These differences are strongly related to physical structures in the brain and to sensory perception. There is an extensive body of knowledge about how men and women process language differently, showing that women use more parts of their brain to consider similar stimuli. Other studies show women's greater cross-hemisphere processing of first and second languages compared with men, who use fewer areas of their brains when processing language(s). (My husband says this is because of efficiency, and some researchers agree.)

Hand Use

There are two main points to be considered related to hand use and hemisphere dominance. First, human beings are predominantly right-handed, though a significant number of individuals, estimated to be between seven and eleven percent of the world's population, are left-handed. Additionally, most of the world—ninety-five percent of right-handed people and seventy percent of left-handed people—have their main language areas in their left frontal and parietal lobes. This means that most people are right-handed, and that most people have language in their left-hemisphere. Many studies about language, and most of the theories about bilingualism, are based on this majority, which does not take into account the five percent of right-handed people and thirty percent of left-handed people do not have their main language areas in the left hemisphere. Either this population has right-hemisphere lateralization, or language is distributed equally between left and right hemispheres. Hand use has also been correlated with reading abilities, suggesting a link between where language is learned in the brain and how successful students are at learning literacy in our traditional, formal education system. Second, multilingualism may lead to a rearrangement of brain areas related to language, with greater reliance on the right hemisphere being noted in several cases. Researchers now acknowledge that important relationships exist between hand preference and the anatomy of language areas.

In summary, the first point in *Raising Multilingual Children* is that every individual will combine the ten factors differently. Such individuality is what gives researchers and educators awe at the human capacity for language, and what challenges policy makers and teachers to emphasize an individualized approach in multilingual classrooms. Each child will take her measure of motivation, opportunity, and natural aptitude and weigh that against the time in her life when she learned her languages, whether or not the child had helpful siblings, and how the child's first and subsequent languages were related linguistically. In other words, every individual will have her own recipe, taking these ingredients and combining them in different proportions. This is just like taking the flour, sugar, milk, and eggs found in your kitchen and mixing them in different proportions.

In one recipe these ingredients give me flapjacks, in another, a crêpe, and, in yet another, a cake. The different results come about through the measurement of the ingredients and the way we mix them in our individual recipes. Let me offer a few examples of children we know, to illustrate this point better.

Take Karina, for example, one of my daughter's friends who became trilingual by having a second-generation German mother who met a Peruvian man of English descent while studying in the United States. They returned to Peru, where the father chose to speak to Karina in English. She had Spanish from the environment and German from her mother and school. Karina's recipe is heavy on the opportunity, motivation to speak her parent's language, and that of the community, and probably a large quantity of aptitude.

Another example is Carlos, who is one of my son's friends. His mother is Ecuadorian, and the father is Dutch, and they speak English as a family language. He receives Spanish, Hebrew, and English at school, and he goes to Dutch school a few afternoons a week to ensure that he is multiliterate as well as multilingual. Carlos's motivation to speak Dutch is low. All the friends he has who speak Dutch also speak Spanish, so the only people he knows who use Dutch resolutely are his father's age. All of these people have limited verbal exchange with him. His need to use written Dutch is very low. Dutch, however, is similar linguistically to English, meaning the two languages have had a positive influence on each other in terms of shared vocabulary and grammar. Carlos is also high on opportunity (use at school and home), has mixed motivation, and average aptitude; he is also left-handed, with some tests of lateralization pointing to his unusual right hemisphere dominance for language. His recipe takes the same factors and measures them in a very distinct way compared to Karina's situation.

A third example of a multilingual child with a different recipe altogether comes from another school friend whose father is Italian and whose mother is Austrian. They speak their respective languages to their child, and English to each other, leaving Spanish to the Peruvian environment and formal schooling. This child goes to school in German and Spanish and has English and French in school as well, totaling five languages at fifteen, all complete with literacy abilities.

Lili's is yet a different case. Lili's parents and two older siblings were born in China and immigrated to California. Lili was born in the United States, but her home life was conducted entirely in Cantonese. She is now an adult, but as a child she grew up in two languages, Cantonese and English, took Spanish as a high school requirement, and later learned sign language to earn her multilingual identity.

Juan's is another distinct case. His parents came to the United States from Mexico, and he was born here, but his entire home life and social upbringing were in Spanish. Like millions of other Americans, Juan was brought up bilingually and biculturally, balancing the input from school and from the dominant community language with an equal or greater number of hours in his home language. As these five cases show, each child took the same ten factors and created his or her own particular recipe for multilingualism.

The first goal of *Raising Multilingual Children* was to emphasize that different families adopt different strategies for languages in their home, school, and community. The children's motivation, opportunities for use, aptitude for languages, and combinations of languages, together with their particular family goals will determine their individual recipes.

The second goal I had with *Raising Multilingual Children* was to take empirical evidence from studies in linguistics, psychology, neurology, cultural anthropology, sociology, and education, and make them easy to read without ignoring the special status of language as the distinguishing human trait. My goal was to make crucial studies about bilingualism and multilingualism available to caring parents and responsible teachers, who might not know the difference between *code switching* (an alternation between two or more languages in the course of a conversation between people who have more than one language in common), and a *switch reference* (a word that signals the identity or nonidentity of the referent of an argument of one clause, with an argument of another clause), but who wanted the best for the children in their lives in terms of language development. I love languages and the opportunities they provide. Languages open the door to a world of cultures, values, empathies, and mentalities. I also love the learning mechanism in the brain: How do people learn different subject matters best? What is occurring in the brain, and how can knowing this help us teach new languages better? Helping parents and teachers understand the most efficient ways of guiding their children was why I wrote *The Multilingual Mind*.

THE MULTILINGUAL MIND

My second book, *The Multilingual Mind*, also had two goals. The first was to tackle curious questions about life with many languages:

In what language do multilinguals do math? Is there a relationship between musical ability and language ability? Are some languages easier to learn than others? Is your stronger language the one you dream in? Does the number of languages you know enhance cultural sensitivity? These fascinating questions were posed in workshops I gave between 1997 and 2007, and it became evident that information on all of these issues was sorely lacking, or at least not readily available to the public. I contacted experts in each area and invited commentaries, compiling their responses to share their answers with the "average" multilingual. The results were a collection of twenty-one essays on the most intriguing questions that multilinguals ask others and themselves.

The second goal of this book was to help elevate multilingualism to its rightful place as a recognized global trend, value, and phenomenon that will shape our world in the coming decades. Most people in the world speak more than one language, but there are very few who are also biliterate. Multiliterates are in high demand in the marketplace, around negotiating tables, and as policy brokers and cultural translators who help us understand people and their values in distinct corners of the world. It is possible that these are some of the few people alive who have the power to actually create intellectual empathy between nations through the knowledge to communicate clearly between peoples. *The Multilingual Mind* celebrates the important role that people who communicate in many languages can play on the world stage as well as in terms of human exchange.

LIVING LANGUAGES

This book, *Living Languages*, has a different focus. After fifteen years of research and watching my own three children grow up multilingually, I want share new information. Both technology and tenacity provide new research findings that not only confirm the ten key factors influencing successful bilingualism and multilingualism, but that also point to a future in which societies cannot afford to ignore the growing need for more people who know several languages. Technology is celebrated in this text through refined brain imagining techniques and groundbreaking studies about the multilingual mind. Today we can actually see how healthy multilingual brains function, and, most importantly, how unique each one is, depending on what languages the person learns and when they are learned. Technology is also celebrated in a discussion of new teaching tools, which we will see in Chapter 7. This book also applauds tenacity, viewing multilingualism across the human lifespan, and sharing fascinating longitudinal research findings. These findings confirm how long it takes people to become fluent in more than one language, demonstrate how people can learn languages at different ages, and point to appropriate methodologies for doing so.

In a practical sense, this book also points to the best practices in education to support the multilingual child. By reviewing the results of different systems, including English as a second language (ESL) programs, pull-out programs in which English language learners are taken out of the regular classroom for intensive English instruction during some part of the day, and dual-immersion programs in which all children learn at least two languages, independent of their first language, we can see how different communities benefit from different structures. This book also recognizes the growing phenomenon of trilinguals on the world stage, and their economic, social, cultural, and political value in a world where communication breakdowns have lead to tragedies in recent years. While in some ways similar to bilinguals, trilinguals are special, and less documented, and they are examined here in detail.

Most importantly, however, this book helps parents to sail through the heavy seas of doubt that can accompany this multilingual adventure at different stages of the voyage. I recall when my second son was slow to speak at thirteen months, and I doubted the wisdom of our choice to be a multilingual family. Our decision was reinforced when I remembered the book *The Moon Is Also Feminine*, in which a woman living in Germany was told to stop speaking her native Italian to her 18-month-old child because he was "obviously confused." She did so, and, *voila*! After six months, he began speaking. She realized that he would have done so with or without her Italian influence, and the only thing that happened when she stopped speaking Italian to him was that she lost her chance to speak to her child in her native language—something she woefully regrets to this very day. I want this book to be like that one, for it to be read as a good friend's well-founded advice, based on nearly 700 reliable, twentieth-century studies and her own children's experiences with languages. This book is grounded in hundreds of families' and teachers' experiences in fifteen countries, experience of people with whom I have had the pleasure of working through the years. After conducting workshops with teachers and parents in Argentina, Australia, Belgium, Colombia, Ecuador, France, Germany, Italy, Japan, the Netherlands, Norway, Peru, Switzerland, Thailand, and the United Kingdom, I have identified several questions in need of answers. Those questions are answered in this book.

Should you worry if your four-year-old mixes her languages? Should you drop biliteracy skills if your son just doesn't get it after three years of schooling? What benefits are there if you try to learn a language alongside your daughter? Is it important to take your child's teacher's comments seriously, even if you think you know more about multilingualism than he or she does? Will your son ever write as well in his native Spanish as he does in his school English? Is your school doing all it can to support your family goal of bilingualism? Is it your place to insist on mother tongue classes at school, or is it your job solely to be sure your child has the correct language skills in your home language? This book will help you arrive at the right answers to these questions and combine them with your own child's unique approach to languages.

This book also puts language in its place. Although multilingualism is literally the gift of tongues that parents, caregivers, and teachers can give, it should be subservient to the relationships we have with the children in our lives. As with anything we want to give our children (our career choice, love of soccer, art, chess, reading, math, ballet, etc.), or our hope of what they will become (fine citizens, successful professionals, good friends), nothing is more important or transmits our messages better than our love. If we attempt to force language on children, we will have the same negative effect as that of trying to shove a certain profession down their throats. They may accept passively, gleefully, or hatefully, but whichever the case, it will be our choice, not theirs, and that is not sustainable. We want the children in our lives to speak several languages for many sound reasons, but they must own this goal for themselves. Unfortunately, we have not successfully done this in our society as a whole. By forcing students into language classes, shaming them into learning, encouraging their rejection of native customs and values in order to adapt to the majority, we detract from their structure as whole individuals instead of adding language that can serve them for life. This has to change. As one of the most multicultural societies in the world, we in the United States have not celebrated bilingualism and multilingualism in proportion to their possibilities.

Finally, this book takes on the challenge of multilingualism in its various stages and forms. Although there are some aspects of language that are similar across the human lifespan, different ages and different levels of language acquisition have particular challenges associated with them. By reviewing each stage separately, and explaining the physical, psychological, and social aspects of each, we are better prepared to use this information to make the most of multilingual opportunities throughout the human lifespan. Newborns, elementary school children, middle school children, high school students, and adults all have unique stages of brain growth, psychological preparedness, and social pressures that influence language learning. This book will consider these different stages and celebrate the most unique of human traits, language, and how it is lived.

We will close this chapter by asking whether language is the key to human intelligence. Language is the single characteristic that differentiates humans from other animals. Although other species communicate, no other being employs complex grammatical structure or utilizes a written guide for memory. Many linguists believe humans are innately prepared for language and point to the fact that children around the world master the complex syntactical structures of all languages, as a natural skill, by about the age of five. Others go so far as to propose that language, unlike other aspects of learning, is special, and follows patterns distinct from those of other humanly acquired abilities. Psycholinguists have pondered the philosophical question as to whether we think in words. That is, do humans rely on language in order to form thoughts? Do we, for example, have different perceptions of time or space depending on the language we use? While these questions remain unanswered, many theorists posit that language is indeed the key to human intelligence, with some even proposing that there is a specific gene for this skill, unique to the human species. Linguists such as David Premack believe that what makes humans unique is not language alone, but that it is more specifically the human drive to form written symbol systems with which we record our histories, transactions, relations, fictions, futures, and follies. In this sense, it can be argued that language is "in many ways the ultimate artifact,"[1] though the point is still in debate.

A social vision of language is offered by Raymond Cohen, who says, "language is best thought of as shaping expectations rather than determining thought," as the original linguistic determinism model claimed.[2] This means that language creates a base for shared meaning and is the glue of community. This makes the developmental aspects of a person's language, such as the person's native language, the cornerstone of the rest of a person's life experiences. Cohen believes that "The mother tongue is the main repository of a community's common sense."[3] The words we use within our communal language are sources of our history, and they are a "community's shared stock of meaning."[4] He goes on to explain that language simply cannot exist in isolation from the community that speaks it: "Languages do not exist in isolation as abstract systems of signs but within unique, organic habits, complex ecologies of sensibility and interaction,"[5] making culture a reflection of language, and vice versa. This is vital to keep in mind as the melting pot of America becomes more and more linguistically diverse.

Whether appraised as the most distinct feature of humanness or as the key to intelligence, language is recognized as a salient aspect of humankind's uniqueness. We now turn to multilingualism's place on the world stage and put language into the global context.

2

The Global Community and Multilingualism: Who, Why, When, Where, and How Being Multilingual Has Grown in the Past Decade, and What This Means for Your Children

THE RECENT HISTORY OF MULTILINGUALISM

Never before in the history of the world have multilinguals been prized more than they are today. In business, government, world politics, cultural domains, communications, media, and international relations as a whole, there is a deficit of qualified professionals who can speak, read, and write in more than one language. *The Economist* and *Business Week* recently acknowledged that the characteristic most valued and least available in new business recruits was the ability to speak more than one language, and other studies go as far as saying that the future of some fields can be jeopardized by the lack of foreign language skills.

Anglophones, most notably Americans and British, have relied heavily on others to speak English, placing competitors at a disadvantage, which they now no longer accept. The language chosen for negotiation has an influence on outcomes. Government officials in England acknowledge that the "lack of proficiency in European languages is one of the main reasons why the UK is not making the most of opportunities offered by EU-funded education and training schemes, . . . and that this has serious implications for UK businesses and future employability for students."[1] This lack of languages could damage the future of UK business in the European market. American officials acknowledged a similar problem, but with political rather than commercial roots, as they scrambled to find native speakers of

Arabic immediately after 9/11, only to find that they had few in their diplomatic corps. English alone is not enough anymore.

ENGLISH DOMINANCE? NOT FOR LONG

Other studies have actually characterized English linguistic hegemony as arrogance and blamed it for impairing international relations. It has even been hinted at, not so subtly, that America's language limitations and poor communication are to blame for the problems with countries in parts of the world in which the U.S. government participates without a thorough understanding of the culture. But language can also play a role in conflict resolution. The United States launched the *National Security Language Initiative* in 2006 to invest more money in foreign language programs in U.S. schools because it recognized that there was a "critical need" for language education in America. Though it may take a generation before we see the results of this gesture, it is a start in recognizing how the languages we speak influence our success as individuals, as well as our progress as nations.

Learning a second language in formal school settings has become a topic of growing debate in recent years because English is no longer the *de facto* language of the United States. Increased immigration and higher birthrates of minority populations means that the Southwestern United States now has a majority of Spanish-speaking families. The number of Americans who speak a language other than English at home grew forty-seven percent between 1990 and 2000, accounting for nearly one in five Americans. Although this phenomenon is new to the United States, Europe has been adjusting to the need for multiple languages throughout most of its history, and it is now routine to find many countries that require three languages for high school graduation. Most countries in Asia require students to learn from two to six languages during their educational journey, as in India, where a child begins with a village language, moves to a community language for grammar school, attends high school within a Hindi or Punjabi structure, but will attend university in English.

In 1999, UNESCO acknowledged the promotion and respect for multilingualism, which insists that all world citizens should learn at least three languages: the native language, a neighboring language (one that shares a border), and an international language, one recognized by the United Nations (U.N.) as an official language (Arabic, Chinese, English, French, Russian, and Spanish). The U.N. believes that the promotion of such a policy would greatly reduce world tensions and the chances of war. The U.N. sees monolingualism as a handicap: "It means you see the world through the inevitably limited dimensions of a single language even if it's a world language."[2] Multilingualism is a modern necessity in the increasingly globalized and interlinked world.

In 2000, more than one-third of the population of Western Europe under thirty-five was of immigrant origin, according to a recent UNESCO report on linguistic diversity in Europe. Some areas have higher immigration rates than others. In Holland, a sample of 41,600 children aged between four and seventeen found that forty-nine percent of primary and forty-two percent of secondary school pupils in the Hague use a language other than Dutch at home. People are more mobile than ever, and this trend will only increase in the foreseeable future.

America's Opportunity

Globalization means that humans need to communicate in the most efficient and effective ways possible in order to coexist peacefully during such times of mobilization. This can be analyzed from an internal country policy perspective as well as from an international point of view. On the national level in the United States, there is an urgency to respond to the growing population who do not speak English at home. The findings of the *National Literacy Panel on Language Minority Children and Youth* recommends that the structure of American schools become more informed to create better policy for improved learning achievement by both non-English speakers learning English, and by English speakers learning a foreign language. Mary Abbott of the *American Council on the Teaching of Foreign Languages* calls for schools to begin integrating foreign language instruction earlier than the current average fourteen years of age. She says this should occur ideally by kindergarten, or at least by elementary school, because that is what most of our international allies do. One of the reasons for an earlier start, aside from being more efficient and using resources better, is the sheer number of years a person then has in a language, and the subsequent ease of learning additional languages. The logic is that if students get a taste of French in second grade, they will find tackling Russian in high school less frightening. It comes as a bit of shock to learn that fewer than eight percent of Americans take a foreign language in college—this at a time when the popular press has begun to communicate what academics have been saying for years: we have been ignoring the importance of languages for too many years.

American linguistic arrogance has had a negative impact on its ability to compete in the business world, and to be compassionate in the diplomatic world. Language ability is the focus of all concerned with the successful growth of individuals and of nations. Commerce leaders say, "The most frequent reason cited by the others for not exporting was a lack of the background knowledge and language skills required to understand foreign markets,"[3] whereas those in diplomacy say that there is a link between language policy and a culture of peace. Attitudes are slow to change, but they are sure to do so. Like most intellectual movements, attitudes begin in the world of academia and spread to other areas of society. It is now a common mantra in higher education that "in today's world, the definition of a well-educated student must include fluency in a foreign language."[4] We now have to try to get this message to filter down into the earlier years of schooling.

Table 2.1   The Benefits of Multilingualism

Cognitive benefits	Enhanced higher thinking skills (metalinguistic awareness, creativity, sensitivity to communication).
Social benefits	Integration, appreciation of other cultures.
Personal benefits	Marketability of bilingual skills, government- and business-recognized need.
Psychological benefits	Psychological well-being, self confidence, sense of belonging, enhanced identity with roots.
Communication benefits	Multiliteracy enables access to wider spectrum of literature and a wider communication network of family and international links.
Cultural benefits	Greater tolerance, less racism, increased intercultural awareness.
Academic benefits	Impact on other subjects. Being able to read in other languages is correlated with wider achievement in other curriculum areas. Easier to learn the third language.

Source: Maher (2002), reformatted by Tokuhama-Espinosa, 2005.

It is ironic that one of the reasons why Americans may be so poor at languages is thanks to the wealth of the nation. When Americans travel, they tend to do so within national borders; there is no need to go any farther, many argue. A trip across country is just as much an adventure as a trip overseas. Only twenty percent of Americans have passports, and only two percent go abroad during college exchange programs. However, this is changing slowly but surely. Americans are traveling more, spurred on by the internal make up of U.S. citizens who now visit family in other parts of the world, or who travel for business needs, military duty, or diplomacy postings— or those who are simply more adventurous.

Changing Demographics

Americans are also more diverse than ever these days. More people are immigrating to the United States than ever before. Between 1990 and 2000 there was a fifty-seven percent increase in the number of foreign born citizens. Whereas migration from Europe to the United States was more common at the turn of the twentieth century, at the turn of the twenty-first century Latinos account for the greatest number of new citizens. This puts an interesting angle on Americans' unspoken language policy because nearly eighty percent of the students who are English language learners (ELLs) speak Spanish at home, totaling over 17.3 million U.S. citizens over the age of five whose first language is Spanish.[5] One in five Americans speaks a language other than English at home. Within this group, roughly three-fifths speak Spanish at home, a fifth speak a different Indo-European language, and almost fifteen percent speak an Asian language. There are 425 native languages represented in the U.S. public schools. "Overall, foreign-language speakers grew by about 15 million during the 1990s, with new Spanish speakers contributing about 11 million people and new Asian speakers almost 2.5 million."[6]

These various facts about the fabric of modern American society bring with them some philosophical questions, which urgently need answering. For example, are our Latino students doing so poorly as a group in school because we are not meeting their language needs? According to Janet Klinger and Alfredo Artiles, "Many cultural minority groups—Hispanic students in particular—continue to underachieve at alarming rates. Hispanic students have higher dropout rates than non-Hispanics. . . . In 1998, only sixty-three percent of eighteen- to twenty-four-year-old Hispanics had finished high school or earned a GED, compared with eighty-five percent of the total population. Although the achievement gap between Hispanics and whites narrowed in the 1970s and 1980s, it widened in the late 1980s and 1990s and remains large today."[7] Not only are non–English-speaking citizens on the rise in numbers, they are also on the move, no longer limited to big cities such as New York or Los Angeles. This has been a growing trend for years, but it seems to be catching up with us as if taking us by surprise. These immigrant English language learners are increasing. At the same time, U.S. mainstream study of foreign language is not as high as some would like.

The State of Language Learning Today

The U.S. Department of Education says that, of all undergraduate college degrees awarded, only one percent are in foreign languages. Of that one percent, only two percent are in languages such as Arabic, Chinese, Farsi, or Korean, for which the government says we have a "critical need."[8] Although this is partially true, some say the choice of language does not matter as much as the willingness to study. Harvard University's *2004 Benefits of Bilingualism Conference* brought together experts from various fields to discuss the ways that knowing many languages promotes various career paths. Then president of Harvard, Larry Summers, said, "It doesn't matter what other language you know; the very fact that you can think in more than one code makes you more flexible intellectually, more stable emotionally, more cautious politically."[9]

At other campuses research is underway, and more people from a variety of fields are beginning to share their knowledge about languages to seek new and better ways of helping people become multilingual. Cornell University's *Language Acquisition Lab and Virtual Center for the Study of Language Acquisition*, for example, manages an ongoing exchange of brilliant minds in the field of foreign language acquisition. Their forum encourages people from linguistics, neurology, psychology, and education to join forces and combine their knowledge in search of improving the language acquisition process. *The Center for Brain Basis of Cognition* at Georgetown University held a monumental conference on the neurocognition of second language in 2006. This historic event brought together some of the most respected names in the fields of linguistics and neurology to discuss how new information about the brain can help advance the ways in which we teach and assist, not only immigrant children in the United States to learn English, but also the ways in which we help U.S. citizens meet with more foreign language enthusiasm and success. As Judith Kroll of Pennsylvania State University remarked during the conference, "Until recently, cognitive science virtually ignored the fact that most people of the world are bilingual. In the past decade this situation has changed markedly."[10] Conferences such as this one bring to light the growing importance multilingualism is playing in all of our lives. But it wasn't always this way.

The Possibilities

I grew up in Berkeley, California, in the 1960s and watched friends begin and end high school in the "ESL track" for English as a Second Language learners, never advancing into the mainstream school culture. This limited their chances for higher educational opportunities and labeled them as less competent than their peers because of their limited English. There were a variety of reasons for why this happened. Some might say the curriculum structure was inadequate, and the ESL teachers were poorly trained. Others might suggest that the social structure lends itself to keeping students where they feel most comfortable, gaining status year after year within the same social group, making it unattractive to cross over into the regular academic track, where they would have to begin from scratch. Yet others might believe that these students had a low level of competence in their mother tongue, impacting the quality of English, their second language.

It saddens me to think that this group as a multicultural whole offers an amazing wealth of language resources that should be celebrated, but that are instead considered a burden on the system. That is, instead of the "ESL kids" and the "Foreign Language nerds" being ostracized, our schools should look to new models of education, such as dual-immersion systems, in which everyone, independent of first language, learns at least a second language. In such a model, immigrants learn English, and native English speakers learn a second, if not a third, language. This would celebrate U.S. cultural diversity in the best sense of its melting pot heritage.

In 2000, the U.S. census confirmed that more people speak Spanish at home than speak English at home in California, Arizona, New Mexico, and Texas. That makes language learning a hot issue as legislators scramble to try to remediate the language challenges that face these states. The bilingual debate in California has been on the back burner for politicians ever since I was a kid and probably longer. Perhaps the reality of a non–English-speaking majority will help force a decision to adopt more equitable, effective, and proven programs that will leapfrog the United States from its poor language abilities into a nation that best uses the natural talents of its citizens. An *American Demographics* article proclaimed that "people who speak foreign languages at home are the fastest-growing group that is now found throughout the country. America's identity as a melting pot now extends beyond multiple races and cultures to also include numerous languages."[11]

It is interesting to consider this from a historical perspective because the language challenge is really nothing new for Americans. Since its founding, the United States has met with a mix of language encounters, including the actual creation of the country with Native American Indians and people from mainly European countries, but built upon labor from Africa and Asia. What is ironic is that by trying to continually improve our institutions and structures, education in the United States has suffered some setbacks as it relates to integration and valuing of all its citizens. In education, as is often the case in other fields, there is a tap dance of one step forward and two steps back before we focus enough on what we truly hope the citizens of tomorrow will be.

The Role of Languages in Forming Tomorrow's Citizens

One of the best collective decisions I have ever seen in education came from the Organisation for Economic Co-operation and Development (OECD) nations (whose members include Australia, Austria, Belgium, Canada, Czech Republic, Denmark, Finland, France, Germany, Greece, Hungary, Iceland, Ireland, Italy, Japan, Luxembourg, Mexico, Netherlands, New Zealand, Norway, Poland, Portugal, Slovakia, South Korea, Spain, Sweden, Switzerland, Turkey, the United Kingdom, and the United States), who agreed that there were three main desirable characteristics of the citizen of the future. To them, by the time a person reaches fifteen years of age, when compulsory schooling ends in many countries, the citizen should know how to work with others (group skills), know how to solve problems, and know how to use tools (such as the Internet, dictionaries, experts, libraries, etc.). I think it's not too far-fetched to presume that the goals of formal education in many, if not all, countries coincide with those goals. For me, group skills include the ability to communicate;

communication implies language, and languages are numerous in multicultural America.

Multilingualism and the Law

In 1968, the *Bilingual Education Act* was signed into legislation by President Lyndon Johnson. In 2003 that act was replaced by the *No Child Left Behind* legislation and Title III, *Language Instruction for Limited English Proficient and Immigrant Students*. For all the good brought about by the *No Child Left Behind* legislation, it is unfortunate that it has created competition for precious school hours that have been taken from foreign languages (and the arts) in order to shore up weak Math and English skills. Doing that might help our students improve their test scores on state exams, but it does little to cultivate citizens for tomorrow's workforce. On the contrary, *Education Week* reported that "because of the intense focus of the federal *No Child Left Behind Act* on reading and mathematics, some schools around the country have reduced the number of foreign-language courses offered or stopped teaching foreign languages altogether."[12] This seems to be exactly the opposite of what should be happening in our schools.

The U.S. Department of Education declined to publish the report on literacy education of bilingual children in 2006. Some people, such as Bruce Fuller of the University of California at Berkeley and James Crawford of the *National Association for Bilingual Education,* say this is because the report indicates that the current practice of teaching immigrant children through English-only classes is inefficient. Additionally, "in recent years, conservatives have pushed to abandon bilingual programs in favor of English-only education, and No Child Left Behind requires that immigrant children be tested in English after three years,"[13] a timeframe that researchers now recognize is two to four years short of how long it actually takes a child to reach academic proficiency in a foreign language. These statistics seem to indicate that we are doing a disservice to both our English language speakers and our limited English proficient students. "What is important is that foreign-language instruction be valued, and that there be more of it."[14] How can we go about achieving this shift, which on one level is a national policy consideration? I believe the answer is to start at another level, by examining how we can maximize each individual child's full potential in foreign languages. We now turn to multilingualism across the human lifespan and look at the best ways of getting people of all ages to improve their multilingual skills.

3
Languages across the Lifespan

People can learn languages throughout their lifetime. This chapter will look at bilingualism from birth; the elementary, middle, and high school years; university study; and adult learning. My biases are clear throughout this exploration. I have witnessed thousands of children learn languages throughout childhood and adolescence and observed how other adults and I have done the same. I believe that languages can and should be learned across the lifespan.

A CRITICAL PERIOD FOR FOREIGN-LANGUAGE LEARNING?

To lay the foundations for this section, we should start by asking whether there is a "critical period" for learning languages. Brian Mac Whinney of Carnegie Mellon University believes that there is no critical period. Rather he has established that there is entrenchment of information over time. "Age effects in L2 [second language] learning emerge from entrenchment, competition, and weak resonance, but not because there is evidence of a particular plasticity in the brain for languages at a specific age,"[1] says Mac Whinney. Other evidence comes from Catherine Snow and Marian Hoefnagel-Hohle of Harvard, who showed that the older the person, the more superior the language learning at all levels. Adults are better second language learners than children because they already have a well-established foundation upon which to make logical references about the new language. "The studies, then, do not point to a critical period for second language learning," conclude Ellen Bialystok and Kenji Hakuta, two other highly respected linguists. "The answer is short and simple: regardless of age, those who attained near-native proficiency in English were able to make abstract judgments with a high level of accuracy. . . . Thus, learners of second language, even adult learners, continue to have 'access' to the ability to learn abstract linguistic structures, even of the Chomskian variety."[2]

Having said this, there is a logical assumption that the younger a person, the easier it is for him to become fluent. This can be explained from two important perspectives, one quantitative and the other neuropsychological. Acquiring a language in the early years gives the learner more time to practice, say bilingual education specialists Thomas Wayne and Virginia Collier. By the time a person is eighteen years old, for example, language ability may differ if learning began at birth or at age thirteen (eighteen versus five years of practice). "On the basis of our findings, the distinction between native and second languages may be less for [people who had] younger ages of exposure to a second language,"[3] confirms Joy Hirsch at Columbia University. But does this explain all the differences in fluency? Not exactly, because the other piece of the puzzle appears to be in neuropsychology. As we will see, the way the brain takes in information about language varies from age to age.

BILINGUALISM FROM BIRTH: WHY STRATEGY AND OPPORTUNITY ARE THE KEYS

Children who are brought up bilingual from birth can normally manage each of their languages with fluency, though the level of proficiency within the languages may vary in each of the sub-skills of understanding, speaking, reading, and writing. The amount of time devoted to each of the languages has a direct correlation in the early years to the ability to later use it efficiently. That is, the more quality time devoted to a target language, the more likely the speaker will have high-level fluency. This is important to remember when parents commit themselves to raising children bilingually or multilingually: fluency does not come without effort. A family strategy for approaching languages should be a conscious decision; simply exposing a child to a language is helpful but not nearly as impacting as engaging the child in constructive play or learning and using age-appropriate vocabulary. We will talk more about strategy after we clarify how bilingualism from birth works.

When a child learns languages from birth, he is effectively learning them as two first languages. Brain scans show that people brought up bilingual from birth have languages in the same area of the brain as do monolinguals, whereas people who learn languages after the first seven months or so actually use different areas for processing sounds, or do not perceive sounds at all that are not representative in their native language.

Children use language as a collection of patterns that regulate social life, according to educational researcher Chet Bowers. This means that a child who is bilingual from birth is learning to manage the world through two social systems, based on the concepts learned, which are represented in two languages. When a child does this from birth, he has the advantage of understanding a single concept, but with two lenses on the world. This is a great advantage over children who become bilingual or multilingual after birth because there are conflicting patterns that regulate social life. A monolingual who learns a new language later in life takes the concepts learned about the world from birth and learns to represent them by two different patterns, or ways of understanding and expressing. Let's look at an example to make this point clearer.

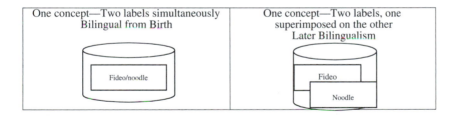

Let's say an eight-year-old English speaker moves to Mexico. "Noodles" is no longer the noodle concept the child had before; it also now becomes *fideo* (Spanish for noodle). *Fideo* arrives with its own cultural baggage. It could be that *fideos* are prepared differently than noodles are. They could have a different taste or smell. *Fideos* might look different, have distinct shapes from noodles, or be eaten under different circumstances. Noodles and *fideos* are two different concepts. This is in contrast to a child brought up bilingual from birth, who accepts the concept of noodle/*fideo* as one. Although the circumstances, shape, or flavor may differ, his understanding of the noodle/*fideo* concept is simply larger than a monolingual's concept would be. Noodles and *fideos* are not laid one on top of the other but rather *are* one. Bilingualism from birth makes learning about *fideos* different from simply accepting that noodle and *fideo* are the same concept with different wrappings.

This English-speaking child who moves to Mexico was monolingual from birth. He has different mechanisms for conceptual understanding from a child brought up bilingual from birth. Maintaining the English home language, once settled in Mexico, would help the child to harmonize his symbolic world built out of internal and external symbols. Learning different languages and cultures influences cognitive processes by exposing individuals to different values, beliefs, and demands. By maintaining the home language alongside the majority language, the child's internal symbol system is preserved, and a broader conceptual understanding of "noodle" or *fideo* can begin to occur. This does not always happen, however. If this child were to be told to drop his first language and concentrate on perfecting Spanish, for example, he would be deprived of his primary conceptual understanding of noodle, making the task of understanding *fideo* more difficult. Parents who feel they are helping by limiting the child to use of the new language are wrong. If the child is forced into only using the majority language, Spanish, and not allowed to link it to an established concept (noodle), the child is being asked, in effect, to build a new concept rather than modify an existing one, something the brain is not apt to do. It is less natural for the brain to be forced to replace existing labels for concepts about the world than it is to ask the brain to add a new label to the concept. This is one of the strongest psychological arguments in favor of additive bilingualism, adding a new language, as opposed to subtractive bilingualism, in which the new language replaces the old.

The process of becoming bilingual from birth is where we turn next. All people brought up bilingual from birth learn to speak their languages, whereas only some go on to learn to read and write. As we said earlier, one of the strongest arguments for bringing children up bilingual from birth is that the brain treats both languages as first languages, and the mechanisms for development follow the natural pathways of language acquisition. Although it is a bit alarming to accept at first, we now know that the child treats bilingualism as a single language at first, borrowing from one or the other until he becomes cognizant of their separate domains, usually at around two to four years old. When a child can begin to categorize languages ("Mommy says *noodles*, Daddy says *fideos*") and then labels the languages by name ("Mommy speaks English, Daddy speaks Spanish"), then the child begins to do what adults do, translate. Until that time, however, the child may mix syntax and grammar, borrow vocabulary, and speak one of his languages at inappropriate times. This is absolutely normal. Does this mean that if we can't bring up our children bilingual from birth we might as well give up? Not at all! It does, mean, however, that there are distinct advantages to being bilingual from birth. Let's further compare the differences between early and late bilinguals.

Although most researchers agree that people of all ages can learn a new language, there are studies that explain why bilingualism from birth is "easier." Several studies distinguish how late bilinguals rely on their native languages as linguistic crutches for understanding, referring constantly to the first language concepts as points of reference for future learning.[4] One study found that even proficient bilinguals "categorize second language sounds according to their first language representations,"[5] meaning that the concepts we are exposed to in infancy influence our ability to learn subsequent new conceptual understandings throughout our lifetimes. This is the most efficient way our brain can work. Imagine, it would be incredibly redundant for the brain to create new concepts for every new word in every new language; it is far easier to attach a new label to an existing concept. But this means that the new label has to pass through the filter of understanding of the original concept in the original language. This is efficient and logical, but it is also less rapid than starting off life with conceptual understandings that have multiple labels attached.

Are multiple languages in a single system in the brain, do they overlap, or are they distinct? Are languages somehow connected to the same meaning system, or are there two different meaning systems related to each language? Evidence from stroke victims shows that one language can be lost but not the other. This implies that the conceptual understanding can remain even if an entire language is lost. This means that there also has to be some kind of inhibition system in order to keep one language available and the other "quiet."

When a child first applies meaning to words and produces speech, there appear to be three steps to the process, according to

Ellen Bialystok and Kenji Hakuta. "First, children need to determine the simple units of meaning that become the basis for more complex ideas."[6] In our noodle example, "noodle" is the basic unit, and the labels spaghetti, lasagna, and macaroni and cheese, can be built upon the basic unit. Second, "children need to be cognitively prepared to represent these primitive ideas in a symbolic system."[7] This can be the actual noodles themselves or the written word "noodle." Third, "the conceptual primitives need to be properly labeled and combined in order to organize the structure of the emerging language."[8] This means if our child misunderstands *fideo* and does not associate it with "noodle," he will be lost. If the child misunderstands *fideo*, he will also misunderstand its subentities as well as the purpose/use of the concept. This means that without understanding "noodle" it us impossible to know spaghetti. This is the core explanation of why mother tongue (or first language) proficiency is so important. This conceptual development of language is explained in part by how the human brain is wired,[9] which we will now review.

HOW TWO LANGUAGES CAN BE REPRESENTED IN ONE MIND

There are many ways to think about how two or more languages can coexist in one mind. I am sure that each multilingual has his own theory about the process. For example, one day while doing homework my youngest child promptly laid down his pencil and told me that "the hole in my brain for Spanish is full now. I can't do any more Spanish. I'm going to start my Math instead." When he said this, he was creating a mental model of how his brain was structured and how information could fill up the different spaces allotted to different disciplines. Ingenious—and maybe closer to the truth than we think! Other slightly more sophisticated models of two languages in one mind are based on an "overlap" hypothesis in which the languages are distinct but have an area where they cross into each other's space. A second view is that the two languages are functionally separate and therefore do not cross over. And a third view is that there is a "mental firewall" that separates the languages. That is, the bilingual can function as a monolingual by putting up a barrier on his other languages. The key to this smooth functioning is in the speaker's ability to quickly identify which language he should be using. In other words, to apply this mental firewall one needs to know which language to access and which to block. Clues about which language should be used are fundamental to the external appearance of the child's effort level when he uses his languages. This is one explanation for why the one-person one-language strategy is so popular. In this strategy children have the best possible clues available and know exactly which language should be used in which context. If the child is not sure about which side of the firewall to access, he hesitates and can appear confused.

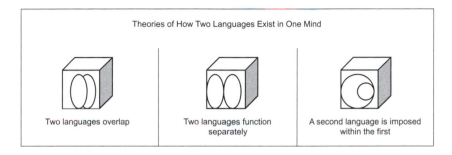

Theories of How Two Languages Exist in One Mind

Two languages overlap | Two languages function separately | A second language is imposed within the first

In her laboratory, Judith Kroll simulated this potential confusion. She asked participants to view pictures and to "name the picture in English if you hear the high tone and in Dutch if you hear the low tone."[10] This created a situation similar to that in which a child is told, "name the picture in English if you see Daddy's face, and in Dutch if you see Mommy's face." Both the tones and the faces are clues that help children decide which side of the firewall to access. Humans as a species are very visually inclined, so it is no wonder than one-person one-language is easy to adhere to. We think to ourselves, see the face, and speak the face's language. Without a visual cue, children seek out auditory triggers to help them decide what language to speak. It is interesting that as the bilingual becomes more proficient, fewer clues are needed, and less inhibition takes place because the action becomes automatic. Brian Mac Whinney believes that both children and second language learners pick up frequent cues and then determine their reliability. When they are found to be "legitimate," they guide the choice of language. This leads to the first of four subelements of language, comprehension; the other subelements (speaking, reading and writing) will follow.

Language Comprehension

The first basic element of language is the ability to comprehend others, which begins with speech and sound perception even before a child is born. Sounds are perceived in utero, and the rhythm of the language, which will surround the infant, is sensed even before he or she is born. Shortly after birth the child begins to distinguish native language sounds from foreign ones. Dehaene-Lambertz, Dehaene, and Hertz-Pannier used functional magnetic resonance imaging (fMRI) to measure brain activity as it related to normal and reversed speech in awake and sleeping three-month-old infants. This experiment showed that although the infants could not yet produce speech of their own, they had sophisticated interpretation methods of others' speech. Their conclusions were that "precursors of adult cortical language areas are already active in infants, well before the onset of speech production."[11] This study shows that by three months of age infants discriminate between real speech and nonsensical sounds in the same way as adults do, even though they are not producing these sounds themselves.

A very intriguing conjecture posed by some theorists in England is that human infants are born universal receivers of all sounds, such as musical ones, and they have the ability to distinguish all human phonemes possible. These researchers suggest that the ability to recognize these sounds narrows drastically in the first months of life, and after approxiately nine months, humans are only able to perceive the sounds that are part of their daily repertoire. For example, if a child is exposed to all the notes in the musical scale and these are rehearsed throughout the first year, he would theoretically not lose the innate perfect pitch we are all born with. In a similar fashion, if the child is exposed to Arabic, English, Chinese, German, Japanese, Hindi, and French in the first year of life, he would be able retrace these neural pathways later on in life and perceive them when formally learning the languages at a later age. Such a suggestion has wide-ranging implications for parenting as well as for all early caregivers. Exposure to language sounds (cassette tapes of songs from other languages, for example) cannot hurt a child's language development, and may potentially help. But does this mean that parents should be encouraged to bombard their children with language sounds from foreign lands just in case they decide to pursue one foreign language in the future? I think most parents would agree that "everything in moderation has its place," and that all things in exaggeration should be discarded. Having said this, a good argument can be structured in favor of using otherwise unoccupied moments (long car rides, for example) to expose infants to sounds they might not normally encounter on a daily basis. As I drove the kids back and forth to crèche or kindergarten in Geneva I remember playing musical soundtracks in the car, sometimes in French, other times in English or Spanish. They were popular children's songs and enjoyable in and of themselves, but by playing a variety of language sounds I believe I was helping strengthen different neural pathways for phonemes in different languages that my children would formally learn in later years.

Manuela Friedrich and Angela Friederici of the Max Plank Institute for Human Cognitive and Brain Science noted another early discrimination procedure of language by infants. They demonstrated that infants not only acquire knowledge about the sounds, intonation, and organization of their native language but also begin to understand the way words and symbols are linked. Additionally, their study showed the dramatic finding that nineteen-month-old infants showed the same discrimination abilities as adults when it came to identifying phonotactically legal (pseudowords) and phonotactically illegal (nonwords) word onsets versus real words. Their study has implications for second language learning after this early age in that words not recognized in the native tongue will be considered "nonsensical" until a conscious understanding and labeling of languages can be made, which normally occurs between two and four years of age. This means that a child brought up bilingual from birth will have an easier time acquiring languages than a child introduced to a second language at nineteen months of age because the older a child gets, the better the brain becomes at filtering out nonnative sounds. Patricia Kuhl of the Institute for Learning and Brain Sciences and the Department of Speech and Hearing Science at the University of Washington goes so far as to say that "infants use computational strategies to detect the statistical and prosodic patterns in language input, and this leads to the discovery of phonemes and words."[12] She hypothesizes that one of the reasons it is believed that children learn languages differently from adults hinges on "the brain's commitment to the statistical and prosodic patterns that are experienced early in life," which, to her, "help to explain the long-standing puzzle of why infants are better language learners than adults."[13] That is, the brain is a pattern-seeking organ; it searches for meanings by finding recognizable patterns that it has seen before and that confirm knowledge about the outside world. The earlier the exposure, the stronger the patterns.

However, some believe that language development is more closely related to the amount of experiences one has than to the stage of natural brain development that the child is undergoing. Work by Barbara Conboy of the University of California at San Diego and Debra Mills of San Diego State University places a higher premium on the experiences of the bilingual infant as compared with developmental changes in the brain to explain bilingual infants' word recognition and use in their languages. They found that studies of nineteen- to twenty-one-month-old bilingual infants "indicate that the organization of language-relevant brain activity is linked to experience with language rather than brain maturation."[14] That is, the more practice and exposure children had to their languages, the speedier the recognition and use of their vocabulary. This study has implications that challenge whether it is important for a child to have early exposure to a language or whether the amount of exposure can offer equal benefits in terms of foreign language learning. The question now seems to come down to whether language proficiency depends more on "when" or on "how much." In a guarded recommendation, it would seem prudent to say that learning a new language is guided by the concept that earlier is still better than later, and that more is better than less.

The more exposure a child has to quality language input from loving caregivers, the better off that child will fare with languages. In summary, quantity and quality both carry weight in determining the eventual fluency of the language learner. In the early years quality translates into exposure to all the sounds found in the child's languages (which can easily be achieved by reading aloud to the child and natural verbal exchanges), along with quantity, which implies that all languages in a child's life get equal time. Offering children exposure to language sounds is only half of the parents' and caregivers' job, however. Parents need to learn to listen to what their children produce and guide their emerging speech. This is where we turn our attention next.

EARLY CHILDHOOD (0–5): THE RACE IS ON, BUT WHO IS IN THE DRIVER'S SEAT? THE REASONS PERSON, PLACE, AND TIME MATTER IN LANGUAGE STRATEGY

Learning to Speak First and Second Languages

After understanding language through the perception of sounds, an infant's natural instinct is to try to reproduce those sounds; thus speech is developed. Human speech evolved with the species. According to Philip Lieberman, "speech anatomy first appears in the fossil record in the Upper Paleolithic (about 50,000 years ago)" and involves "species-specific anatomy deriving from the descent of the tongue into the pharynx."[15] Humans, unlike their ape counterparts, have the unique ability to speak because of the physical attributes of the tongue's shape and the pharynx and voice box structures. Chimpanzees lack a vocal tract capable of producing certain sounds that facilitate both speech production and perception. Although not all evolutionary scientists agree, some believe that speaking evolved from other motor development, such as walking upright and running, not from the existence of Broca's and Wernicke's Areas, which they say are consequential to speech. As we will see in Chapter 6, this links aspects of motor delivery and coordination to eventual speech processes.

Choosing to raise a child bilingually or multilingually from birth takes a great deal of commitment on the parents' part and relies heavily on parent-child interactions as well as the consistency of those interactions as they relate to the strategy parents use with their child. As the child's speech develops, parents play a huge role. How exactly does this speech development occur?

There are two main schools of thought about how children develop language. The overall debate is beyond the scope of this book, but it is helpful for parents and teachers to understand the basic mechanisms of each. In the early history of linguistics it was believed that children learned languages by imitating the models surrounding them. Later, the cognitivists, lead by Noam Chomsky, demonstrated how children actually have innate language ability. Chomsky had a profound impact on the way theorists viewed the process of language development. From his work it was determined that language is "part of the brain's mental equipment. . . . Children learned language because it was their biological destiny to do so," as Ellen Bialystok and Kenji Hakuta summarize.[16] Others contributed to this argument by demonstrating how parents actually do little grammatical correction of their children, primarily concerning themselves with the content of the child's message as opposed to its grammatical structure. That is, when Mary says, "Daddy am a girl!," the parents are more likely to correct Mary by saying, "No, Daddy is a *boy*," rather than "No, Daddy *is* a boy." This has important implications for second language learning because it points to a key aspect of communication in which nouns play a bigger role than correct grammar. Some schools of thought encourage the child to learn as much vocabulary as possible and presume the grammar will follow naturally. This tactic is based on the belief that parents don't normally correct these kinds of errors in the first place, and the child eventually self-corrects as his clarity is compromised if he does not learn to use correct grammar. Others go so far as to believe that even if the child fails to learn the correct grammar for the language, people will still understand him if his vocabulary is large enough. That is, the person will know enough words to make his point clear, despite the lack of grammar. This is contrary to a growing trend in schools these days in which there is a return to overt grammar instruction. For a decade and a half there was a slow drift away from formal grammar instruction in the United States; it was considered "old fashioned" and tedious. Many international and bilingual schools have found that overt instruction of grammar in new languages actually has distinct benefits for students. The schools may be filling in a gap for parents when they do this, because parents are less likely to pay attention to these problems. Success in school is more reliant on grammatical perfection than on informal communication, so grammar becomes the school's responsibility by default.

MacWhinney and colleagues have devised a beautiful visual representation of how children develop vocabulary. They show that initially, when a child has a vocabulary of roughly fifty words, nouns are the primary content, making up about ninety-five percent of a child's speech. Nouns remain the dominant unit of vocabulary throughout the child's life. Later, when the child has a vocabulary of around 150 words, nouns still dominate, representing about seventy-five percent of the child's vocabulary; the rest is about twenty percent verbs and five percent adjectives, adverbs, and other parts of speech. When the child grows to have 250 words, nouns still remain the dominant vocabulary at about eighty percent, with verbs reaching about seventeen percent and adjectives growing as well. By the time children enter schools they employ more and more verbs, but their propor(on as compared with nouns is always smaller. By grade school, verbs are about twenty-five percent of the child's vocabulary, whereas nouns are roughly sixty percent and the rest of the words are the other parts of speech. This graphic bears witness to the importance of vocabulary building in both first and subsequent language development, and the key role that nouns and naming objects play.

Language Strategies

The most popular bilingual parent strategy is one-person one-language in which each parent speaks a single language to their child. This is an efficient strategy primarily because it is the easiest to be consistent with, but it does not necessarily yield superior results. Though effective, one-person one-language is only an option for families in which the parents speak distinct languages. This strategy is not an option for a family in which both parents speak the same language. For example, if both mother and father speak Spanish at home and leave English to the community, the family language strategy will be based on place, not person. Other families choose to use time to set the parameters for language use, for example, weekends are always in the second language, or story time is only conducted in the first language. There are a myriad of combinations possible, but it should be remembered that they all fall into three simple categories or strategies: Person, Place, or Time (see Table 3.1).

It is important to remember that no one strategy has been proven superior to any other. There has been more research on one-person one-language, but this is probably because it is easy to document. Think about it. It's easier to observe who should speak which language to the child than whether or not it is the right time or place to do so. I have had the pleasure of meeting hundreds of families who choose strategies other than one-person, one-language who have found success as well; consistency is the key in all cases. Any strategy in which there is consistency has a far greater chance of success than a random approach to language. Another plus in favor of one-person one-language is that many parents feel it is more natural and allows them to express themselves to their children in a free and normal manner.

A constraint of successful strategies is that they also have to be realistic given the child's developmental stages. For example, I once met a woman in Switzerland who devised an ingenious but utterly ridiculous strategy. She told me she spoke five European languages and wanted her children to be able to do the same because it opened the door to a myriad of job possibilities, guaranteeing work and well being. I told her that was an admirable goal and asked her just how she was going to go about ensuring this. She told me, "Simple. On Mondays I speak Italian. On Tuesdays I speak German. On Wednesdays I speak English. On Thursdays I speak French. On Fridays I speak Greek." "That's very ambitious of you," I told her, beginning to think she had really thought out how to give each language equal time. "How old are your children?" I asked. "Two and three," she replied. Hmmm, I thought to myself. Now, while using time as a marker for languages is a realistic strategy, it is only valid when the

Table 3.1 Person, Place, or Time

Person, Place or Time	Parent 1	Parent 2	Community	Plan
Person	Language A (some B)	Language B (some A)	Language A or B	The parents each speak their native language to their child.
	Language A	Language B	Language C	The parents each speak their native language to their child, who learns a third language from the environment.
	Language A / Language B	Language A	Language A	Parent 1 always addresses the child in his or her non-native, second language.
Place	Language A	Language A	Language B	Both parents speak Language A to the child, who is only fully exposed to Language B when in school.
	Language A	Language B	Language C / Language D	The parents speak their native language to the child who studies in a third language. The environment is a fourth language.
	Language A	Language A	Language A	Parents speak their native language to the child. The child associates the second language with certain places, such as special classes or visits with relatives.
Time	Language A / Language B	Language A / Language B	Language A	The parents speak their native language to their child except during specific times (such as meals or weekends), when they speak their second language to the child.
	Language A	Language B	Language A	Language B, which normally receives the least amount of exposure, is always used during story time.
	Language A	Language A	Language B	Language B is only used during special classes (religion, sport, after-school activity, etc.).

Source: Based on Tokuhama-Espinosa, 2000.

language receiver understands the concept of time. Normally, two-year-olds are not very good at grasping the days of the week, and they are often even challenged by "before" and "after," let alone abstracts such as Monday, Tuesday, and Wednesday. Clearly, this was a strategy doomed to failure, at least until the children were old enough to understand how their languages were being divided.

Different strategies work for different family circumstances. One-person one-language would also not be very successful if one of the parents was not around with enough frequency to give his or her language sufficient time with the children. In such a case, it might be more effective for the family to decide that Mom always speaks her native language with the kids, except when Dad is home, when the family language switches to Dad's native language. Or if Mom is not proficient in Dad's language, then decide that storytime on the weekends is Dad's time and in his language. Or optionally, the family could adopt a strategy in which vacations are spent in the father's home country if resources permit. Different options, depending on family resources and goals, will meet different family needs. Regardless, a good strategy is imperative in successful multi-lingualism so that a space for quality language input for the child is guaranteed.

An aspect of quality language input relates to the speech production that the child is able to achieve. For example, a concerned father once asked me, in his thickly Turkish-accented English, what I thought about him speaking only English with his son. I politely told him it depended on his family's language goal. Language input is language output in the early years, what goes in is what comes out. That is, if the family's goal was that the son speak the same level of English as the father, then so be it. But the family has to accept that unless there were others also speaking English to the son, his only source would be his father, and if his father had an accent, grammatical errors, pronunciation problems, or otherwise imperfect speech patterns, this would be what his son would end up producing. This does not make this a "bad" strategy, on the contrary, it if meets the family's language goals, then it is a good one. However, parents need to understand and accept the limits of their influence on their child's language abilities. If English is a goal, and this Turkish family lives in Swiss-German speaking Switzerland, the father could potentially use his English to give his son a leg up on basic understanding, but he also might consider whether this might be detrimental. Perhaps he should leave the English to the school when his son begins this as part of the regular curriculum in about the fifth grade. Different families will evaluate this situation in different ways and make different choices about their personal strategies. For this particular family, if the father spoke in English and the son learned English with a strong Turkish accent, this might be inconsequential, but many families prize bilingualism in early youth precisely because it reduces the chances of having an accent.

Accents

It is well established that speaking is contingent on being able to hear—you can't produce a sound with the mouth if you have never perceived it with the ear.[17] When this happens, the brain registers each sound as different electrical impulses, in distinct parts of the brain. In studies of individuals learning foreign languages, István Winklerand and colleagues, who studied Hungarians learning Finnish, noted such distinct neural firings. They concluded that "learning to speak a new language requires the formation of recognition patterns for the speech sounds specific to the newly acquired language."[18] This is one explanation for why foreign language learners often have accents; they simply cannot perceive the subtle sound differences and therefore cannot reproduce them. An example of this can be seen with Japanese speakers who do not differentiate between *r* and *l* or between *fu* and *hu*; Japanese has a single written character for each of these pairs, making it very hard for Japanese native speakers to distinguish them in their own speech within new language.

Another reason people often have accents in a foreign language is that the tongue is a muscle, and it is trained to vocalize sounds in harmony with the throat to reproduce sounds it has practiced. Like other muscles, it can be built up to do things it has not yet practiced. This means that if I "work out" my tongue and ear, I can eventually learn to speak a language without an accent. However, many people don't worry about having an accent; they simply care about communicating a message.

Another key reason for accents relates to the number of sounds in the native language compared with the number of sounds in the second language. Some languages have a large phoneme scale, whereas others have a small one. Japanese has just a few phonemes, making native Japanese speakers highly likely to have accents. This is in contrast with Dutch speakers who have a large number of phonemes in their language, meaning the likelihood they have an accent is fairly low. English has twenty-six letters, which can be combined in approximately 1120 manners to produce forty-nine phonemes. This contrasts with Italian, for example, which has the same twenty-six symbols, but just thirty-three letter combinations to produce twenty-five sounds. This kind of a hierarchy of phonemes implies that if you are a native Swedish speaker, for example, and you want to learn Japanese, the likelihood that you can speak that language without an accent is quite high as you already hear and use all the sounds in the phoneme structure, save one (*tsu*). On the other hand, if you are a native Spanish speaker and you want to learn English, the chances of having an accent are high, because there are several sounds that are used frequently that you have never practiced before, (such as *th*). The total number of phonemes in a person's native language versus the number in subsequent languages influences how likely a person is to have an accent.

Others have demonstrated the importance of language typology in successful, accent-free adult foreign language acquisition. Salim Abu-Rabia and Simona Kehat[19] reviewed the critical period hypothesis, which supposes that people past a certain age will never be able to speak a foreign language without an accent. However, their study documented ten cases of late-starter English-Hebrew bilinguals who learned native-like Hebrew pronunciation in an attempt to challenge the critical hypothesis theory. This study reinforces the belief that people can learn to pronounce sounds in foreign languages without accents even later in life. English and Hebrew share some phonological basis; the likelihood of speaking these languages interchangeably with little accent is high. Similar findings are seen with Dutch and Swedish speakers, whose languages have a very broad phonological band; they are able to speak nearly any other language with little perceptible accent.

Another reason that people have accents is because they like them. As I wrote in *The Multilingual Mind*, "Foreign accents let the listener know that something non-native, unnatural, even difficult is being undertaken," and many people want it to be known that they are going to some trouble to communicate with others in a foreign tongue. Accents are cultural markers that let others know where they are from, which implies something about their beliefs and values. Some people like their accent because it identifies their cultural roots. In the opposite case, it has been noted that some people quickly perfect the native accent in the new target language in order to avoid being identified with a particular group.

This information makes it clear that people have foreign accents for a variety of reasons, some of which are related to age, training of the ear, or practice with the mouth. In other people, the desire to lose foreign accents is more important. Let's return now to the basic stimulation of speaking in young multilingual children.

The Power of Storytelling

We all love a good story, whether read from a book or pulled from the imagination. My kids often ask, "When you were a kid . . . ?" in the hope that I will tell them something about my childhood that they can compare with their own. Some cultures are built around stories. Some Native American Indian groups begin the day telling the stories of their dreams. The Japanese-Americans in Hawaii often "talk story" and swap the news of the day. African cultures and Greek myths built their morality lessons around stories. In a similar vein, storytelling offers us another way to bring a second or third language into a natural context with children. "We know that children are active participants in their acquisition of language. Their language patterns are learned in social contexts while they are interacting with other children and adults. Studies continue to confirm that the development of vocabulary and syntactic complexity in language are more advanced in children who are frequently exposed to a variety of stories."[20]

By sharing stories with our children, and getting them to develop their own, we nurture growing language skills. Storytelling is a powerful tool that parents use instinctively. "What did you do at school today?" we anxiously ask as we pick up the children. We also know to frame these inquires to draw out information: "Did you get to paint again today? Was everybody there, or were some of the children still sick with a cold? How did you like the sandwich I sent you? Was it enough food, or do you want me to give you a yogurt tomorrow? Did Miss Annie say anything about the song you're practicing?" When we give children guidelines for a broad array of responses by asking about a certain part of their school day, we are not only more likely to get an answer from them but are also helping develop a certain domain of vocabulary. If the child attends school in a language that is different from the home language, then this kind of storytelling is an opportunity to build vocabulary and make links between conceptual understandings. For example, when my three-year-old came home from the German School where he had just spent the past five hours and I asked him what color he used to paint the house in his drawing, his mind probably races to the German word. But then, in a split second, he realizes he is speaking to me, and he will rethink his response and seek out these words in English. By telling me the story of his painting, he is reinforcing not only the newly learned German vocabulary, which he reviews in the split second before he responds to me, but he is also applying past knowledge of English and making a conceptual link between the two.

"Human planning abilities may stem from our talent for building narratives. We can borrow the mental structures for syntax to judge combinations of possible actions. To some extent, we do this by talking silently to ourselves, making narratives out of what might happen next and then applying syntax-like rules of combination to rate a scenario as unlikely, possible or likely."[21] This makes listening to the children in our lives as important as instructing or modeling for them. Great parents and teachers know how to bring out narratives from the children themselves. For example, when teachers show children a series of pictures that tell a story, and then ask them, "What do you think happens next?" they are helping students anticipate, project, and plan, while simultaneously developing proper syntax and increasing vocabulary. Similarly, when we get near the end of a story and ask the children what they think will happen next, we are helping them understand the logical course of actions, and encouraging their use of proper language, to express conjecture.

Narratives are also a major foundation for ethical choices. William Calvin believes that "we imagine a course of action and its effects on others, then decide whether or not to do it."[22] When my son was seven, I recall that he once brought home a series of three pictures. His homework was to draw the fourth picture and write the ending to the story. The first picture showed a boy carrying his books and a sandwich. The second picture showed the boy's sandwich falling on to the ground as he tried to balance the books and his food without success. The third picture showed a group of children pointing and laughing at the boy who was staring sadly at his sandwich on the ground. This simple series of pictures sparked off a very long conversation as my son thought about the various things that could or should happen next. We talked about how the boy must be feeling. We discussed what the other children were doing, and why. Then he told me several ways the story could end. After several minutes of possible and probable ideas floating around, he (thankfully) decided that another child would walk by and pick up the sandwich and give it back to the boy, and offer to share his lunch as well. This was an ethical and morality-building exercise, mediated through language. After deciding on the ending, he drew the picture and then wrote his response in German, meaning that this critical thinking, ethics-forming exercise was also a writing lesson in a foreign language.

Many of us can remember how we as children listened to teachers or our parents read to us. Before being able to read on our own, all of us were read to. One of my favorite activities as a child was the weekly visit to the public library, where the librarian would pull out a delicious book with colorful pictures and read to us. Similarly, I remember Ms. Houston, my fourth grade teacher, saving Friday afternoons for a good book in the corner of our classroom. Reading stories aloud to small children can help instill a love of literature at an early age and creates a habit of mind about how messages are stored through written text. Stories help children develop predictive skills about logic and order as well as enhance vocabulary and identify salient aspects of life narratives. Storybook reading in multilingual and multicultural classrooms is also a way of enhancing recall. Parents and teachers can pause at different points in the book and ask about things that occurred on previous pages, giving children the chance to use appropriate vocabulary, and stimulating their working memory. This carries over into the next stage of development in which school-age children begin to learn to read, which we'll turn to next.

Strangely enough, when taken with the insights about the complexities of language in the brain, being able to speak a language without an accent remains a more prized goal than being able to read in a foreign language, which is cerebrally a far more challenging mental task. The distinction between spoken forms of language and reading show complementary yet distinct systems, and they are explained in the following section as we look into the elementary years.

ELEMENTARY SCHOOL YEARS (6–12): WHY LANGUAGE IS A GAME WHERE WE CAN ALL LEARN THE RULES

Learning foreign languages can seem like a lofty goal to adults. The more we know about languages, the more daunting a task it appears. Luckily young children do not know enough to be scared. As I wrote in *Raising Multilingual Children*, small children have small egos and this is a generally wonderful time to introduce a second language to a monolingual child, or a third language to an already bilingual child.

Small children treat language as a code to be broken or a game to be played. Like a game, children gather up all the pieces they have handy and make up the rules as they go along. After they start to play they are corrected by their peers or parents and so modify these rules until they perfect their game. Learning to speak is a game in which the child is guided by parents, and then friends and teachers. By the time the child enters school, the game becomes more complex, and although the rules never change, the level of difficulty does.

In the elementary years children may continue with imaginary play, but this slowly gives way to other more formal structured games, which can also lead to language enhancement. For example, giving kids *The Game of Life* or *Monopoly* in the target language gives them practice reading and following directions. Games can also enhance peer teaching, which we will see more in Chapter 7. A scene I witnessed between children went something like this:

Tomás:	"You got a four: move ahead four spaces and take a card."
Geronimo:	"It says, 'If you own electric utilities pay a $50 tax.' What's a *utilities*?"
Tomás:	"It's like the gas and the water thing you just bought. You gotta pay $50!"

Tomás subtly teaches Geronimo new vocabulary and models correct sentence patterns. While not the Webster's Dictionary, as they make their way around the board, what Tomás says will probably stay in Geronimo's mind far longer than the dictionary definition of "utilities." Informal peer instruction is one of the most powerful ways of getting young learners to use language in appropriate ways. Parents often ask me if they should pay a tutor to give their young children extra classes in the target language, and I tell them they would be far better off taking time to arrange play dates. In the elementary years, one of the best sources of language instruction comes from the natural interactions children share with similar aged peers. Good schools also know this and their curriculum structures encourage authentic learning experiences that model natural peer exchanges.

Formal Schooling

There is general consensus that theme-based syllabi are more effective than traditional grammatical syllabi when teaching foreign languages. This is not to say that grammar should not be taught, but rather that the lessons should gravitate around themes rather than points of grammar. This is something that both parents and teachers should take advantage of when trying to promote the use of second or subsequent languages. Rather than insisting that Johnny read in Spanish (or Thai or Arabic or Swahili), why not encourage him to learn more about soccer (or dinosaurs or trains or animals) in that target language? This way parents and teachers use the natural interest of the child and the language is merely a vehicle toward learning. In pedagogical terms this means the structure is based on two basic ideas: syllabi should be "based on systemic versus schematic knowledge in language learning" and founded on a "two-dimensional concept of language proficiency, involving basic interpersonal/communicative skills and cognitive/academic language proficiency."[23] This method guides learning through authentic activities in which students see immediate applicability for their studies. We have all heard (and probably said so ourselves), "When will I ever use *that* in my life?" When children learn a new language they need to see its immediate applicability, usefulness, or benefit in order to maintain a high level of motivation for the task. Although this is true for any subject taught in school, language has the distinct advantage over other areas in that our world is mediated through language, meaning it should be easy to find applications in real life.

Language is also played at several different "levels." Babies first begin to babble in reaction to the sounds they hear around them; they gain their first words in their languages and move on to learning to read and, the toughest level of all, write. Whereas speaking is something *Homo sapiens* have done for thousands of years, reading and writing are relatively "new" skills in the human repertoire. We will now turn to literacy, the highest level of language.

Reading in First and Second Languages

We take reading and writing for granted in our school systems. What we often forget is that the expectation that all people will learn literacy skills is just three or four generations old. Before that time, reading and writing were limited to the educated elite and to the clergy. It is rather recent that all people, poor and rich, lower as well as upper class, are expected to learn how to read and write. Adamson and colleagues reported extensively at the *European Conference on Reading*, which sought to clarify the relationship between reading, writing, and thinking. They pointed out that although verbal communication has been part of human exchange for thousands of years, the expectation that average citizens should reach levels of universal literacy is only about two hundred years old. As a "new" cognitive task, the location of reading in the brain is of particular interest to evolutionary biologists, who can actually trace the changes that have occurred in the human brain due to the demands of reading and writing, something we will explore further in Chapter 6.

In cross-linguistic studies, it has been documented that literate societies train children to read sometime between three and eight years of age. Americans and the British seem to push literacy earliest, with many programs teaching preliteracy skills starting as early as infancy, and formally by around three-and-a-half. The Nordic countries tend to begin later, and generally begin teaching literacy skills around age eight. Interestingly enough, it has been documented that by the age of nine there is virtually no difference in the accuracy with which children read between these two extremes. That is, learning to read at three or learning to read at eight makes no difference in the level of reading by age nine.

Two basic schools of thought drive literacy policy around the world, phonics and whole language. Phonics basically treats languages as a code: teach the code, and then teach the student to decipher it. Whole language asks learners to approach the text as a single entity, filling in gaps of understanding through context. Although extremely popular in the United States in the 1990s, whole language is giving way to phonics at present (it is interesting to note that the Europeans never abandoned the phonics approach). It is no wonder that recent studies confirm the efficiency of phonics as compared with whole language. Constance Holden reported in *Science* that tutoring students in phonics actually changed the way brains were wired for language. This article documented the Yale study by Sally Shaywitz and Bennett Shaywitz, which imaged the brains of poor readers aged six to nine years old as they underwent an intensive eight months of phonics as opposed to the whole language approach. They found that the children gained ground through the use of phonics, which had long-lasting results, as compared with whole language approaches, and that the physical structure of language areas of their brain changed through the process. Some researchers have accepted these findings and have tried to adapt teaching methodologies to respond to the poor reader by concentrating on the social context of learning how to read.

Materials That Enhance Reading Motivation

Landis reported in the *Reading & Writing Quarterly* that when the context of the reading material was more closely related to the lives of the children being taught, their motivation to learn was higher. This finding has implications for the selection of initial reading material for emergent readers and refers to a broader area of educational development concerning multiliteracy skills. This means that success hinges on the ability of children to relate to what they are reading. Books that children connect with personally stimulate more interest than books about places or things that they have no connections to. This reminds me of the English textbooks used in Lima, Peru, which were filled with vocabulary and pictures of snowstorms and rain. There is less than a third of an inch of rainfall a year in Lima. Many of the children had a very hard time digesting the vocabulary related to English winter weather, let alone snowstorms, as they had no point of reference to these concepts in their real lives.

This leads to two pieces of advice for parents and teachers of new readers. Choose books by focusing on the content or theme of ideas, and when possible, remember that the more emotionally engaging the books are for the children, the more likely they are to read them. This means different things to different people. My son Gabriel fell in love with the *Guinness Book of World Records* series, which he first received in Spanish in 2003. The next year I bought the book in German and he continued to be engrossed by all of the strange facts and stories. The following year we returned to Spanish, and the next year back to German. In this way, we were able to encourage extra reading time in his target languages through a specific interest area he had.

Other responses to multiliteracy demands have emerged as a result of technology. Cruickshank found that youngsters in Sydney, Australia, who spoke Arabic at home were aided more in their emerging reading skills by the Internet than by their parents. Such self-directed structures suggest that home language reading skills can be developed as elaborately as school language reading if and when the individual feels sufficiently motivated to use technology as a surrogate classroom for such skills. I have watched some of my children's friends experiment with language via e-mail and messages before opening their mouths to speak. For example, some of my daughter's friends in Switzerland recently began formally studying English in school. Their usual message chats suddenly changed from

Spanish to English as they sought to apply what they were learning in the classroom to their real life contexts. These friends have never attempted to speak to my daughter in English, however.

Reading involves the mind's ability to perceive symbols, relate them to a "code," interpret their sounds, and then combine them with other symbols to create words and eventually derive meaning, all through the filter of a second language lens. Although this is challenging, it is actually less so than the feat of writing, which we will now explain.

MIDDLE SCHOOL YEARS (12–15): THE TEACHER IS THE KEY, BUT DOES SHE KNOW THE BEST WAYS TO TEACH FOREIGN LANGUAGES?

Writing is a mental challenge in any language. To give an example, we will speak about a specific group of students in the United States who must learn a second language. We should remember that there are two large and distinct groupings of people who learn to read in a foreign language in the U.S. public school system, though similar situations can be found around the world. First, there are individuals who are native English speakers who must learn a foreign language as a school requirement, and, second, there are non-native English language speaking students who join the school system in their teen years. Let's explore the U.S. example further.

Unlike other industrialized nations that begin second language instruction in primary school and through oral skills, the U.S. public schools leave foreign language instruction to middle or high school and link literacy skills to oral skills. Not only does this put Americans at a disadvantage for learning a new language but it also requires a great deal of creativity on the part of teachers to maintain student interest and attention at this age compared with younger learners who are often more willing to participate. We will turn to this later. First, let's consider the second population of students: immigrant English-language learners who arrive in an English-speaking school and begin learning to speak, read, and write in English. This population is also at a disadvantage as compared with their younger peers because the older the child, the bigger the ego. As students get older, they are less likely to jump into the cold shower of integration of a new language. Judith Rich Harris writes that it is also more likely that peers guide each other's choices the older they get, as humans are social beings. It is for this reason that researchers such as Lies Sercu suggest that teaching foreign languages is not only a linguistic task, but teachers "are now required to teach intercultural communicative competence,"[24] meaning rote grammar lessons and spelling tests on irregular verbs are *not* at the heart of good teaching. Good language teachers understand that learning their subject for its own sake is no longer good enough; best practice related to creating significant learning experiences means that the information students take in best is colored by their perception of its usefulness. Whereas it was previously acceptable to ask students to do things because "the teacher knows best," nowadays, teachers are responding to the demands of a savvier student body. Paloma Castro and colleagues at the Universidad de Valladolid in Spain write that foreign language instruction used to be mainly tied to teaching a linguistic code against the backdrop of a majority culture, but now "teaching has reflected on language and culture in an integrated way with a view to preparing learners to use the foreign language in intercultural contact situations."[25] This trend in teaching means that more great teachers are applying the "sense versus meaning" rule[26] to classes: the course structure, order of concepts, and information needs to not only make sense to the learner but it also needs to have meaning in the student's life.

This means foreign language instruction demands more creativity than it used to. One of my favorite article titles of all time was written by Patricia Heasley, a Pennsylvania librarian: "Reading and language arts worksheets don't grow dendrites."[27] Such a comment takes a stab at the common practice in multilingual classrooms of giving students worksheets upon worksheets until the hour finishes, which she argues should be banned from serious classrooms. Some believe that a social cultural approach to learning strategies is best suited to mixed language classrooms. The social cultural approach consists of "children's mediation of their own and each other's language learning within and across languages, focusing on strategies that support learning." In dual language programs, for example, the goal is centered on the children's ongoing negotiation of how to learn, giving the student control over certain aspects of his or her work and making each assignment personally important. Middle school children thrive on control, and by giving them space to elect some of their own materials, teachers can appeal to their independent nature.

A spin-off of this concept is peer teaching. Caroline Linse and Kathleen White describe a project they conducted in an elementary school in which fourth grade students who spoke English as their second language (ESL) taught monolingual English speakers about language diversity. The bilingual children visited the monolingual children and told stories about how it felt to learn a new language. By instilling empathy from monolingual peers, ESL students gained emotional ground and self-confidence in their own skills by speaking in English to their peers and sharing the challenges and successes of the bilingual students.

Technology in the Middle School Classroom

Let's face it, our children are far more versed in technological issues than we are. Although it is prudent to be cautious about how far we want to let computers take over the classroom, we have to admit that there is some pretty amazing software out there, and the truth of the matter is that our children's teachers are often not as entertaining as some of those programs. The application of some of these programs and the use of digital media in multilingual classrooms are in infantile stages, but their potential is great. Some school districts are investing in software that helps overcrowded classroom situations by giving the teacher a chance to work individually with some children while the others are gainfully occupied on foreign-language learning tasks. When resources permit, technology can be a great help to teachers. Alison Taylor, Elisabeth Lazarus, and Ruth Cole share a brilliant idea in which English speakers who were learning to write in German were given feedback by their teachers via computers: "Students used a simple yet highly effective electronic learning tool to facilitate extended, more complex, more accurate and more imaginative writing."[28] Some argue that the new dynamics of virtual classrooms lead to freer expression by students and a greater level of experimentation, which enhances the level of learning.

Other successful activities with middle school students include the use of authentic texts and narrow reading to enhance interest levels. The use of self-selected reading material, including newspapers, can help middle school students develop a sense of autonomy about their language. Terry Meier believes that "children learn to use language in culturally specific ways" and encourages teachers to link children to their texts. This could, for example, take shape as a search for a certain verb tense as found in fashion or sports magazines in the target language. Or it could take the form of students submitting a letter to an advice column of a local newspaper. Eventually, this can move from popular press to book assignments. Meier writes that by "choosing books that relate to children's lives; teaching book reading behaviors explicitly; and making books come alive," teachers can make foreign languages more directly related to the lives of students.[29] This implies that teachers know how to integrate a certain level of choice in assignments, something many authors point to as part of authentic learning experiences.

Patrick Manyak of the Department of Elementary and Early Childhood at the University of Wyoming suggests that encouraging bilingual students to engage in translation in the classroom also represents a practical and powerful way to draw on linguistically diverse students' sociocultural resources to facilitate their language and literacy learning. We know that translation activities involve negotiation with words and push children to seek out new vocabulary, making such tasks highly beneficial to the learner. For example, a bilingual class newsletter would help students improve writing skills, help students learn vocabulary in both languages, and help those that do the translation improve their own bilingual skills. By translating each other's work, a deeper metalinguistic awareness of all languages is also stimulated.

Struggling readers are bound to be struggling writers, says Gail Tompkins. To stem this problem in multilingual classrooms she suggests that (1) teaching the writing process, (2) participating in writing workshops, (3) sharing published writings, (4) teaching mini-lessons on writing skills, and (5) providing support and guidance for students will ensure that writing becomes a celebrated classroom activity.[30] This is very similar to suggestions from other authors in which they encourage sharing final writing projects by internal class publishing or public postings. This enhances self-esteem in emerging—as well as proficient—language learners. Such an activity is basically cost-free (the cost of a tack on a wall), but it does wonders to boost the self-esteem of language learners and their motivation to continually improve. This is very much in line with what other experienced researchers in the field say. Cummins and colleagues assure us that by affirming the identities of English language learners, they are increasing the confidence with which these students engage in language and literacy activities.[31] These authors believe that improved school achievement is a byproduct of "identity investment." In the middle school years parents and teachers need to remember that self-esteem is deeply correlated with language success. How a child feels about his or her own identity as a multilingual impacts learning for the rest of his or her life. We will explore this further as we view language in the high school years.

HIGH SCHOOL YEARS (16–18): MOTIVATION, SENSE, AND MEANING IN FOREIGN-LANGUAGE LEARNING

In the high school years, research points to three crucial steps in foreign language success. The teacher's ability to relate to the students, the enhancement of critical thinking skills through language, and the creation of authentic learning experiences are all important in creating learning environments that are stimulating to older teens. Each of these aspects is briefly described below.

Student-Teacher Relations

Zoltan Dörnyei is a well-known author in the field of foreign-language learning and a proponent of differentiated teaching methodologies. He believes three things must be kept in mind when teaching a student a foreign language. The teacher must consider the learner's (1) personality, (2) ability/aptitude/intelligence, and (3) motivation, mood, temperance, attitude, and values. Too often, teachers rely too heavily on textbooks and do not take enough time to get to know their learners, which Dörnyei says is a mistake. Although personally getting to know students is one of the most time-consuming aspects of teaching, it is the only sincere way to understand student personalities, abilities, aptitudes, intelligences, motivations, moods, temperance, attitudes, and values. By considering the needs of learners at each of these levels, Dörnyei has documented how teachers can become more effective in their practice. This view is hard on "old school" teachers who feel that their job is simply to deliver the subject matter. It was common belief just a generation ago that teachers fed students information, and the students needed to do the work. In other words, the teacher should not be obliged to know the students, only their grades. This belief has changed drastically in recent times, mainly because of our growing understanding of the learning process.

Enhancing Critical Thinking

Another general practice that serves high school students well is enhancing critical thinking skills throughout the language learning process. Critical thinking means getting students to move beyond superficial knowledge (memorization of terms, grammar, and vocabulary) and to seek deeper, enduring understanding about language (what it means to communicate in another language). Through the art of questioning, teachers can help students elevate their level of thinking. In her article entitled "What If and Why? Literacy Invitations for Multilingual Classrooms," Sara Simonson points out that good teachers are always sure to posit *What if?* and *Why?* questions in order to make ordinary conversations extraordinary learning experience.[32] When students were challenged to use language in this way, classroom experiences were made more authentic and the language used is more sophisticated. Critical thinking should exist in all facets of education, but it plays a special role in high school language classes in which there are hundreds of opportunities per class to capitalize on developing this kind of logic. Teachers aren't the only ones to guide students in this way, however. Parents play a tremendous role in their children's learning experiences. By modeling good critical thinking, parents can help children. This means parents should ask children questions for which there are no right or wrong answers. For example, instead of saying, "Did you like the movie?" say, "What did you like about the movie?" These subtle word variations in the daily exchanges we have with our children elevate their level of thinking.

An overall best practice concept in foreign-language learning is called content-based instruction (CBI). CBI views "the target language largely as the vehicle through which subject matter content is learned rather than as the immediate object of study."[33] This means "an approach to language instruction that integrates the presentation of topics or tasks from subject matter classes (e.g., math, social studies) within the context of teaching a second or foreign language."[34] CBI is also what most successful bilingual or international schools do. The curriculum of these schools uses language as the means of teaching another subject. For example, if Mario studies math in Spanish, the Spanish language is learned through the math subject.

Authentic Learning Experiences

In his book, *Creating Significant Learning Experiences*, L. Dee Fink writes extensively about his belief that there is no academic growth without personal growth. To be successful, teachers must know their students well. Understanding differences in student personalities means knowing who the introverted and extroverted students are, who is likely to lead and who will follow, and who prefers intuiting information versus who needs to sense it, creating learning experiences that cater to all learning styles. By identifying and then meeting individual growth goals, teachers give students the power to achieve academically as well.

High school students are social creatures. It is logical to presume that activities that cater to this need for social interaction will also enhance language. For example, theater activities are a brilliant way of getting students to fall in love with another language while building up tremendous self-confidence. Theater activities stretch the learner to cross psychological boundaries with their language(s).[35] Not only does theater push students to their limits of self-confidence by making them perform in front of others, it also teaches them to express themselves in another language in an appropriate way. Through performances about overarching cross-cultural themes, students learn the appropriate contexts, body language, facial expressions, and tones of voice that accompany different exchanges. Theater performances are also team-building activities. Being a part of a group with a single purpose is a great way to learn language in a dynamic way that engages high school students on linguistic, psychological, and social levels. This is supported by findings by Nilsen and Nilsen, who feel that "there is nothing more motivating than to feel you have something to contribute to a group situation." They encourage "activities that teach all students about the connections between languages"[36] and to each other. Theater has the ability to teach human lessons that override individual cultural beliefs. Such themes as honesty, loyalty, responsibility, citizenry, respect, trust, and caring cross cultural boundaries and are understood in all languages. Using theater to bring these messages to others develops a type of vocabulary all students should possess. By linking authentic learning experiences based on solid content, such as a theater production, second language teachers are more likely to be successful in creating significant and long lasting learning experiences for high school students. Other authentic experiences include travel to other countries, if possible.

Some high school students are given the opportunity to study abroad and live with a host family in another culture. Thousands of American high school students participate in international student exchanges every semester, and language is often one of the primary goals for which they go abroad. Speaking from my own personal experience as a Youth For Understanding exchange student to Japan when I was sixteen, I can say that it is very hard to match the intensity and reward of using a language in its authentic country context.

Many study abroad programs are subsidized, and some even often scholarships for highly qualified learners. If this is an option for students, it is a highly recommended language experience. Other study abroad programs are promoted through the university system in which "Junior Year Abroad" has become more and more common. We will turn next to the challenges and opportunities of learning a foreign language at the university level.

UNIVERSITY YEARS (18–24): THE MARKETABILITY OF MULTILINGUALS

Many people who have not had the opportunity to learn a language earlier in life realize the value of a foreign language when they are in college. As we saw in Chapter 2, there is growing demand for people in all professions to communicate in other languages. Although this demand is led by corporations, other professions, such as medicine and the technology fields, also value multilinguals and prize them for these skills. Traditional fields, such as the diplomatic and military corps, translators, and educators, continue to encourage professionals in their fields to be able to manage at least one language other than English. There is a huge demand for teachers willing to go abroad who have foreign language experience. The trend for international school growth is widening and will only continue to expand in the foreseeable future.

Some university students are wary of the prospect of learning a language "late" in life, because they have heard if they did not learn another language as children, it will be painfully hard as adults. There is no doubt that there are distinct neural mechanisms that accompany different-age learners, as we discussed earlier in this chapter, but linguists have actually demonstrated that adults are far more efficient than children when learning a new language. Such news is encouraging if it is understood thoroughly.

How Children and Adults Differ When They Learn Foreign Languages

It is indisputable that adults learn languages differently from children and that children appear, in terms of brain use, to be more efficient, but it is also acknowledged that humans can and do learn languages across the lifespan with success. Shiro Ojima, Hiro Nakata, and Ryusuke Kakigi of the National Institute for Physiological Sciences in Okazaki, Japan, studied the process of postchildhood second-language learning by comparing event related brain potentials, a type of brain imaging technique.[37] They found that some aspects of language appear to follow similar processing patterns in early and late bilinguals, although others were distinct. They demonstrated that equal language efficiency could be achieved through multiple channels in the brain. University students should not hesitate to undertake a second or third language based on their age.

Ojima and colleagues studied university-age students learning a second language as they perceived new sounds. It was not surprising that they found that increased repetition decreased brain activity. That is, the more rehearsed the function, the less energy it takes to distinguish different sounds. This means that during relatively early stages of acquiring a second language the brain works harder and shows greater activation when hearing the native language alone or the second language alone consistently. Presumably late learners need to "get their head into" a foreign or native language mind frame to do well on this task. It was also found that during early learning stages, priming using the second language followed by first language translation was more effective in teaching new sounds. Adult learners rely more heavily on the native language translation to consolidate new learning than a child brought up bilingual from birth, for example. In contrast, during late stages of learning, first language words followed by second language priming were most effective. This means as the brain becomes more accustomed to the new language it is most helpful to go from the native language to the new language, rather than vice versa.

University students learn best with the following system. In early stages of learning, hearing the new word and then its translations helps the learning process. In the later stages, using the native language to prompt the new language works best. This shows two key differences between how infants perceive new language sounds as compared with how adults perceive new language sounds. This also proves that infants' strategies for learning new speech sounds rely on first language brain areas, whereas adults use different areas of the brain to perceive new sounds. New learning for both infants and adults relies on first perceiving the new sounds and then relating that sound to a concept. That is, giving a sound a lexical label is subsequent to distinguishing the sound in the first place. This seems a reasonable finding if we presume that one cannot assign a meaning to a sound (or group of sounds) if those sounds are not first perceived. University-age learners are typically in an academic environment. How do other older adult learners, who may not have the luxury of a stimulating university environment, cope with new languages? We turn to older adult learners next.

ADULT FOREIGN-LANGUAGE LEARNING (24+): WHY ADULTS LEARN LANGUAGES DIFFERENTLY

Research says that given the same language, an adult will learn faster than a child. Although children may be more efficient at using their brain when it comes to language, adults can actually use what they know about their first language to speed up their learning in the second language. The difficulties adults may face when learning a second language do not have to do with grammar, or at least it is not any more problematic for an adult than a child; adults and children tend to learn vocabulary and syntax at similar rates. Michael Ullman assures us that "evidence suggests that native-like abilities in L2 [second language] can indeed be attained, even for grammar."[38] The real problem for adults is related to phonology, or accents. As we discussed in the previous section on accents, this is a small but distinguishable area of language expertise in which adults and children differ.

Children are often "forced" or coerced into learning foreign languages either due to family structures, moves, or as a course requirement at school. Adults that I have known, on the other hand, take on a foreign language for different reasons. Some adults feel highly motivated to learn a new language because they are emotionally attached to someone who speaks that language. Others may want to learn a language as a hobby. Still others have jobs for which promotions require knowledge of another language. The biggest distinction between children and adults in terms of motivation, then, is that children are bound to a social structure in which learning the new language is central to their integration, whereas adults tend to take on languages either as a hobby (for which there is no external pressure), for work (for which there is basically only external pressure), or for love (for which there is positive internal motivation). Given what we know about learning, positive internal motivation leads to the best learning. This is why adults who fall in love with a native speaker of another language are more likely to be successful than a person who needs to learn Chinese for a job promotion. How can we find ways to make the obliged language learning situations of most adults convert into an intrinsically motivated endeavor? It's important to know first how adults learn, and, second, to analyze whether those needs are met through current learning options.

How Do Adults Learn Best?

Dorothy Billington proposes seven characteristics of highly effective adult learning environments that are easy to imagine in the language learning context. She believes that adults learn best when they (1) feel safe (both physically and psychologically), (2) enjoy intellectual freedom, (3) give and receive respect, (4) are allowed to be somewhat self-directed, (5) are provided with paced challenges, (6) enjoy participative learning activities, and (7) receive constant quality feedback. With little imagination, most of these characteristics of a good learning environment for adults can be easily adapted to the multilingual classroom. Educators Carl Rogers and Jerome Freiberg speculate that given the freedom to learn, adults will be able to do so. Adult educator Sharan Merriam identified this as a call for self-directed activities. Whereas self-directedness appears to be beneficial to all learners, adults and children alike, adults are better at managing this freedom. For example, it is one thing to create a self-directed learning experience with adults in which the mentor provides limited guidance and allows the adult to craft an assignment to their liking, and quite another to give a four-year-old a self-directed activity in which far more scaffolding would be required. This highlights the importance of models and mentors in human learning for children as well as adults.

Laurent Daloz believes that adults learn best through mentoring situations, in which desired behavior, knowledge, or skills are modeled. He writes that adults can be transformed by such experiences, and he places a great deal of emphasis on how mentors come into adult learner's lives. The powerful impact of mentors cannot be disputed, and in the multilingual context this takes the shape of instructors or other models in the learner's life who demonstrate abilities that the learner desires, such as fluently holding a conversation in another language.

Assessment of Adult Learners

One of the main differences between pedagogy (teaching children) and andragogy (teaching adults) is that evaluation in adult learning is more collaborative, and self-assessment often plays a greater role. This means that adult learners often want to be a part of the development of the criteria by which they are being judged, or at a minimum, informed clearly about how they will be graded. Many adults tend to exercise high levels of critical thinking, and it is easy to engage them in self-assessment exercises and independent projects as well. Adults are far better than children at self-regulation and the ability to stay on target during the learning processes.

Jack Mezirow, perhaps one of the greatest figures in adult education, believes that the heart of successful adult learning is in transforming the learner. This means that if languages transport the learner to a higher mental ground, or transforms his worldview, then the learner will pursue that knowledge. It might be hard to find situations in which learning a foreign language for work would give us such a pleasant jolt, unless we are learning languages out of love or a feeling of self-realization. Some language packages or adult learning programs try to capitalize on this sense of self-realization and accomplishment. They do so by trying to stimulate the learner's own identification and self-identified needs and capitalizing on the goals attached with learning a new language. For example, the texts in these programs are full of useful vocabulary and dialogues that are helpful in managing work situations, which brings us back to what we know about the importance of authentic experiences.

SUMMARY

In summary, successful adult language-learning programs do seven basic things well. They (1) need to show the student how the information will meet needs, (2) give the freedom to evaluate progress, (3) respect the student on equal status with the professor, (4) value the learner's past experiences and what they can bring to the class, (5) allow students participation in their own goal-setting, (6) give students the possibility of working with strong mentors, and (7) teach within a positive environment.

Foreign languages can be learned throughout the lifespan. Each age group has different learning strategies that can be employed to maximize potential, whether being bilingual from birth or learning a new language in elementary school, middle school, high school, university, or beyond. There are many reasons in favor of starting foreign language instruction early, but there is also evidence that no matter what your age, foreign languages are an achievable goal and multilingualism across the lifespan is attainable. In the next chapter we will consider how long it actually takes a non-native speaker to become fluent.

How Long Does It Take a Non-Native Speaker to Become Fluent in a Second, Third, or Subsequent Language?

LANGUAGE FOR SCHOOL, LANGUAGE FOR PLAY

This chapter is devoted to the questions on every parent's lips and in every teacher's mind as they work with multilingual children: How long does it really take to become fluent in a foreign language? Is my child normal? Should I seek help? Is it time to give up? In this chapter we review the evidence and offer guidelines about the normal time frame for language acquisition. We will also look at the process of learning multiliteracy skills and how this also impacts the speed with which people reach their fluency goals in a foreign language.

Acquiring a Second Language for School

There is a distinction between languages used for play and verbal information-sharing situations and languages used for school or academics. First, language used in play is primarily verbal and supported by visual cues, whereas language for school requires a literacy aspect and is often de-contextualized. To make matters even more complex, learning a second language for school is not just a linguistic challenge; it poses social and cultural obstacles as well. When children learn languages solely for academic purposes, they often miss emotional links to language, including personally relevant ties that made learning their first languages so easy. The time it takes a child to learn to play in a new language is far less than the time it takes to learn a second language for school. Jim Cummins found that on average, it takes approximately two years to reach native language fluency orally, though this is highly influenced by the age and motivation level of the learner. The same study showed that it takes a child between five and seven years to reach native language fluency in an academic setting. That is, although verbal skills are relatively quick to form, literacy skills require far longer cultivating. And according to Wayne Thomas and Virginia Collier, "Research shows that even the most effective programs require five to six years to bring English learners to full parity with average native English speakers in English proficiency and in mastery of the curriculum to high standards."[1]

Why does it take double or even triple the amount of time to learn a language for school than for simple social exchanges? One of the reasons is probably because verbal, playground language is supported by clues, such as gestures, facial expressions, and intonations, whereas reading and writing are experienced without a specific context. For example, read the following sentence: "I am pregnant." Can you think of at least three different intonations you can apply that would change the significance completely? Surprise? Doubt? Excitement? Without the context in which this is said, the written words might mean many things. To complicate matters even further for English language learners, Simon Elmes notes that a majority of English verbal language is actually of Anglo-Saxon origin, whereas written English is primarily Graeco-Latin based (see Table 4.1). This means that although a child may speak English fluently, there is no guarantee he or she will write it fluently because the foundations are actually different in each case.

Table 4.1   Verbal versus Written Language

	Oral Skills (Basic Communication)	Literacy Skills (Academic)
Time[1]	Average two years to reach native language equivalent (however, this is highly influenced by the age and motivation of the learner)	Average five to seven years to reach native language equivalent
Definition[2]	Playground language	Classroom language
Characteristics[3]	Supported by interpersonal cues such as gestures, facial expressions and intonation	De-contextualized language
Origins	Anglo-Saxon	Graeco-Latin

Sources: 1. Cummins (1993); 2. Gibbins (1999); 3. Elmes (2000). Tokuhama-Espinosa 2007.

These findings draw attention to at least two important questions: (1) Does the structure of our school's language program lend itself to five to seven years of study (if, indeed, the goal is fluency in a foreign language)? (2) Are we as parents patient enough to give the children the time they need to achieve academic language, or should we be content with verbal skills? In the first case, schools need to recognize that they cannot expect to produce students with high-level academic language skills if they do not provide the time, space, and personnel in the curriculum. In the second case, parents cannot expect a child to develop literacy skills at the same rapid pace at which they develop oral skills. Other evidence about the time it takes for people to learn languages based on the level of difficulty comes from the American Foreign Service Language Institute.

The Language Research Center of the University of Calgary conducted a review of the literature on second language learning. Their document includes a table based on the Foreign Service Institute (FSI) of the U.S. Department of State's evaluation of the length of time it takes for a native English language speaker to become fluent in different languages. This is an intriguing table that has been developed over several decades, and it deserves attention. It should be kept in mind, however, that it is applicable to the average Foreign Service Institute student, who is profiled as being almost forty years old, with high aptitude and experience studying foreign languages. Those enrolled in the program take the course intensely, twenty-three to eighty-eight weeks straight for several hours daily. This is an interesting guide, but parents and teachers of "regular" students in school should realize that the circumstances for learning are very different for this group than for their children. According to the University of Calgary report, the FSI's "240 hours correspond to approximately three years of [regular class] instruction, while 480 hours correspond to five years."[2] This is an interesting addition to the information about how long it takes for someone to become fluent in a foreign language, because it is actually longer than the five to seven years indicated by Cummins in the study mentioned previously. This is presumably because learners in the FSI program are expected to reach full, native-like fluency and literacy skills in the language. According to the FSI, language difficulties are ranked as follows (Table 4.2):

Table 4.2   Language Difficulty for English Speakers

Category I: Languages somewhat related to English 23–24 weeks (240–720 class hours)		
Afrikaans	French	Portuguese
Creole	Haitian	Romanian
Danish	Italian	Spanish
Dutch	Norwegian	Swedish

Category II: Languages with some significant linguistic and/or cultural differences from English 23–24 weeks (480–1,320 class hours)		
Bulgarian	Hindi	Persian (Dari, Farsi, Tajik)
German	Indonesian	Swahili
Greek	Malay	Urdu

Category III: Languages with significant linguistic and/or cultural differences from English 44 weeks (1,100 class hours)		
Albanian	Hebrew	Serbo-Croatian
Amharic	*Hungarian	Sinhalese
Armenian	Icelandic	Slovak
Azerbaijani	Khmer	Slovenian
Bengali	Lao	Tamil
Bosnian	Latvian	Tagalog
Burmese	Lithuanian	*Thai
Croatian	Macedonian	Turkish
Czech	*Mongolian	Ukrainian
*Estonian	Nepali	Uzbek
*Finnish	Pashto	*Vietnamese
*Georgian	Polish	Xhosa
Greek	Russian	Zulu

Category IV: Languages that are exceptionally difficult for native English speakers 88 weeks (second year of study in-country) (2,200 class hours)		
Arabic	*Japanese	Mandarin
Cantonese	Korean	

According to the Foreign Service Language Institute, the languages preceded with asterisks are slightly more difficult for native English speakers than other languages in the same category. This information is interesting to consider, but it should not be used as a definitive guide unless the learner's characteristics are identical to those of the Foreign Service Institute students.

How Long?

In an interesting longitudinal study of U.S. bilingual programs, Collier and Thomas sought to find a correlation between the type of English-language program a student participated in and the number of years it took to reach native-like fluency. They confirmed hunches by others in the field that most effective English-learning programs in U.S. schools were dual-immersion programs. They found it took children an average of five to seven years to reach native-level test scores and perform academically on par with English-speaking peers. This implies that a child could begin as a five-year-old Spanish speaker in an English school and by age twelve have a level of English language fluency similar to the native English speakers. It also means that a Spanish speaker could start learning English at ten years of age but would not reach native-language proficiency until seventeen years old. Or, the student could start as a teenager, say fifteen years old, but would not reach proficiency with native English-speaking peers until twenty-two years old (and only if continuing language instruction past high school in a formal, structured setting). Although these studies were conducted in the United States and based on English-language learners only, they provide an interesting platform for discussion about the way foreign language programs are designed around the world.

Some schools provide mother-tongue instructional support for students, which has proven to be very effective in obtaining spin-off benefits in academic achievement. Other schools teach the second language through academic content, which has also been proven as one of the best ways to support both subject content knowledge and second language content. General coaching in critical thinking and problem-solving skills has become popular among schools in the past decade, and such skills not only benefit the average student but also deeply enhance the second-language learner's ability to develop metalinguistic awareness about languages possessed. Additional recommendations from Collier are that "continuous support for staff development emphasizing activation of students' prior knowledge, respect for students' home language and culture, cooperative learning, interactive and discovery learning, intense and meaningful cognitive/academic development, and ongoing assessment using multiple measures"[3] all contribute to the speed with which students reach fluency in a second language. We will see more specific strategies, methodologies, and activities in Chapter 7, but for now, suffice it to say that successful language programs also incorporate a variety of activities that include authentic reading material, stimulate the multiple intelligences, value the learner's cultural background, and use all these for a basis of instruction.

PREDICTORS OF RAPID FOREIGN LANGUAGE SUCCESS

There have been dozens of studies about the possible predictors related to foreign language learning and achievement within the normal time frame. After reviewing hundreds of studies, the top eight predictors that are most supported by research follow.

1. *Native language proficiency:* A student's native language proficiency when beginning studying a new language is the strongest predictor of academic development.
2. *Language aptitude:* People with high aptitude for languages learn them faster than people without high aptitude.
3. *Affective variables (anxiety, motivation, attitudes, self-concept):* How students feel about their languages is a primary factor in their success.
4. *Personality (competitive vs. cooperative; interactive styles):* People with open and driving personalities who have no fear of failure, seek out cooperative relationships, and are interactive generally have greater success in learning new languages.
5. *Demographic features (age, gender):* Starting age when learning a foreign language impacts success with the language (the younger the better). Additionally, girls tend to be more verbal than boys, though both genders can eventually achieve the same levels of success.
6. *Learning strategies (self-reward; learning modalities):* When languages are approached through intrinsic motivation and self-reward they are learned faster than when people rely on others to give them praise.
7. *Learning styles:* People who are auditorily inclined have an edge on those with visual or kinesthetic preferences when it comes to learning languages, presumably because language production and comprehension both rely heavily on the ability to perceive foreign sounds.
8. *Language typologies:* The more similar the languages, the faster they are learned.

All eight of these factors influence the speed with which a person learns a new language. The eighth factor, however, has the greatest amount of research backing it and deserves further exploration. We will examine language typologies in detail next.

Language Typologies

According to Murphy of the Teachers College at Columbia University, typology is "the most important variable in determining the likelihood of language transfer."[4] Languages that share grammar, vocabulary, or a similar phoneme base are easier to learn. Those of us who have experimented with foreign languages ourselves recognize that similarity between languages appears to facilitate new learning. For example, someone learning Spanish after already learning French would find the task far easier than someone who only knew Korean, because Spanish and French share historical roots but Korean does not.

Language typologies refer to structural similarities between languages that make them easier to learn, something that has to do with either the historical roots of the language or the linguistic structure. Languages that "grew up" together historically are easier to learn. For example, Latin, or Romance, languages that developed side by side include Italian, French, Portuguese, Spanish, and Romanian. A native speaker of Italian will find learning Portuguese or Spanish relatively easy when compared to learning Chinese, for example, which shares no roots. This is due to the fact that languages from the same family to varying extents share roots and structure of words, as well as vocabulary elements. They often tend to share the same linguistic structure as well, though this is not limited only to languages from the same families. Let's look at how this occurs.

All of the world's languages have subjects, verbs, and objects, though they vary in order. Let's call subjects "S," verbs "V," and objects "O." Joseph Greenberg created a typological ensemble classification of the world's languages in which he noted there are only six possible word orders (SVO, OVS, SOV, OSV, VSO, VOS). What he found most interesting, however, is that only three are commonly found in the world's languages today: SVO, SOV, and VSO. What is equally intriguing is that this language classification is unrelated to language genealogy, which means although the historical roots of languages play a part in typology similarity, the structure does so as well. Therefore, some multilinguals may find their learning facilitated by similar linguistic typologies. For example, English, which is a subject-verb-object language, may facilitate easier learning of Greek, which is also a subject-verb-object language, because the word order seems "logical" to them. Conversely, individuals may have a harder time learning new languages when the conceptual organization of the language is different.

For example, let's suppose I speak Japanese, a language that does not enjoy historical roots with any other language, unique in terms of grammar, vocabulary, and some aspects of its writing system. If I want to study Hindi to do business in India, or Basque to work with a company in Barcelona, Spain, I might presume that because Japanese has no shared history, I would be at a disadvantage. However, Japanese is a subject-object-verb (SOV) language, as are Hindi and Basque. I could potentially use what I know about my own language typology to learn faster. If such a presumption were true, it would probably be more common to find multilinguals knowing language combinations based on their ensembles:

VSO (verb-subject-object)	SVO (subject-verb-object)	SOV (subject-object-verb)
Arabic (ancient), Berger, Gaelic, Hawaiian, Hebrew, Irish, Maori, Masai, Swedish, Tagalog, Tongan, Welsh	Arabic (modern), Chinese, English, Finnish, French, German (and SOV in past tense), Greek, Guarani, Khmer, Indonesian, Malay, Russian, Spanish, Swahili, Thai, Vietnamese, Yoruba	Armenian, Basque, Korean, German (and SVO in present tense), Hindi, Japanese, Manchu, Mongolian, Navajo, Persian, Quechua, Turkish

History (geography, colonization, and trade) and grammatical structure (VSO vs. SVO vs. SOV) of languages, however, do not always lend themselves to our individual realities. Though I can say that in my own family's case all four of our languages are SVO (English, German, Spanish, and French), and my husband and I studied Japanese (SOV) and found it much more challenging than our earlier languages, this may not be the case for all multilinguals. When pursuing a multilingual lifestyle, language typologies should be considered and understood but they shouldn't dictate our language learning choices. There are thousands of multilinguals who do not rely on a similarity between their languages and still find success. This information might explain, however, why some people find becoming multilingual easier than others.

Another individual aspect of multilingualism that impacts the speed with which a person learns a language relates to goals. Some people are content being able to just speak a foreign language. Others, however, want to be able to reach multiliteracy skills. We will now consider how this impacts the amount of time it takes to learn a new language.

MULTILITERACY SKILLS: HOW AND WHEN TO INTRODUCE READING AND WRITING TO MULTILINGUAL CHILDREN

When we decide to pursue literacy skills in more than one language we are adding years to the total time it takes to master a second or third language. Having accepted that, we also know that learning to read is an exciting time in a child's life, and doing this in more than one language is doubly or triply so. Something that zealous parents should remember, however, is that although speaking more than one language is widespread (most of the world does so), reading and writing skills in more than one language are not so common. To make matters even more complex, learning to read and learning to write are complimentary but distinct skills in the brain. The following is a summary of key ideas related to multiliteracy skills.

To be a good reader in two or more languages, a child must give time and practice to each of them. This is different from oral skills. Whereas learning oral vocabulary in the first language usually parallels increased vocabulary in the second language, the same spin-off benefits do not exist for reading and writing. To become a good reader in a foreign language, one has to devote time to that language separately. A child with strong oral skills in Spanish and English who then learns to read in Spanish has a very good chance of becoming a good reader in English as well—but it does not happen automatically. Each language has to be given time to develop.

There are five basic steps to assuring multiliteracy skills (being able to read and write in more than one language):

1. Understand the use of the written word.
2. Learn the phonemic alphabet.
3. Acknowledge exceptions in sound to letter relation.
4. Acknowledge exceptions between languages.
5. Practice familiarity, repetition, and frequency.

Let's look at these five steps in the context of an example. Kate is an American married to a Spaniard, living with their two children in Spain. She speaks English to her children, and her husband speaks Spanish to them. Their four-year-old son, Pedro, goes to a Spanish preschool. Pedro is beginning to learn the vowels, recognizing the written letters and also the sounds of English as well as Spanish.

Understand the Use of the Written Word and Learn the Phonemic Alphabet

If this is an ideal situation, Pedro's mother, Kate, has been reading and speaking to him in English since he was born, and his father has done the same in Spanish. Around age three, when Pedro began showing a natural curiosity for letters, they encouraged this interest and helped him label the symbols that corresponded to letters. Kate did this using her native English, whereas her husband did the same in Spanish. When Kate wrote his name, she told Pedro that it starts with a *pee*, not *peh*, as in Spanish, for example.

At this stage there are many ways natural curiosity about language manifests itself. For example, Pedro might see a "P" on a billboard or in a newspaper or book and ask, "Hey, Mom, is that *my* letter?" This is similar to a situation I had with my youngest son when he was three. I remember Mateo told me he "read" the McDonald's logo. He had matched a symbol to the word and basically mastered a conceptual understanding of reading by doing so. "That is *my* letter. It says McDonald's!" In a twist, a four-year-old friend accompanying us at that moment said, "That's nothing," as she pointed to the four circles that are the Audi car logo, "That says a-u-d-i!" This sophisticated matching of symbols (logos) to words (concepts) is a huge first step toward building literacy skills. At this stage, children learn that written language can be used to label things and, especially, to record information, such as in stories or making lists.

"Mateo's letter"   "A-U-D-I"

Acknowledge Exceptions in Sound to Letter Relation as Well as Between Languages

Ideally, when Pedro starts preschool in Spanish, he does so with a working knowledge of pre-literacy skills in English *already in place*. Then, when Pedro begins to learn letters and their corresponding Spanish sounds at school, his mom continues to read in English at home but stops (temporarily) explicitly teaching the names of the letters in the alphabet and their corresponding sounds in English. Why stop? It is very hard for a child to learn biliteracy skills simultaneously, especially from two different trusted sources: "But, my *mother* says something different," or "My *teacher* corrected me and said it was like this." When the child is slightly older and has a cognitive understanding of the different languages and can label them by name, then Kate can begin again to point out that, "Yes, in Spanish we say *eeee*, but in this English word, the letter "E" sounds like *ehh*," helping the child understand not only the exceptions in the letter sound-to-symbol correspondence but also the exceptions between languages. Having said this, it is important to recognize that many school systems begin teaching literacy skills simultaneously. The schools that do so successfully are those that separate the processes by person, place, and time. Ideally, a different person, a different physical space, and a different time are used for each language. In the best-case scenarios, time means a separation by a number of years, whereas in other cases it means the difference between morning classes and afternoon classes.

It is important to note that most consonants are very close in sound, independent of languages. The exceptions are usually found in the vowels (a, e, i, o, u). If Pedro's mother has not yet taught him the phonemic alphabet in English before he starts learning Spanish, she should not try to do so until he gains a firm grasp on the Spanish alphabet and can clearly label and distinguish between Spanish and English. She should, however, continue to strengthen Pedro's mother-tongue vocabulary by reading to him in English frequently. In other family cases when languages have different alphabets, it is important for parents to realize that understanding the different symbol systems and giving time to practice each one is perhaps the most important factor in literacy. For example, a child whose home language is Russian might learn the Cyrillic alphabet before entering school and not find conflict learning the Phoenician (ABCs), but he or she will still need to give each language time and practice to ensure fluency.

Practice, Familiarity, Repetition, and Frequency

Good readers read a lot and give time to each of their languages. My daughter learned pre-literacy skills in English with me before she started reading in German at school in the first grade. About two years later she told me it was "too bad" she had never learned to read in Spanish (her father's language). When I asked her why she thought she couldn't read in Spanish she said because she had "never had a class in it." Excitedly, we took advantage of this opportunity and my husband began to read more with her in Spanish, pointing out the sound-to-symbol correspondence, and I explicitly pointed out that the vowels in Spanish were very similar to those in German (which she found easy by that point). She began to read in Spanish more fluently. We lived in Switzerland at the time, and Spanish books were expensive and not commonly found. We had more English books available than anything else (thanks to my mother and the nearby American library), so she spent more time reading for pleasure in English than in Spanish or German. When she got to the third grade, however, German began to dominate based on the amount of school reading. Spanish did not gain equal footing, however, until we returned to South America when she was in the fifth grade. Because of the equal amounts of opportunity (country, school, and parental presence), availability of resources (books in all languages), and personal motivation (friends and relatives who highly recommended books in each of her languages), she now reads at or slightly above age level in these three languages. Practice, familiarity, repetition, and frequency were vital factors. Her writing skills, however, are another story.

To my chagrin, my daughter Natalie's English spelling is still pretty atrocious, but because English and Spanish are school subjects, she accepts corrections from her teachers, something she never did well with her parents, and her writing has improved in a consistent manner over the years. It is worth mentioning an observation about timing and writing in our personal family case, which is admittedly anecdotal but consistent with projections by experts. In sixth grade Natalie blossomed as a student (seven years after being in the German school system). It was at this point that her English and Spanish writing began to catch up with her German. It appears that her writing achievements were staggered in time and developed in direct correlation to the amount of time spent practicing writing in each language. She first needed to consolidate her first language literacy base, and then move on to the second and third.

An additional factor about writing that did not exist when "we" were kids is the computer. My daughter argues endlessly with me about the need to learn to spell: "The computer can do that later!" To her credit, her teachers (English, Spanish, and German) now generally comment on her sophisticated content—just before they slam her awful spelling. I have faith, however, that with time and practice, her writing skills will continually grow just as aspects of her oral language did.

I feel that one of the reasons my children have made good strides with their languages is their emotional links to each of them. The people who love them most in the world, their parents, grandparents, and cousins, speak English and Spanish. This gives these languages an important emotional status in their life. Additionally, their best friends come from school and the community, giving German and Spanish an elevated status. Finally, the years we lived in Switzerland were extremely important in the formative years of my children, and the relationships they formed there, many in French, impacted us all in a very positive way. The overwhelmingly positive links made to these languages have contributed greatly to the speed with which my children learned their languages. We have been fortunate in this respect as I have seen more than a few unsuccessful attempts at a second language thwarted by negative emotions. Let's look at the link between how emotions impact memories and how memories form the basis of learning.

EMOTIONS, MEMORIES, AND LANGUAGE LEARNING

Historically, psychologists and neurobiologists steered clear of considering emotions a serious influence on learning. However, "in recent years both neuroscience and cognitive neuroscience have finally endorsed emotion" and research "has shown that emotion is integral to the process of reasoning and decision making."[5] With the blessing of these prestigious fields, we, too, will consider the importance of emotion in foreign language acquisition, especially as it impacts the speed with which a language is learned.

Emotions in their extreme states have been recognized in psychology as playing a role in memory formation. William James, the father of psychology, wrote, "An experience may be so exciting emotionally as to almost leave a scar on the cerebral tissues."[6] It has since been recognized that even subtle emotional experiences can also "leave a scar" and, furthermore, that the scars are real, especially in the negative sense. Human experiences are rarely emotion-free, says Antonio Damasio, one of the most respected neurologists specializing in emotions. Emotional memories are triggered by the experience of feelings that are cemented into the memory system through the release of certain neurotransmitters, as we will see in Chapter 6.

We all know from experience that we like doing the things that make us feel good, and we avoid doing the things that make us feel bad. When languages are used within a context that is full of love, those languages are given permission to thrive. When languages are learned under stress or are attached to people who make us feel badly about ourselves, we withdraw, and the learning is stunted. There are a number of people who attest that they learned a second language because they fell in love. Similarly, many share how they "hated" a language teacher who made them detest the language. Emotions, memory, and learning are inextricably intertwined in the human brain.

The environment in which we surround our children impacts how they feel, and how they feel impacts how well they learn. A negative learning environment is one in which children sense anger, fear, sadness, or disgust. A positive learning environment is one in which the participants sense joy, surprise, curiosity, and acceptance.[7] "Emotion plays a clear role in learning the behavior," say neurologists Christian Balkenius and Jan Morén.[8] The choice to use a new language is a desired behavior that we as parents and teachers hope to encourage. Studies of the brain, best practice in education, and good parenting all recognize that learning is both cognitive and affective, involving both the head and the heart. Negative as well as positive emotions impact learning. Mel Levine shares case studies of older adults who continually have anxiety symptoms when asked to recall learning experiences that involved being publicly embarrassed by a parent or teacher. He feels strongly that humiliation of this sort is the worst experience a learner can have, often impairing future learning. At the other extreme, we all learned our first language compelled by the love we felt for our parents. Though it may seem counterintuitive, emotions are very cerebral.

I recently wrote to some of the most respected names in the field of bilingualism in an attempt to gauge their view of emotions and language learning. Ellen Bialystok (*Language Processing in Bilingual Children*), Colin Baker (*Foundations of Bilingual Education*), Edith Harding-Esch and Philip Riley (*The Bilingual Family, A Handbook for Parents*) all responded by saying that they acknowledge that emotions are important in language acquisition. Baker, Harding-Esch, and Riley have all raised their children bilingually (Riley, trilingually), though they were not raised bilingual themselves. Harding-Esch says, "The issue of emotional factors is of course essential for parent-child relations whether bilingual or not!"[9] Baker echoed how emotional ties also impacted his own experiences raising his children in Welsh and English. Bialystok also acknowledged the importance of social and emotional dimensions of language and language learning.

How does emotion impact the speed of learning? Emotions are felt in the heart but regulated by the brain. Neurobiological reactions to negative emotions can, at the least, hinder the uptake of new information, and at the worst, cause permanent blockage for the uptake of information. Positive emotions do the opposite, triggering dopamine and other "happy" neurotransmitters in the brain, which can facilitate the cementation of memories in the brain, including new language skills. It stands to reason that any learning environment that causes a child to feel fear, anxiety, or stress will not be as conducive to learning as one that cultivates language through joy, surprise, curiosity, and acceptance. How we make our children feel about their languages is more important than how many opportunities in the day we give them to speak. As with all skills, if we want to ensure that our children learn another language, it should be taught with love.

As said earlier, both neurology and best practice in education acknowledge that learning is both cognitive and affective; that is, learning is done with the heart and the head. Specific examples of this related to "math anxiety," "science traumas," or "writing anxiety" can be found in abundance in the literature. On the other hand, using what we know about the brain and learning as it relates to reward, motivation, and extroversion, could also be used to create positive guides for creating good learning environments. Patricia Wolfe conducted a study involving many of the most influential neurologists of modern times to make the case that all learning is emotional learning at some level.[10] Her works highlight the impact that negative emotions, such as stress, anxiety, and fear, can have on classroom learning experiences. Along with others in the new field of neuro-education, which unites neurobiology with pedagogy, she documents how feelings such as humiliation often cause long-term damage to an individual's ability to cope in formal class settings. On the positive side, Wolfe notes that educators should "recognize the power of emotion to increase retention, and plan classroom instruction accordingly."[11] Emotions impact learning when they facilitate the creation of memories; emotions are only as important as the memories they make because memory is the key to learning—not emotion *per se*. As the emotions-memory link and the memory-learning connection become more documented in the literature, it seems a natural outgrowth to propose an emotions-memory-learning connection as it relates to foreign language acquisition.

Part of best practice in education presumes that the teacher has influence over the creation of the learning environment, and in a similar way, parents orchestrate good home environments. Simple acts by teachers and parents, such as facial expressions, have been studied and shown to stimulate emotional reactions and enhance or create resistance to learning. A sincere smile can go a long way in motivating students. Similarly, a nod of approval from a work colleague or boss can spur on adult language learners because their internal motivation levels are positively impacted by such gestures. Good emotional environments are made, however, not found. Teachers, parents, and work colleagues can take a number of steps to improve the ambiance for learning. Small things can be done to create a better emotional setting. Some psychologists suggest the use of music to reduce tension levels, but this presumes that the same music triggers similar emotions in all people, which is not necessarily true. Others recommend plants or fish in the classroom to bring a sense of balance and nature to enhance an authentic environment, while others say the only necessary physical decoration of the class is student work that celebrates the learners. Setting the mood for formal instruction and varying activities help both children and adults create good environments for language study. These activities and others that we will see in Chapter 7 are useful in lowering stress levels and elevating achievement potential. On another level, we parents must acknowledge that we can also be the source of stress in our child's life. Unrealistic expectations, unresponsiveness, or even physical absence can stress children. If we have the lofty goal of multiliteracy in mind, we would do well to temper our enthusiasm with realistic and feasible expectations.

In summary, the time it takes for people to learn a foreign language varies for many reasons, but several studies suggest that between five and seven years are typically needed for a non-native speaker to reach native language fluency depending both on the type of academic program in place as well as the individual's abilities. Other factors can also influence language learning success and speed. These include native language proficiency, general intelligence, language aptitude, affective variables, personality, demographic features, learning strategies, and learning styles. Although all of these factors are important, there is a great deal of evidence to suggest that language typology is the greatest influence related to how much time it takes a learner to become fluent. If multiliteracy skills are a goal for learners, the time frame for learning is longer than for simple conversation skills, which can often be achieved within two years. Finally, the emotions people attach to their language learning experiences influence not only the speed but also the quality of acquisition.

All of these factors are magnified when the goal goes from bilingualism to trilingualism. In the next chapter we will consider the special case of individuals who learn not just two but three languages or more.

5
A Special Word about Third Languages

WHEN WE WANT MORE THAN BILINGUALISM

When families decide to go beyond one language, they jump into a sea of bilingualism shared by millions of people around the world. Most people in the world speak more than one language, and as a consequence of this there are many books, research documents, and case studies on bilingualism. However, when a family decides that its needs are best met by trilingualism or multilingualism, they find their sources, support systems, and information bases far more limited.

There are millions of people in the world who speak three or more languages, and this population is on the rise. Children brought up bilingual from birth often take on a third language in the course of their formal education. More monolingual families live overseas than ever before, and many of them send their children to a local or international school that has a second language requirement, meaning the children have a second language as the primary school language and then a third language as their "second language" school requirement. Many once-monolingual businessmen recognize how a second language has benefited them, and they are less fearful about launching into a third. Though their level of competency may be limited to a conversational level, they can be categorized as multilinguals (bilinguals have varying levels of competencies and the definition of bilingual ranges from "mumbling significant utterances" in a language to "perfectly balanced vocabularies and spoken abilities"; the same is true for multilinguals). Others, such as academicians, doctors, and technology engineers around the world speak a home language, have a second language as a university requirement, and then find they spend much of their time as "passive trilinguals," reading articles in an international language. Trilinguals have also emerged from two types of historical exchanges between countries. First, historical linguists can attest to the outgrowth of modern languages from a handful of primary ones. Second, history documents the spread of languages through colonization and trade.

There are more trilinguals whose languages have similar language roots than trilinguals who learn unrelated languages. That is, individuals who know many historically related languages—such as the Latin family of Spanish, French, Portuguese, Italian, and Romanian or the Germanic family of languages, which includes German, English, Dutch, Danish, and Swedish—are more common than those who know three languages from distinct families, such as Japanese, Arabic, and Russian. It is logical to presume that geography and historical roots go hand in hand;[1] most language families are found close to one another, facilitating their learning. For example, Hindi, Urdu, Bengali, and Nepali are all spoken in India, and they all share Indo-Aryan roots; it is not uncommon to find multilinguals who speak these languages. This is similar to finding many Chinese who speak a Chinese dialect, Tibetan, and Burmese because all share Sino-Tibetan roots and can be found in geographically similar regions. Therefore, it would be more common to find trilinguals who speak languages with shared roots than trilinguals who speak languages with distinct roots. However, we know from experience that this is not always true.

Two modern factors changed the "typical trilingual case" from those who spoke historically similar languages to those who spoke a *lingua franca*: colonization and trade. Several countries have languages with distinct historical roots because of colonization. For example, Afrikaans and English are spoken in South Africa alongside the native Sesotho and Zulu, and Japanese is spoken in Korea because of a former occupation. Colonial languages are often the formal school languages in many countries (for example, English in Kenya, French in Lebanon, Portuguese in Brazil, or Dutch in the Netherlands Antilles), and though normally unrelated in a historical linguistic sense, they are linked by social-historical events.

In more recent times, language study has been influenced by trade, not colonization. A current trend in globalization is that "everyone speaks English," because the largest consumer market in the world is the United States. "Necessity is the mother of invention," and when communication demands include learning a new language, many feel compelled to oblige. Because the United States is the strongest economic power in the world today, many people have learned English to gain access to American trade partners. Additionally, the United States does not have a particularly strong reputation for teaching foreign languages, meaning that waiting for Americans to learn other languages would perhaps be a lengthy task. Global linguistic expectations are changing, however, as new markets such as China and the European Union gain more and more strength; the days of English as the world's lingua franca will undoubtedly change in the coming decades.

Types of Trilinguals

There are five basic scenarios whereby people become multilingual, according to Hoffman:

1. *Bilingual families (two home languages) who live in a community where a third language is spoken:* For example, Salman, who speaks Arabic, and Mary, who speaks English, moved to Russia with their children for job opportunities. The children attend an American School, learn Russian as an elective and as part of their community life, and speak Arabic with their father.

2. *Monolinguals who live in bilingual/multilingual communities:* For example, an American journalist who lives in Belgium, where French, Dutch, and German are spoken, finds that her life in Brussels requires at least two of these languages in order to communicate socially as well as professionally.

3. *Students who go to multilingual schools:* Hundreds if not thousands of international schools around the world teach the local language and an international language and often require a third language for graduation. For example, David, a native German speaker, goes to school in Japan, where he learns English and Japanese and has the option of taking French.

4. *Bilinguals who move to a third language community for work:* For example, Canadian Louise knew French and English before moving to Mexico for work, where she had to improve her Spanish skills in order to advance.

5. *Citizens of multilingual communities:* Many countries are multilingual in themselves. For example, while growing up in Lebanon, Hannah learned Arabic, English, and French as part of the normal school system. Similarly, Max grew up in Switzerland, where his first language was Swiss German, followed by French and then English with an option of Italian (see Table 5.1).

Table 5.1   Multilingual Countries

Region	Country	Number of Languages	Language Names
Africa			
Central Africa	Cameroon	11	English, French (official), Cameroonian Pidgin, Basaa, Bikya, Bung, Fula, Kanuri, Ngumba, Yeni, Bamum
	Central African Republic	2	French (official), Sango
	Chad	103	Arabic, French (official), Chadian Arabic (national trade language), more than 100 tribal languages
	Democratic Republic of the Congo	243	French (official), Lingala, Kongo, Swahili & Tshiluba (national languages), 238 other languages
	Equatorial Guinea	2	French, Spanish
	Republic of the Congo	3	French (official), Lingala, Kituba (national languages), Kikongo, Kituba (Kikongo creole)
Eastern Africa	Burundi	3	French, Kirundi (official), Swahili
	Djibouti	4	Arabic, French (official), Somali, Afar

Table 5.1   Multilingual Countries (continued)

Region	Country	Number of Languages	Language Names
	Eritrea	13	Arabic, Tigrinya, Tigre, Dahlik, Afar, Beja, Blin, Saho, Kunama, Nara, English, Amharic, some Italian
	Kenya	2	English, Swahili (official), other indigenous languages
	Rwanda	3	English, French, Kinyarwanda (official languages)
	Seychelles	3	English, French, Seychellois Creole (official languages)
	Somalia	3	Somali (official), Arabic, English
	Tanzania	4	Swahili (national), English, Gujarati, Portuguese
	Uganda	6	English (official), Arabic, Luganda, Swahili, other Bantu languages, other Nilo-Saharan languages
Northern Africa	Algeria	4	Arabic (official), Tamazight (national language), other languages, French
	Egypt	3	Arabic (official), Egyptian Arabic, English, French
	Libya	5	Arabic (official), Tamazight, Tamahaq, Italian, English

Table 5.1   Multilingual Countries (continued)

Region	Country	Number of Languages	Language Names
	Mauritania	3	Arabic (de facto), Hassaniya, French
	Morocco	5	Arabic, French, Amazigh, Moroccan Arabic, Berber
	Western Africa	4	Hassaniya, Moroccan Arabic, Spanish
	Sahrawi Arab Democratic Republic	2	Arabic, Spanish
	Sudan	4+	Arabic, English, indigenous languages
	Tunisia	5+	Arabic (official), Tunisian Arabic, French, several Tamazight languages
South Africa	Botswana	2	English (official), Setswana (national)
	Comores	3	Arabic, Comorian, French
	Lesotho	2	English, Sesotho
	Madagascar	2	French, Malagasy
	Malawi	2	Chichewa (national), English (official)
	Mauritus	8	English (official), French (administrative), Mauritian Creole (lingua franca), Hindi, Hakka, Bojpoori, Tamil, Urdu
	Nambia	5	English (official), Ovambo, Afrikaans, German (former official languages), Portuguese

Table 5.1 Multilingual Countries (continued)

Region	Country	Number of Languages	Language Names
	South Africa	11	Afrikaans, English, Ndebele, Sepedi, Sesotho, Setswana, Swati, Tsonga, Venda, Xhosa, Zulu
	Swaziland	2	English, Siswati
	Zimbabwe	3	English (official), Shona, Ndebele
Western Africa	Benin	3	French (official), Fon & Songhay (indigenous languages)
	Burkina Faso	2+	French (official), indigenous Sudanic languages
	Cape Verde	2	Portuguese, Cape Verdean Creole
	Cote d'Ivoire	61	French (official), 60 indigenous dialects
	Gambia	5+	English (official), Mandinka, Wolof, Fula, others
	Ghana	80+	English (official), Akan, Dagaare/Wale, Dagbane, Dangme, Ewe, Ga, Gonja, Kasem, Nzema, 70 others
	Guinea	4	French (official), Arabic, Fula, Susu
	Guinea-Bissau	4+	Portuguese (official), Kriol, indigenous languages
	Liberia	21+	English (official), 20 ethnic group languages
	Togo	4	French (official), Ewe, Mina, le Kabiyé

Table 5.1 Multilingual Countries (continued)

Region	Country	Number of Languages	Language Names
Americas	Canada	62	French, English, Inuit dialects of Inuktitut and Inuinnaqtun, 18 First Nation Languages, 42 minority languages
	Guatemala	24	Spanish, 23 distinct Mayan languages.
	Mexico	63	Spanish, Nahuatl, 62 indigenous languages.
	Netherlands Antilles and Aruba	4	Dutch, Papiamentu, Dutch, English, Spanish
	Paraguay	3	Spanish, Guaraní, Jopará.
	United States	337	English (*de facto* language, but not official), Spanish, Cantonese, French, German, Italian, Tagalog (close to 1 million speakers each), 155 minority languages, 176 native languages
Middle East	Afghanistan	2	Arabic, Persian
	Lebanon	3	Arabic, French, English (official languages)
	Iran	2	Persian, Arabic
	Israel	3	Hebrew, Arabic, English
	United Arab Emirates	2	Arabic, Hindi

Table 5.1   Multilingual Countries (continued)

Region	Country	Number of Languages	Language Names
Asia	China	236	Putonghua (Chinese), Wu (Shanghai dialect), Cantonese (Chinese), Tibetan, Mongolian, dialects in all regions
	Hong Kong	3	English, Cantonese, Putonghua (Chinese)
	Macau	4	Portuguese, Cantonese (Chinese), Putonghua (Chinese), English
	India	23	Hindi, Urdu, Bengali, Nepali, English, 18 other official languages)
	Indonesia	200+	Indonesian languages (over 200 native languages)
	Korea	2	Korean, Japanese
	Malaysia	4+	Malay, English, Tamil, several Chinese dialects, ancestral languages, Indian dialects
	Philippines	3	Filipino, English, Tagalog, Spanish
	Singapore	7	English, Mandarin (Chinese), Malay, Tamil (official languages), Japanese, French, German

Table 5.1 Multilingual Countries (continued)

Region	Country	Number of Languages	Language Names
	Sri Lanka	2	Sinhala and Tamil (official languages), English
	Taiwan	3	Mandarin (Chinese), Taiwanese (Southern Fujian), Hakka
Europe	Belgium	4	Dutch, French, German (official languages), English
	Finland	3	Finnish, Swedish (official languages), English
	Greece	2	Greek, Armenian
	Ireland	3	Irish and English (official languages), Goidelic, Welsh, Ulster Scots
	Italy	6	Italian, German, French, Slovene, Ladin, Sardu, Friulian, Occitan
	Luxembourg	3	Luxembourgish, French, German (official languages)
	The Netherlands		Dutch, Frisian, German, French, English
	Norway		Norwegian, German, Swedish
	Belarus	4+	Georgian, Russian, Tartar, Abkhaz
	Ukraine	4+	Georgian, Russian, Tartar, Abkhaz
	Poland	2	Polish, German
	Czech Republic	3	Czech, Slovak, German
	Slovakia	3	Slovak, Czech, German

Table 5.1   Multilingual Countries (continued)

Region	Country	Number of Languages	Language Names
	Switzerland	4	German, French, Italian, Romansh (official languages), English
	Spain	4	Spanish, Basque, Galego, Catalan
	Sweden	3	Swedish, Tornedalen, Haparanda, Finnish
	Scotland	4	English, Scottish, Gaelic, Welsh
	Slovenia	6	Slovene, Italian, Hungarian
	Serbia	3	Serbian, Croatian, Bosnian
	Turkey	5	Turkish, Kurdish, Dimli (or Zaza), Azeri, Kabardian
	Croatia	3	Croatian, Bosnian, Serbian
	Bosnia	3	Bosnian, Serbian, Croatian
Oceania	New Zealand	2	English, Maori

Defining Multilingualism

UNESCO adopted the term *multilingual education* at its General Conference in 1999 to mean "use of at least three languages in education—the mother tongue, a regional or national language and an international one."[2] Mother-tongue education, or the right to be educated in one's native language, is promoted by the United Nations as part of best practice in language learning and general education. In 1999, February 21 was proclaimed International Mother Language Day and meant to encourage education in the home language, alongside bilingual or multilingual education. This day is dedicated to three goals: (1) promoting education in the mother tongue to improve the quality of education, (2) encouraging bilingual and/or multilingual education at all levels of schooling as a means of furthering social and gender equality and as a key part of linguistically diverse societies, and (3) calling attention to languages as a central part of inter-cultural education.

BENEFITS OF BILINGUALISM THAT PERSIST INTO TRILINGUALISM

As we saw in Chapter 2, there are many social, cultural, and economic benefits of being multilingual. In the cognitive realm, trilinguals enjoy even more benefits.

Multilinguals Deal with Levels of Abstraction Earlier Than Monolinguals[3]

Both Suzanne Flynn, professor of linguistics and second-language acquisition at the Massachusetts Institute of Technology, and Ellen Bialystok, professor of psychology at York University in Toronto, established that bilinguals are better at managing abstract concepts than are monolinguals. This means that people with many languages can exchange concrete, tangible information for less physical evidence, and the world of ideas can serve in its place. There is reason to believe that if bilinguals do this well, then trilinguals do it even better.

Multilinguals Have More Flexible Minds

Adele Diamond, director of the Center for Developmental Cognitive Neuroscience at the University of Massachusetts Medical School, says that bilinguals learn how to switch back and forth between tasks when the rules change and do so at a faster pace than monolinguals. This is easy to see when one considers how the rules of language shift and how bilinguals manage to adjust almost simultaneously. Does this mean that flexibility increases with the number of languages learned? Though this has not been answered conclusively, many theorize there is a correlation between mental flexibility and the number of structures one learns to work within—whether language rules or logical, mathematical constructs—meaning that the more languages you know, the more flexible your mind is.

Multilinguals Learn How to Inhibit Previously Learned Skill Sets

Knowing when *not* to access information is also a part of learning. The ability to keep unnecessary information out of the mind when accessing only vital information is a skill that develops over time and practice. It would be chaos if everything we knew about each topic were perceived every time something related to that topic came up. This also applies to languages. The prefrontal cortex is charged in great part with managing the executive functions of the brain, letting us know when something deserves attention and when it should be ignored in order to maximize learning. Memory, planning, and multitasking are all managed by this function and help the multilingual mind focus on the appropriate language in the appropriate context, says Flynn. The spin-off benefit is that multilinguals can multitask better than monolinguals.

Multilinguals Use More of Their Brains Than Monolinguals

As we will see in Chapter 6, a multilingual brain uses more areas than a monolingual brain does. Is more necessarily better? This is not known with certainty, though it can be argued that speaking more languages brings cognitive benefits, which may be associated with increased use of the brain. One of possible spin-off benefits is creativity.

Multilinguals More Creative Than Monolinguals in Thirty Out of Thirty-Three Studies[4]

Lena Riccardelli defined thirty-three different types of creativity (problem solving, painting, musical composition, etc.) and found that multilinguals scored higher on thirty of thirty-three of these tests. What is not known is whether this is because of right hemisphere use or the cultural experiences of the language learning. Some suggest it may be due to the schooling of people raised in many languages. Are multilinguals more creative because their brains are wired differently, because they are more culturally savvy, or because the type of education they received encouraged open-mindedness or gave them specific training in creative skills? Although the origins of the phenomena are not clear, it appears that people who speak multiple languages are more creative in almost every way, from artistic expression to problem solving.

Multilinguals Have Transferable Cognitive Benefits

Ironically, people who learn English as a second or third language score higher on English proficiency tests than their Anglophone, monolingual peers. Kenji Hakuta found that bilinguals tested in English showed better results than monolinguals in four of five measures: listening, speaking, writing, vocabulary, and grammar.[5] This could be because of their overt grammar instruction in English, or it could be that bilinguals are better prepared for exams of this sort because of their school training—we do not know for sure. The reason behind the scores is not yet known, but the fact remains that multilinguals have an edge on Anglophones in English testing.

Multilinguals Are Superior at Cultural Integration

The ability to speak several languages opens the doors to cultures. Ludwig Josef Johann Wittgenstein once said, "If we spoke a different language, we would perceive a somewhat different world." The ability to understand others through their own language is the first step in gaining understanding and eventually integration of cultural perspectives. This cultural sensitivity increases the possibility that differences between different nations can be overcome. By using another language we have a different lens on the world. Empathy begins with such perspectives.

Multilinguals Have Enhanced Intellectual Empathy

We know that empathy, or the ability to see the world through another's eyes, is increased when individuals feel closer to the culture of the "other." People feel closer to other cultures when they speak the language. Although extreme linguistic determinism is questionable, its founder, Benjamin Whorf, is known for expressing many accepted truths in the field, among them that "we dissect nature along lines laid down by our native language. Language is not simply a reporting device for experience but a defining framework for it."[6] By understanding several languages, we can understand several frameworks and thus develop empathy for speakers of other languages who are representatives of other cultures. The benefits of trilingualism are overwhelmingly positive. Why, then, aren't there more people who pursue this? We turn to the elements that can influence successful trilingualism and the problems that can stand in the way of achievement.

WHAT INFLUENCES SUCCESSFUL TRILINGUALISM?

Seven Elements and Ten Factors

Successful trilingualism is influenced by several elements that piggyback on the ten key factors that influence multilingualism, which are discussed in *Raising Multilingual Children*. After a review of hundreds of studies, I suggest that there are seven aspects of bilingualism that directly influence trilingualism:

1. First-language proficiency
2. Linguistic awareness and metacognition
3. Time spent on task
4. Educational level of the learner
5. Parent involvement
6. Teacher qualifications
7. Learner's self-esteem

These seven elements should not be confused with the ten key factors that influence successful multilingualism, though each of those factors is *also* important when considering the difference between bilingual and trilingualism. Timing, aptitude, motivation, strategy, consistency, opportunity and support, the relationship between languages, siblings, gender, and hand use are all important for trilingualism, but the research shows that the seven elements mentioned also are vital for success.

As with the ten key factors, these seven elements influence successful multilingualism in children, and all are important but not all are necessary in the same individual. For example, a person who enjoys a high level of similarity between language and a high degree of parental support and enthusiasm can be just as successful as someone who enjoys none of these factors but has a high degree of self-esteem and excellent teachers and spends years on the learning task. The key is to recognize that all ten factors and all seven elements are important and that each person will combine them differently (see Table 5.2).

Table 5.2   Influences on Trilingual Success

Ten Key Factors Influencing Multilingualism (Raising Multilingual Children)	Seven Additional Elements
1. Timing and the windows of opportunity	1. First-language proficiency
2. Aptitude	2. Linguistic awareness
3. Motivation	3. Time on task
4. Strategy	4. Educational level of the learner
5. Consistency	5. Parent involvement
6. Opportunity and support	6. Teacher qualifications
7. Relationship between the first and second languages (language typologies)	7. Learner's self-esteem
8. Siblings	
9. Gender	
10. Hand use	

Why Call the New Evidence *Elements* When the Others Are *Factors?*

Astute readers will quickly question why the new evidence is labeled as "elements" whereas the original groupings were called "factors." The reason for this categorization is primarily because several elements can form a factor. For example, the ten key factors include "opportunity and support" for language use, which could theoretically break down into the elements of "parent involvement" and "teacher qualification," among others, which are found in the trilingual influences. Whereas the evidence in the research on trilingualism does not identify "opportunity" or "support" as factors, there are several articles that point to the importance of parent involvement and teacher qualifications. Likewise, the element of "time on task" could be seen as a small piece or result of "motivation." Similarly, "first-language proficiency" and "linguistic awareness" could be seen as subelements of the factors of either "timing" or the "linguistic relationship between languages." The point is that the importance of these elements cannot be denied in their impact on trilingual proficiency, though in most cases they are parts of the larger factors.

In addition to these seven elements, two of the ten key factors also have a great deal of trilingual literature supporting them. The two factors of language typology and of the age of the learner, or window of opportunity, complement the seven elements to create each individual's particular recipe for multilingualism. Language typology is an extremely important factor. However, we reviewed this in Chapter 4 as it related to the length of time it takes a non-native speaker to reach fluency, so we will begin with a description of each of the seven elements and conclude this section with a review of the role that age of acquisition plays in trilingualism.

First-Language Proficiency

This element is concerned with mother-tongue or native language proficiency of the learner. The basic question is, "Can a child develop strong second or third language skills if he or she has a weak mother tongue?" Tove Skutnabb-Kangas conducted some of the early substantial research in this area in a Finnish study concerned with children of migrant workers in the 1970s. Skutnabb-Kangas noted that many of these transient workers had a weak record of sending their children to school. When they did attend, they performed poorly in Finnish. She suspected that this was not due to the poor preparation of the Finnish schools, but rather to the generally lower education level of the students in their mother tongue. Similar suspicions were evident in Switzerland, which experiences an influx of gypsies at harvest time. The Swiss authorities in the Geneva and Vaud cantons oblige these migrant children to attend school, and they have found that they tend to do poorly, despite being given extra help in French. It is suspected that this occurs due to the children's poor foundation in their first language, including lack of formal literacy training. That is, despite being given personalized tutors and extra help, the children do not manage to learn grade level French because their first-language skills are so weak that they have no points of reference from which to create new learning, or they are missing basic concepts about the purpose of language as a whole.

A simplified analogy of this concept is that when we learn languages, we are building a house. The foundation of the house must be strong in order to continue to build the floors on top of it; if it is weak, we have nothing substantial to build upon, and eventually the floor literally falls out from underneath us. If a person is not proficient in his or her first language, the likelihood that he or she will be capable of learning subsequent languages successfully is low. In recent studies in the United States, there is more and more emphasis placed upon getting at-risk students (including those with impoverished home language environments) into early intervention programs. In a specific longitudinal study by Kathryn Whitmore and Caryl Crowell, the importance of early intervention for children with impoverished language environments was studied in a dynamic bilingual school setting. The long-term results were a powerful testimony to the importance of strengthening the mother tongue in order to give children a leg up on future foreign language study. Students in this program were given extra home language support and intense bilingual training at school. The results were students who were more highly prepared for formal schooling than their monolingual counterparts, and were apt to go on and learn third languages with similar success.

Humans become more efficient at learning languages as they practice. The more languages you know, the easier it gets to learn an additional one. Studies show that prior linguistic experience facilitates new learning of additional languages. Cristina Sanz at the Center for Language Science at Pennsylvania State University believes that the efficiency of bilinguals to learn a third language is based on both internal and external factors. The internal variables relate to the amount of prior second-language experience and the level of bilingualism achieved, the age of onset of exposure to the second language, and the cognitive capacity of the individual, including the level of working memory and aptitude, as well as the learning strategies employed. The external variables, which can be manipulated, include the amount of grammar lessons prior to practicing the third language, the amount of explicit feedback the learner receives, and the amount of practice devoted to the task.[7] Additionally, Sanz notes that the potential for achievement in the third language is mirrored by levels of achievement in the second language, which in turn rests on first language fluency.

Research shows that there is a direct link between academic results and the time spent learning in the mother tongue; that is, the stronger the mother tongue, or native language, the better the student does academically. This means that success in school in a second or third language relies heavily on the first years of life when parents are the primary teachers. Additionally, a child's proficiency level in the native language relates to the speed and extent to which the second language develops, which in turn has implications for third language learning. This means that not only quality, but also the speed with which a third language can be acquired, is related to proficiency in the mother tongue. Although the focus here is on learning a third language, the importance of mother-tongue proficiency is related to all levels of linguistic prowess, from simple communication in one language to sophisticated study in multiple languages. Much of the importance of the first language relates to a child's ability to develop linguistic awareness or a basic understanding about the purpose of human communication through words and linguistic awareness.

Linguistic Awareness and Metacognition

A variety of elements influence multilingualism. According to Jasone Cenoz and colleagues Britta Hufeisen and Ulrike Jessner, metacognition plays a primary role in an individual's goal to learn new languages. Despite Sanz's just-mentioned research about mother-tongue proficiency, Cenoz and colleagues' research with trilinguals shows that although mother-tongue proficiency is vital, it is not always the point of reference in the trilingual mind. They found that "first languages do not necessarily play a privileged role in the acquisition of subsequent languages. . . . Despite the claims in the literature, first language does not seem to have a determining role in the development of a third language."[8] They agree that bilinguals rely heavily on their first language initially, but they found that when these bilinguals go on to learn a third language, "both L1 [first language] and L2 [second language] have a role: L1 is the default supplier during transfer lapses and L2 during interactional strategies."[9] This means that when looking for the right way to say something, a trilingual will not automatically fall back on a native language and then translate but may equally draw from a second language. This is called "parasitism," similar to the term in biology. A parasite is one thing that lives off another. When a trilingual learns new words, they are words "integrated into [the] existing lexical network with [the] least possible redundancy and as rapidly as possible in order to become accessible for communication."[10] This means that it is natural for the brain to refer to the easier accessible word based on its structure rather than on whether it is the individual's first or second language.

Michel Paradis, one of the most renowned authors in the field of bilingual aphasia, has studied language for three decades. He announced in 2006 that

> [T]here are two ways of speaking: the controlled way (using explicit metalinguistic knowledge) and the automatic way (using implicit linguistic competence). . . . The controlled use of metalinguistic knowledge may be speeded up, but metalinguistic knowledge never becomes linguistic competence. . . . With increased proficiency, the use of metalinguistic knowledge is either speeded up or gradually replaced by the use of implicit linguistic competence, hence switching from relying on one set of neural substrates to relying on another.[11]

Paradis' statement means that we may begin by consciously reflecting on just how to use our many languages, but this soon becomes automated as we become more and more comfortable with our multiple tongues (see Table 5.3).

Linguistic awareness is an understanding of the basic structure of language. Murphy says this covers all aspects of language: "Awareness is not limited to linguistic structure and semantics but also affects phonological, pragmatic, and sociolinguistic knowledge,"[12] meaning that every dimension of verbal and written communication is involved. Whereas very small children can use language, most do not understand the linguistic structure, semantics, sounds structures, or grammar they are applying. (Even older adults are often limited to the basics of language comprehension without a full understanding of the grammar.) Metalinguistic awareness implies knowing how language is pieced together, however, and the use of this deciphering practice to understand new language structures. In a trilingual context this means being able to compare mental schemes about the different languages in order to use them correctly. For example, the table below gives an example of an English–German–Spanish trilingual's possible metacognitive processes.

Table 5.3   Linguistic Awareness

Mental Schema	English	German	Spanish
"All languages use verbs"	Verbs usually come immediately after the subject	Verbs usually follow the subject but are also often at the end of the sentence	Verbs usually immediately follow the subject
"Adjectives describe things"	Adjectives usually come before the object	Adjectives usually come before the object	Adjectives usually come after the object
Example:	I drive a red car.	Ich fahre ein rotes Auto.	Yo manejo un auto rojo.

Metalinguistic awareness can come about through formal instruction in school, in which grammatical structure is taught, or it can come about with experience and practice in the language. Typically, fluency in foreign languages creates the platform for metalinguistic awareness. The level of fluency influences successful trilingualism in that mental schemes are broadened with each new language. That is, what we know about language in general can be applied to a new language specifically. This was shown by Barry McLaughlin and R. Nation's work in which they showed how "novice" language learners differed from "experts" in their ability to quickly generalize concepts about language. They showed that increased familiarity with many languages made it easier to learn additional ones. Why? Because the general awareness of language composition (words, grammar, sounds, gestures) is applied to each new language, meaning there is a cumulative base of information upon which we can learn a third language. It was found that "third-language learners are highly successful; they learn more language faster than second-language learners of the same target language; and (2) their behaviours are those of the self-directed learner,"[13] all presumably based on their greater linguistic awareness. Overall, learning a third language means that the individual spends more time thinking about "language" as a whole. Time spent on any task also increases proficiency, and time is what we turn to next.

Time Spent on Languages

The more quality language input is practiced, the more proficient one becomes in the language. According to the Language Research Center of the University of Calgary, "A limited amount of instruction will not lead to trilingual proficiency, but any amount of instruction time in a L3 [third language] will enable these students to develop their language learning skills."[14] However, we should also remember that the old adage "practice makes perfect" is somewhat flawed and that a more accurate statement would be "practice makes permanent." That is, if the original learning is valuable, then practice does indeed make perfect, but if the original learning is flawed, practice only makes poor information stick. We have to be careful about the quality of the input because the "amount of exposure has a strong effect on the likelihood of both positive and negative language transfer"[15] when learning a third language. Once we ensure that the quality is good, timing is a key to learning. The role of linguistic exposure functions similarly in second and third language acquisition. The quality of the mother tongue has an influence on the second language, and the second language and mother tongue together influence the third language. As mentioned in the section on first-language proficiency, without the building blocks and strong foundations, new languages will be difficult or impossible to achieve. If the foundations are good, however, the success of trilingualism hinges in part on the amount of time the individual devotes to the new language. This is perhaps the greatest challenge related to third versus second languages; it is far easier to divide language time in half than to divide it into thirds. Think about it. In a given twenty-four hour period how many languages can actually be pursued and given quality time? This is especially true in school settings.

If we expect that school will provide the structure for a third language, we have to expect that the curriculum structure provides enough time for this to occur. I have seen a number of schools promise a multilingual education, only to examine their curriculum to find that foreign language time is limited to a few minutes each morning, or to music time, neither of which is sufficient to reach a proficient level of language. Similarly, in a family setting, parents need to be mindful of their role in promoting the best quality mother tongue or native language experiences possible. This includes bilingual families, in which children are brought up bilingual from birth and both home languages are considered "native," whereas a third language is left to the school. Each language should have its quality time carefully delineated. Whereas vocabulary in one language tends to have a positive effect on increased vocabulary in the second and third languages, literacy skills do not enjoy this correlation. In order to be a good reader in a language, the learner has to devote time and practice; there is no automatic transfer of reading and writing abilities from language to language. Being multilingual can be limited to oral skills, but often trilingual goals mean literacy skills as well. This leads us to the important element of the level of education of the learner.

Education Level of the Learner

As we saw in the section about first-language proficiency, the impact of a learner's knowledge about their mother tongue, or native language, has a direct influence on the quality of subsequent languages. Proficiency is also influenced by the level of schooling one has in each of the languages. Two things about education and language success should be highlighted related to trilinguals: the first has to do with intelligence and the second has to do with the number of years in school.

First, in general, though it is controversial, many feel that learning is not linked to overall intelligence but to the ability to memorize. It's interesting to consider that one can have memories without learning, but it is impossible to learn without memory. This means that one does not have to be exceptionally smart to learn a foreign language, but smart people tend to pick up languages easier mainly because they have a great deal of practice with the art of memory because it is required for formal school success. I can think of many very smart friends who don't speak foreign languages and a lot of people of average intelligence who do. Also, I know many learning-disabled and Down's syndrome trilinguals. Yet all of the smart friends who ever attempted a language *could* learn. Smart people tend to have highly developed language skills. The research shows that these first-language skills will facilitate second- and third-language acquisition. Highly developed skills such as reading and writing normally occur within school settings. The more educated a person, the more acquainted that person is with the general tenets of learning, which can be applied to foreign languages as well as other subjects.

Second, the more time spent on a language, the more proficient a person becomes in that language, which makes it logical to assume that fluency increases with education in the language. Collier and Thomas's work in this field is hugely important, because it points to the necessity of a minimum of five to six years in a new language before native-like fluency can be reached, as we saw in Chapter 4. This means that although better-educated people are better candidates for foreign language learning success, those who undertake foreign languages are also more likely to stay in school and become better educated. The earlier the start, the more years a person has in the target languages. Both overall intelligence as well as the total time in the target language (as reflected by education level) are important in trilingual success. Another element influencing trilingual success is related to children's first teachers—their parents.

Parent Involvement

As with all types of new learning, a positive home environment plays a large role in successful trilingualism. The most important thing that parents can do for their children when they decide to embark on the multilingual journey is to agree on a family language strategy (who speaks what to whom and when) and then consistently follow it. A well-thought-out strategy will include an evaluation of the time that can be devoted to each language. For example, if one parent works more than the other and spends less time with the child, has a strategy been devised by which that language can "make up" time when the parent is present? A good strategy will also consider players outside the home, such as the community language in the dominant culture outside the home. If the community language is the same as one of the parents' languages, then perhaps less time can be allotted within the home for proficiency. A good strategy will also include the teachers and other caregivers in the child's life. The school should share the same language goals as the family or frustrations will abound. For example, Katrin's family moved from Germany to Peru for a three-year work contract. Her three children joined the German School. All but a few courses were in the children's native German language, but the three Spanish courses caused her children far more problems than she could have anticipated. Unlike schools in Germany, the school in Peru offered no extra classes in Spanish to support her children. This mismatch of expectations caused more than bad will and for the first year caused a tremendous amount of financial, as well as emotional, turmoil on the family. Each of the major players' roles will be discussed more in Chapter 7, but for now, it is sufficient to call attention to the importance of all the players in a learner's life. Let's focus on the family for now.

If the first and second languages are part of the home setting, as when the child is brought up bilingual from birth, and the third language comes from the community, this means that the home language(s) are minority languages. Deborah Ruuskanan, from the University of Vaasa, Finland, writes:

> Parents who want their children to learn their mother tongue must realize that it will take work, beyond simply speaking their mother-tongue all the time to their child. . . . This means things like reading out loud . . . singing to them and teaching them the songs and nursery rhythms, showing video films . . . and having other adults and children speak to the child . . . taking the child for a visit in the country where the language is spoken.[16]

Other researchers have suggested that parents honestly review their own motivations for wanting to maintain their native languages, because these can impact success levels. Many parents are motivated to keep their native languages with their children "in a more general attempt to maintain traditional cultures,"[17] which may not be enough to get a child to take it on. For the greatest trilingual success, parents and children have to share language goals in common.

Characteristics of good parent involvement are multiple. Catherine Snow of Harvard and colleagues offer some very sound advice in their book *Unfulfilled Expectations: Home and School Influences on Literacy*,[18] where they suggest healthy ways for parents to support their children's literacy endeavors. For example, showing interest in a child's work, including monitoring homework, is very helpful. They also recommend making links with the school to support the child's academic success, not just waiting to be called in about disciplinary problems. High-level parent involvement has a direct correlation to third language success. Schools can assist with this by identifying clear parental roles. Some schools that I have worked in use parent contracts at the beginning of the school year to establish parameters of cooperation. For example, one school outside Milan, Italy, understood the importance of a strong mother-tongue background in order to be a successful bilingual and asked the parents to sign an agreement in which they promised they would *not* help their children with English. Rather, the parents were asked to read with their children in Italian daily. Parental support in ensuring native language fluency and literacy is a key to multilingual academic success. Clear expectations become even more important as a child moves from bilingualism to trilingualism, especially in terms of what the child believes the parents feel about the languages.

Another area in which parents can help relates to beliefs and values. Parental use of and attitudes toward home and school languages directly impacts the quality of their child's learning. If a child's parents have a low level of respect for their child's school language, then that child will be hard pressed to develop it independently. Derogatory comments about languages, jokes about accents, and comments about their perceived difficulty can lower the motivation of children to study the school or community language. Similarly, if the parents speak two different languages but choose to use a third between them, this can send the message that one or the other parent language is less important. In the same way, if parents never make the attempt to learn the school or community language but insist that the children do, this also sends mixed messages. Teachers can often help stem these negative feelings by guiding families in subtle but clear ways. Next, we look at the importance of the teacher and his or her qualifications when it comes to encouraging trilingualism.

Teacher Qualifications

In their research on third language acquisition, Cenoz and Lindsay highlight the important role of the teacher in this process. They found that teachers who have more graduate education and more specialized training for working with language minority children are more successful. Whereas this may not come as a surprise to anyone, the details of what "specialized training" means are often a mystery. Cenoz and Lindsay found that teachers with greater knowledge of the student's home language(s) are more successful than monolingual teachers. Why? Because knowledge of other language structures helps teachers understand student errors better. For example, if I, the teacher, know that Vietnamese speakers use classifiers more than articles, I can better sympathize with the struggles of my students who can't seem to get their heads around "the," "a," and "an." With this in mind, I can develop remedial activities to help them. Or, if I teach Spanish and know my native English speakers rarely use reflexive verbs, I can take measures to highlight their awareness and reinforce their learning in this area. Awareness of the structure of other languages is one of many ways to measure teacher qualifications. A complete review of teacher training programs follows in Chapter 7, but a few ideas include being versed in appropriate teaching methods and student-centered learning activities. Additionally, successful teachers understand different learning styles ("there are no two brains alike"). They also show respect for other cultures. If they know a variety of teaching methods, empathize with different learning styles, and show respect for other cultures, teachers can be more effective.

A key concept in good teaching, especially as it relates to languages, is that the person who does the work is the person who does the learning. Well-trained teachers know that if they want a student to learn how to speak correctly (or read or write correctly), they will need to let the students practice these skills. It is hypothesized that parents who are successful at getting their children to learn several languages are simply successful parents. Similarly, teachers who are successful at helping their students learn several languages are simply good teachers. In both cases, the child is the center of the discussion.

According to Canales and Ruiz-Escalante's report on best ingredients for successful multilingualism, what is essentially needed then is a teacher who understands, appreciates, and respects the cultural background of the child; who knows the phonic and grammatical differences between the child's native language and that of the second language being taught so that he can help the child with his linguistic needs; and who is knowledgeable concerning the various reading approaches so that he will be able to select and utilize those that best meet the particular needs of the bilingual child.[19]

Teacher qualifications will be discussed in more detail in Chapter 7. We now turn to the last element of successful trilingualism: self-esteem.

Learner Self-esteem

Does success with languages lead to higher self-esteem, or does higher self-esteem lead to success with languages? It is most likely that both are true. People with a high level of self-esteem have personality characteristics that allow them to march through to success even against the worst of odds. At the same time, people who enjoy success and have a taste of achievement can use those as building blocks to develop higher self-esteem. Mel Levine, author of *A Mind at a Time*, believes that teachers owe it to their students and to their profession to help each child find some kind of success each day. Why? Success breeds success. Self-esteem is enhanced through the acquisition of new languages because it celebrates an achievement.

Enhanced self-esteem may be inherent in all successful language learners, but it is more likely that it is developed as a consequence of good parenting and/or school programs, which recognize the importance of self-esteem in learning. For example, in the United Kingdom, some teachers are evaluated on their knowledge base, including "the role of self-esteem in developing communication and self-expression and how to promote the self-esteem of pupils through the support [teachers] provide."[20] These kinds of criteria show that quality programs value and seek to enhance self-esteem in students. Although not universal by far, it seems that most quality multilingual programs understand the importance of self-esteem.

So do languages come about as a result of high self-esteem, or do multilinguals have high self-esteem because they have many languages? If languages come about due to high self-esteem, then we can take advantage of the potential that high self-esteem renders and take care to cultivate the psychological well-being of the children in our lives. If the answer is that after learning a language, self-esteem is enhanced, it means that we may contribute to building self-esteem through language instruction. It has been speculated that children are born with a natural curiosity and self-confidence that can sadly be crushed by unrealistic parental expectations or teachers' snide comments. To understand how this occurs, we turn now to children's developmental stages and how age impacts successful trilingualism.

Age When Language Is Learned

The general rule with foreign languages is the earlier the better, as we discussed in Chapter 3; this is primarily true for two reasons, one psychological and the other chronological. Psychologically, we know that young children have small egos and they see language as a game to be played, not an exam to be passed. I remember teaching a small group of children a song in Japanese only to find that the under-fives happily chimed in while the older students observed cautiously from afar. Small children and their small egos experiment more with language than big children with big egos do. However, it is not just self-consciousness that spurs on younger children, more mature minds take more time to reflect.

In a comparison of children in second, sixth, and ninth grades, it was found that the older children used more language transfer, displaying greater metalinguistic awareness. This also indicates that the older a child is, the more likely he or she will rely on the first and second language to learn the third. Now, this is not necessarily a bad thing, because it reflects an understanding of how languages work and a resourcefulness in finding missing information to communicate in the most effective way possible. It means that as each of the three language systems matures, the learner is more and more aware of different languages learned and knows to pull information from one system into another when the need arises. In real life, this means that when fourteen-year-old Julie, who grew up bilingual in German and Spanish (her mother is German but has worked in San Salvador and Ecuador since she was a baby), is faced with learning English in the German School as a third language, she will rely more heavily on her native German and Spanish to learn English than would her ten-year-old younger brother. This also confirms the "younger the better" premise in another way, because the younger the child, the less likely to draw on the first language while learning the third. The languages mature independently in younger children—which can be a positive thing—but they rely on each other in older learners.

Age is also important for reasons discussed in *Raising Multilingual Children*, which are related to the windows of opportunity. There are three main windows, and a window-and-a–half, that apply to all cases of multilingualism, including trilingualism, as shown in the following table.

Table 5.4   Windows of Opportunity

The First Window: Birth to 9 Months

(A Window-and-a-Half: 9 Months to 2 Years for High Aptitude Learner)

The Second Window: 4 to 8 Years Old

The Third Window: From Old Age and Back

Language Milestones

2–3 Years old: Normal mixing stage
3–4 Years old: Labeling of languages
5+ Years old: Cognizant of translation concept
4–10 Years old: Syntactic conservationism

Source: Charles L. Glenn, "Two-way Bilingual Education," *Education Digest*, 2003; 68(5):45.

Many parents raising multilingual children can confirm what Steven Pinker at MIT has documented related to key language milestones in child development. Children raised in more than one language experience a normal mixing stage (two to three years old) when they use words and grammar from all of their languages interchangeably and without discretion. This occurs in trilinguals in the same way as it does with bilinguals. This is followed by a separation of their language systems and an eventual labeling period (three to four years old) when the child can actually name his or her languages. Although this usually begins with, "Mommy says it like this," it concludes with the child being able to label his or her languages by name ("My teacher speaks French"). At this stage children will begin "syntactic conservationism" and generally stick to a single grammatical structure while they consolidate linguistic awareness of their languages. For example, my son Mateo began to use English grammar in all of his languages (English, Spanish and German) when he was six. This subsided for awhile but suddenly returned when he was nine. We helped him recognize when he was doing this, and he slowly broke himself of the habit. Though some estimates say this can last until ten years of age, I suspect it is more a process through which children have to pass than a fixed age. In other words, some children probably have so much practice with their languages that they can stop clinging to a single grammatical structure when they are six, whereas others need several more years to adjust to properly switching between languages. One indication of this is that around five years of age, children become cognizant of the "translation concept" and begin doing what adults do: think about what language they should be using, and then translate. Pinker reminds us that these are general guidelines, and children can vary as much as a year in either direction. For example, my daughter, Natalie, was pretty good about separating her first three languages by about six years of age. She was lucky to have a great amount of stimulation in all three languages and spoke nonstop as a child, practicing her languages with great frequency. This practice perhaps sped up the "syntactic conservationism" process. I suspect that the total amount of time spent practicing the management of access to different languages can speed up the passage through this milestone.

As is evident by a review of these seven elements that influence trilingualism, there are many things that both parents and teachers can do to help the children in their lives with the process. To make these point clearer, let's look at the flip side—what discourages trilingual skills.

WHAT DISCOURAGES THE ACQUISITION OF TRILINGUAL SKILLS

I hate to dwell on the negative, but I feel it is important to share some factors that discourage trilingual skills. Five of the most documented detractors are listed as follows:

1. *Discouragement from parents, teachers, or peers.* Whereas multilinguals may produce more initial errors than their monolingual counterparts, they progress faster and eventually are superior. The initial error-making stage may prompt some parents or teachers to discourage continued multilingual development. Additionally, telling children it's just too much for them can lead them to believe trilingualism is impossible.
2. *Contrived rather than authentic experiences with the language.* Successful learning comes from authentic communication. Use of language in real-life contexts encourages trilingualism.

3. *Insufficient time-on-task.*[21] Language proficiency increases over time. Many parents and teachers give up on their children before the necessary five to seven years of language study take place (see Chapter 3). Additionally, there are only twenty-four hours in a day, whether you have one, two, three, or more languages. Fluency comes with practice, and practice takes time.

4. *Status perception of third language.* Languages that have a higher status, or social appraisal, are learned faster than lower status languages, which have less appeal in society. When language heritage is not a priority, then minority languages can be lost when a new higher status language is learned. It is not uncommon that trilinguals often drop their home language in favor of an international one.

5. *Negative interlanguage transfer.* A person who has more than one language can experience interference from one language when speaking another, and the possibility of this occurring is proportionate to the number of languages a person speaks—the more languages, the greater possibility of confusion if the child is younger and/or if the learning was not conducted with a consistent strategy.

6. *Quality of mother tongue or native language fluency impacts the quality of subsequent languages.* As we explained in previous chapters, if a child has a weak language foundation, it may make it impossible to learn a new language fluently.

I would like to close this chapter with an intriguing question posed me in the Netherlands, in Rotterdam, at an experimental school in 2005. This school had a high minority language rate because of the country's notably high immigration rate. Over sixty-six percent of its population joined the community in recent years from Turkey and several North African nations. Many of the children had not received proper schooling before arriving in Holland and had poor mother-tongue knowledge. The question from the authorities of the school was, "Can English as a third language serve as a social equalizer without having negative metacognitive consequences for the child?" This query was born of the reality that the children entering their school had a home language, in which they were normally only orally proficient (no reading or writing skills). They would join the Dutch language system and struggle. Normally, they would also start English in the early primary or even kindergarten years. This at first sounded like a recipe for disaster, but what they actually found is that English began to play an unexpected social equalizing role within the schools. Whereas the new immigrant children knew they would always be at a disadvantage in Dutch compared with their native-language peers, they saw they could accelerate at a similar pace to their peers in English. This gave many students a leg up academically as well as integrating them through a common third language. After spending time at the school and watching their marvelous program, I understood that their question was born out of the mother-tongue dilemma; the children were starting school with poor skills in their native languages, but the demanding Dutch curriculum would not let them drop English in favor of Berber, or Turkish. What could be done? The school proactively solicited members of the community to work with them and called many parent meetings in which they explained that the school expected parents to help their children speak their native language and not to help with Dutch or English homework. They found that by involving the parents in this way they also showed how they valued not only the students' native languages but also their cultures. Parents were encouraged to share holidays, customs, and foods in order to celebrate their language in an attempt to elevate the status of these languages in the community. They also avoided the frustration of parents "helping" their children with languages in which they were not fluent. After-school programs were started to help parents learn more Dutch, but they were always encouraged to retain their home languages. In doing so the children began to shore up their first-language skills, making the job of teaching them Dutch and English easier. They actually answered their own question: English could be used as a social equalizer without negative metacognitive consequences, *if* the home language was given equal status and parents were assigned the role of improving mother-tongue fluency in order to give children the foundations for new language construction.

SUMMARY

In this chapter we began by looking at the five basic ways people arrive at being trilingual, reviewed the countries that are multilingual, saw the UN definition for multilingualism, and considered the benefits of bilingualism that transfer to trilingualism. We then reviewed the ten key factors (timing, aptitude, motivation, strategy, consistency, opportunity for us, typology, gender, siblings, and hand use) and the seven elements (first-language proficiency, linguistic awareness, time spent on language, educational level of the learner, parent involvement, teacher qualifications, and learner self esteem) and how they influence successful trilingualism. We ended by considering factors that discourage the acquisition of trilingual skills, including discouragement from parents, teachers, or peers; contrived rather than authentic experiences with the language; insufficient time-on-task; status perception of the third language; and negative interlanguage transfer, and we offered a special perspective on the importance of mother-tongue or native-language fluency.

As this chapter shows, language is a beautiful, albeit complex, process and multilingualism is riddled with challenges that all have the possibility of becoming opportunities. Some of these challenges are social, such as those related to language status, others are psychological, as with terms of self-esteem and motivation. Yet others are neurological and have to do with brain structure and the complexities of learning more than one language at different points in life. We now turn to Chapter 6, which is devoted entirely to how the brain handles multiple languages.

6
The Brain and Languages

OUR UNIQUE ABILITY

This chapter is meant to give parents and teachers a better sense of language and the brain. Why? Because understanding the complexities of the brain and language helps us better appreciate the myriad of multilingual skills our children are developing. This in turn helps us more accurately identify when "problems" are part of the natural milestones of language acquisition and when they are related to true learning problems or conflicts between language typologies. We need to get away from the overly simplistic diagnoses of children's problems in school by blaming things on language ("The child is confused because he has too many languages. Drop a language and he will be fixed"). No one should ever say a child has a problem "with language" unless they identify the subfield of language they are referring to. For example, does the child have good receptive language skills (listening and reading) but is poor at productive language skills (speaking and writing)? Does he or she have poor pronunciation and articulation but can write perfectly? Or is the child capable of humor and analogies in his or her second language but incapable of putting them into print? Concerned parents and teachers should know enough about language and the brain to steer clear of oversimplified diagnoses. They should also understand how the brain handles multiple languages because it gives us further reason to celebrate the awesome feat of multilingualism.

Language is what separates humans from other animals. As the most complex of mental tasks, language is managed by various interconnected parts of the brain (written language uses more parts of the brain simultaneously than perhaps any other mental task).[1] In fact, language skills in the brain are so complicated and overlap so many areas that Peter Indefrey and Marlene Gullenberg summarized their attempts to neatly separate them by asking rhetorically if it would not be more effective to ask which areas of the brain were *not* involved in language, as opposed to which were. Using available studies, we will try to piece together this complex puzzle by first explaining what is known to date about the brain and languages in general, and then we will specifically address multilinguals.

WHAT LITTLE WE KNOW

Despite overzealous claims in the popular press, knowledge about the human brain is in its infantile stages. Very little is known about this organ, and of what is presumed, most still remains to be confirmed. Despite these limitations, however, one of the richest areas of brain research relates to human language development, which yields a wealth of fascinating, though incomplete, facts. Neuroscience, psychology, and linguistics have posited explanations for an overall language system involving a myriad of brain areas that perform independent functions in a symphony coordinated by a multifaceted conductor, the mind. Today it is now possible to view a functioning healthy brain in vivo as it processes different language-related activities. These studies help us determine which language problems appear to be congenital (from birth) versus which seem to be developmental, and we can distinguish those that demand the use of one area of the brain more than others.

The most documented aspect of language and the brain is first-language acquisition. By understanding how infants acquire their first language, we can then compare and contrast this with how second, third, and subsequent languages are learned. "With the advancements of the last 30 years, we are ready to combine basic research in first-language acquisition with research in brain imaging and apply that to questions of how children become multilingual," says Barbara Lust, a professor in the Department of Human Development at Cornell University. Happily for existing practitioners, most early beliefs about language related to word learning, reading, and grammar comprehension are being confirmed by these new techniques. We start with a general overview of findings about the brain in the past twenty years.

WHAT WE CAN SEE

Brains may be thought of as analogous to faces; they have the same basic parts, but no two are exactly alike. This fact explains why it is impossible to say, "language is located in X area" of the brain, let alone identify where multiple languages are located. It also helps educators and parents appreciate the uniqueness of each child. The 1990s was the "Decade of the Brain" when tremendous headway was made in analyzing how the brain functions. The 1990s also clearly documented how brains differ between individuals. Barbro Johannson is a linguist at Wallenberg Neuroscience Center, Lund University in Sweden. He says "current neuro-imaging and neurophysiologic techniques have substantially increased our possibilities to study processes related to various language functions in the intact human brain,"[2] the result of which is that we can identify the main language areas of the brain with a high level of accuracy. This means that we have been able to gain an increased level of generalization about what appears to be similar in all brains, although we acknowledge that each is unique. Just as we can say that each face has two eyes, a nose, a mouth, and two ears, we can say that people incorporate general areas for language as well, though no absolutely identical patterns of use are found. Just as there are no identical faces, there are no identical brains. Deciphering this is complex. Experts in the field, such as Michael Ullman of Georgetown University, nurture our growing understanding of the brain and bilingualism and its complexities. Ullman believes it is not enough to view physiological or chemical aspects of the brain in isolation when studying multiple-language learning, and he encourages a more holistic view of the brain that takes into consideration all of its systems. Ullman's work takes into consideration "knowledge of the cognitive, computational, neuroanatomical, physiological, cellular, endocrine, and pharmacological bases of these systems [as each] leads to specific testable predictions about both first and second language."[3] To understand this complexity further, we now turn to some of the better known language areas of the brain.

THE MAIN LANGUAGE AREAS OF THE BRAIN

Broca and Wernicke's Areas

Most people have their main language areas in the left frontal and parietal lobes, bridging Broca's area (commonly referred to as the part of the brain that selects appropriate words, structures sentences, and is related to grammar, naming of objects, and articulation) and Wernicke's area (commonly understood to be responsible for the actual content and meaning of what is said), two regions of the brain named after famous neurologists of the nineteenth century who documented different types of language loss (aphasia) when these parts of the brain were damaged. However, language substructures are numerous. Within this general left-hemisphere area, it is well documented that distinct areas of the brain are employed when an individual hears another language, thinks about what is being said, considers what to reply, chooses the appropriate words, moves the mouth to speak, or picks up a pen to write. What is even more intriguing is that the parts of the brain normally associated with certain language functions are activated even when we simply think about those functions. For example, when we imagine we are going to say something, our brain lights up Broca's area in the same way that actual talking does. Other studies in the field show even

Figure 6.1   Some Areas Associated with Language in the "Average" Human Brain

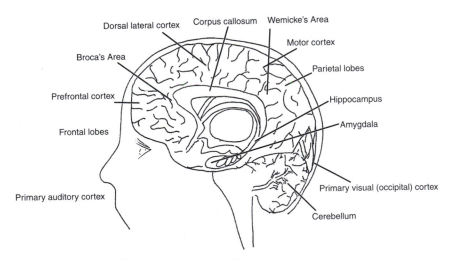

Source: Drawing by Natalia Espinosa Tokuhama.

more intricate details of language in the brain. Spelling, for example, is shown to be associated with a small, specific area in the brain, which is involved in choosing appropriate symbols to spell a word.[4]

But this does not mean that language is neatly documented "down to the letter" in every case. For example, researchers Marian, Spivey, and Hirsch found that the way the brain works when it is *learning* to read is different from how it works when it already *knows* how to read. Although there appears to be shared cortical structures when one starts to learn to read, "the two languages may be using separate structures at later stages of processing."[5] This means that brain use for language changes as the brain becomes more used to the task, meaning that "reading" in the brain cannot be pinpointed without knowing the proficiency level of the learner. Angela Friederici of the Max Planck Institute for Human Cognitive and Brain Sciences has done extensive research using brain-imaging techniques to identify the different areas of the brain that distinguish between semantic errors and syntactical errors (or between errors of word choice and word order). She found that the brain manages semantics, or words, through different systems than it manages syntax and grammatical structure. This explains why some second-language learners may find it a breeze to memorize long lists of vocabulary but do miserably learning a new grammar. This means that because of the way our brains are structured and our memories function, lexical knowledge, or our set of personal mental dictionaries, is easier to cultivate than is grammatical knowledge, or rules about word order. These subtleties and differences grow with the number of languages a person manages. Early bilinguals, for example, appear to use the same parts of Broca's area when speaking different languages, effectively treating first and second languages both as "first" languages. In contrast, late bilinguals use a different segment of Broca's area to process their different languages, according to Joy Hirsch of Columbia University.[6]

Working closely with Broca's area is Wernicke's area, also located in the left hemisphere, just behind and above the ear in the parietal lobe. Wernicke's area is responsible for understanding spoken words as well as fluid speech. People who suffer strokes in Wernicke's area suffer what is known as "fluent" aphasia in which they appear to be talking with the appropriate intonation and grammatical structure, but their word choice is pure jargon and completely incomprehensible. The importance of this area when considering multilinguals can be illustrated by simple curiosity. Children can appear to be fluent in a language because they have the appropriate intonation and gestures. They even sing beautifully, but they have no idea what they are saying and/or upon closer observation, may actually not be saying anything at all.

Executive Functions

Touch your forehead. Behind your fingers is the foundation of the brain's executive functions. Your frontal lobes, as this area is called, help make decisions for the rest of the body. Choosing the right verb to use or deciding how to make yourself understood in a new language takes place here. This is also where choices are made about which languages to use. Physical parts of the executive function include the dorso-lateral prefrontal cortex and the anterior cingulate cortex. These serve as the primary firewalls between our languages. They help us gain access to the right language in the right moment with the right person. These parts of the brain "facilitate the processes of selection, switching, and inhibition" or suppression,[7] which involves how we choose what we say. This is hugely important for multiple languages, because this part of the brain helps us shut out one language and use another or search for a specific word in a specific language.

The Visual Cortex and the Motor Cortex

Other areas related to language include the occipital, or visual, cortex, which is responsible for receiving and processing sensory input, such as written text or emotional cues from faces. Without the ability to properly see such stimulus, an individual would be handicapped in their understanding of language. Though primarily related to vision, the occipital cortex is fundamental to proper language functioning. In a similar fashion, the motor cortex is normally related to movement, however it is intimately involved in language as well. Without a properly functioning motor cortex, an individual would be incapable of producing actions needed for speaking and writing.

Some Right Hemisphere Functions

To make things even more complex, although the primary areas for language in an "average" brain are in the left hemisphere, there is research that points to counterintuitive information in this field, indicating that there are other functions primarily in the right hemisphere. Take humor, for example. Sophisticated uses of language, including humor, analogy, and the choice of intonation, are probably located in the right, not left, hemisphere. Humor and laughter trigger the release of neurotransmitters that aid in the solidification of memories. In a like fashion, negative emotions can block the uptake of information.

Emotions and Language

Another area of the brain related to languages is the amygdala, the seat of emotional memories. The amygdalae are two small almond-shaped orbs in the middle of the brain just atop the hippocampus that mediate as well as store affective memory and emotionally bound contexts. If you point your right finger at your head through your ear, and your left hand points to just between your eyes, the intersection should be at the amygdala. Whereas the right amygdala seems to be related to emotional memory and production, studies have shown that the left amygdala is activated by facial expressions and helps interpret the emotional content of spoken words.[8] There is also evidence that the amygdala is the physical location of certain stored memories, though it is not yet conclusive. In humans "the impairment in remembering emotionally charged words (e.g., *rape*, *terrorist*) is correlated with the extent of damage to the amygdala."[9] In practice, this means that what we remember we felt about a situation impacts how well we can remember what happened in that context. For example, a child who sees the French teacher and remembers how she was humiliated in class the day before will connect that feeling to her next encounter with that teacher. Basic psychology confirms that one's emotions can change other people's mental states. In the positive sense, for example, when someone gives you a smile it can change your mood from being sad to happy. People react to external stimuli in emotional ways, from a teacher's humiliating comment to a friend's encouraging smile. The amygdala's job is "to ensure that emotional responses are appropriate to the external stimuli and social context."[10] The amygdalae are key in using how we feel about a language to learn better. When a concept fights with an emotion, the emotion almost always wins.[11]

This has implications for learning in both the formal and informal educational contexts. For example, although fear has been identified as a survival value, and anxiety is closely related to fear, a "modern" emotional state that has received a great deal of attention lately is stress. Ongoing anxiety results in stress. When managed well, individuals use "good" stress to remain focused and pay attention.

"Good" stress can be seen in classrooms, where students are alert and attentive, or in the work place, where everyone is on task. When stress is out of control, however, it results in the release of hormones that impede learning and can even damage the brain.[12] Some intriguing research points to a greater use of the amygdala in second-language acquisition, which indicates the role of emotions during the learning process.[13] An understanding of this function can positively influence the creation of good learning environments through the management of positive emotions to enhance the overall excellence of learning. Knowing this and understanding the impact on language acquisition is a powerful tool for both parents and teachers. When we acknowledge that language learning is emotionally bound, we can begin to take advantage of this information to structure learning situations in better ways. We can help make positive links toward the emotions if we are more conscious of their impact.

The amazingly complex structure of language in the brain seems to work seamlessly in the majority of people who learn to use language as infants, as well as those who learn second, third, or fourth languages as adults. Some argue that love, the strongest of emotions, is behind the ease of first language learning. Others say that humans have an innate ability for language. How are languages learned? What is different between first- and second-language acquisition? These intriguing questions are where we turn next.

HOW LANGUAGES ARE LEARNED

The Pieces of Language

There are an estimated 7,000 languages in the world, about 1,000 of which have been studied in detail by linguists. All languages have similar basic elements. They are composed of both receptive abilities (hearing and reading) and productive abilities (speaking and writing), they are composed of sounds, and many are based on a written symbol system. This means that the world's languages are more similar than they are different, which lends credibility to the belief that humans have an innate ability for languages, whose natures differ mostly because of culture. The four main aspects of language seen across the world, which are also hierarchical in terms of developmental stages, are the abilities to understand, speak, read, and write. Whereas less than half of the world is literate (can read and write), all non-physically impaired, average-level intelligence individuals can understand their own language and, barring any physical restraints, speak it. This means that although the majority of the world is at least bilingual (if not multilingual), most are illiterate and do not read or write fluently in even one language.

Cross-linguistic studies confirm that infants begin cooing and then babbling, then attempting to echo syllabic utterances; words appear by about the first year, says Dan Slobin, renowned cognitive linguist at the University of California–Berkeley. Bransford and colleagues, confirm that "by 6 months of age, infants distinguish some of the properties that characterize the language of their immediate environment . . . [and] around 8–10 months of age, infants stop treating speech as consisting of mere sounds and begin to represent only the linguistically relevant contrasts."[14] Infants must first perceive and understand language before they can attempt to imitate it, which is why understanding precedes speaking. After understanding language and then speaking it, one can learn to read and, then, to write. Many studies have documented that these four elements of language are distinct, but often overlapping, sub-systems in the brain. There are strong arguments that the way first languages are remembered in the brain differs from how subsequent languages are remembered.

Theories of Memory and Languages

It is argued that a person can have memories without learning but that it is impossible to have learning without memories. Psychologist Alan Baddeley of the University of Bristol in the United Kingdom offers a splendid model of working memory that distinguishes language messages from visual ones. He posits that working memory, or the ability to remember something for just long enough to execute an associated action, is a temporary storage system in the brain. Working memory is what we use when we look up the phone number for the pizza delivery, remember that Johnny has a preference for pepperoni, that Mary also wants garlic bread, and then keep this all in mind as we dial and then talk to the operator to make the order. However, working memory can be exercised and extended to last far longer than a few moments with practice. (As a teacher, I can only wonder if it is actually a form of working memory that students use to keep information in their minds just long enough to take a test, after which everything is then forgotten. After all, this can't be called long-term memory, which is presumed to be permanent.) As we saw in Chapter 4, multilinguals have better working memory capacity than monolinguals, presumably due to the need to maintain one language in the mind while quickly retrieving the second. Our central executive function, or control center of the mind, manages three types of information in this working memory system. The first is for visual imagery, the second is called the episodic buffer, and the third is the phonological loop. This phonological loop is used for maintaining auditory information in the mind for a short period of time, usually by repeating it over and over quietly to ourselves. This is important because it helps us understand how a child can keep foreign words, whole phrases, or even a dialogue in the mind long enough to execute a task ("repeat after me"), but this does not mean it goes into long-term memory or results in real learning. Although children may appear to be "getting it," the only thing we are assured of is that they are getting better at exercising their working memories. The key to real learning is moving information from working memory to long-term memory.

Long-term memory is broken down into memories that are procedural, or implicit, (such as remembering to breath and how to walk), and memories that are learned, which are called declarative (things that have to be learned, like how to subtract, or the capital cities in Europe). Michel Paradis of McGill hypothesizes that second-language learning is managed primarily by the declarative memory system. Many declarative memories often, but not always, require strategies. ("How can I get that information inside my head?"). However, according to Ullman, not all declarative memories "are even explicit (that is, can be brought to conscious awareness."[15] If declarative memories do lead to strategies, however, this means that it is possible that when we learn a second language, we are relying on conscious metalinguistic strategies. ("This is German. And this is past tense. In German the verbs are often at the end of a sentence in the past tense. I should put the verb at the end of this sentence.") This process is less automatic than using our first language. According to Paradis, metalinguistic knowledge is gained through declarative memory, whereas linguistic knowledge is procedural, because "explicit knowledge cannot be 'converted' or 'transformed' into implicit competence."[16] This could be the core difference between how first and subsequent languages are stored in the brain.

The prominent second language theory related to declarative and procedural memory comes from Ullman. Ullman's Declarative/Procedural (DP) model states that use of lexical knowledge depends on the declarative memory system, whereas grammar relies on the procedural memory system.[17] This model helps explain the difference between first-language and second-language users. Although first-language learners are taking in language as an essential skill (such as walking), second-language learners are, at least initially, taking in language as a skill similar to memorizing all the European capitals. The key tenets of Ullman's model are explained in brief below.

Different types of memory are related to different language tasks, which vary over the course of our lives. "The declarative/procedural model posits that L2 [second language] learners have more difficulty with the procedural acquisition of grammar than with the declarative memorization of lexical knowledge, as compared to young children."[18] Ullman documents that "adults can indeed acquire knowledge in procedural memory," and he believes that with increased experience with a language, second-language learners should eventually "show procedural learning of grammatical rules, and rule-based composition in language processing."[19] This means that as second-language learners become more and more proficient at learning both lexical and grammatical aspects of their new language, they will do so using different types of memory systems. These memory systems are hypothesized to relate to different parts of the brain: "According to the declarative/procedural model, the mental lexicon depends on declarative memory and is rooted in the temporal lobe, whereas the mental grammar involves procedural memory and is rooted in the frontal cortex and basal ganglia."[20] Eventually, late bilinguals will increasingly rely on the same brain systems as native language speakers: declarative memory for words and procedural memory for the implicit grammar, says Ullman. The better the brain gets at processing language, the faster that skill can be retrieved and used. When a skill becomes habituated, it is relegated to an area of the brain requiring lower maintenance. "Thus, with sufficient experience with L2, the language is expected to become L1-like in its grammatical dependence on the procedural system, the potential for a high degree of proficiency."[21] Studies suggest that "greater cognitive effort may be sub-served by less well-tuned neural representations that require greater neuronal activity."[22] This means that a lot of brainpower is needed to learn something initially and that the brain becomes more efficient with practice. Theoretically, the closer to "fluent" a person becomes, the more "native-like" language learning becomes. The declarative/procedural model is also important because it explains why adults and children learn languages differently from a neurological perspective and helps us understand the natural learning process for languages in the brain.

Learning Your First Language

Over the past decade there have been several studies that confirm that first-language acquisition is formed very early in a newborn's development. For example, studies by joint researchers at the Departments of Psychology at New York University and Amherst College pointed to a seven-month threshold by which time infants identify structures in their native language(s). Their study implies that seven-month-olds already grasped the basic structure of their native languages and attended curiously to new ones or those that broke the patterns of expectations. This means that before children are one year old, they already have engrained perceptions of their native language(s). Infants less than three months old were breast-fed while listening to their native language and while listening to a foreign language. When the foreign language was played the babies tended to stop suckling and listen curiously. They knew the sound was a language, but they also realized it was not *their* language. Other work by Debra Mills, Janet Werker, and colleagues showed that language in the brain varied between 14- and 20-month-olds when it came to phonetically similar words. Ironically, older infants were less successful at distinguishing similar sounds. This study is one of many that suggest that humans are universal receivers of all language sounds (they are born with the ability to distinguish all sounds in all languages), but they quickly lose this ability before their second birthdays, after which time they have a hard time recognizing any sound that is not part of their native language. This implies that at birth children are primed to learn any language without an accent, but the older they get, the less able they are to perceive foreign sounds. Without hearing the sound, they are unable to reproduce it (and therefore have an accent). As explained in *Raising Multilingual Children*, it is for this reason that birth to nine months is identified as the first window of opportunity for language acquisition. At this age, the brain is identifying language patterns it can adhere to for life. However, ironically, the stage of permanency is also one of plasticity.

Although the brain is noted to be dynamically reshaping itself in early childhood, it can also heal itself in a similar fashion. Brian Mac Whinney reports, "Bones, muscles, cell walls, mitochondria, and immune system[s] [all] become stronger after periods of use and breakage. Neurons work in the same way,"[23] related to language. The more they are stretched, the more they grow. For example, children who suffer strokes before they are seven years of age tend to recover language abilities fully due to the brain's plasticity. This does not mean that the brain heals itself in the same way a cut on the skin would heal but rather that other areas of the brain take over the functions of the damaged area. Researchers have noted that some young stroke victims with left hemisphere damage "recruited the right hemisphere into language processing networks during early development, presumably in response to congenitally aberrant circulation."[24] This means that when the brain's "normal" language areas became damaged, parallel structures in the right hemisphere take over their work. This reminds us how generalizations about the brain have a myriad of exceptions with many different root causes and that this information should be reviewed conservatively.

SECOND, THIRD, AND SUBSEQUENT LANGUAGES

This History of Bilingual Brains

The very first story of bilingual aphasia on record was "Johann Gesner [who] in 1770 probably provided the first description of dissociation in reading ability in different languages in a bilingual patient, who after brain damage was able to read Latin [his second language] but not German [his first language]."[25] Since that time, many well-respected neurologists suggest that first and second languages may differ in their location in the brain. Neurologists are divided as to whether this means there is increased right brain hemisphere use by bilinguals. The greatest number of studies about bilingual brains originally came from evidence provided by stroke patients, who are not consistent in how they lose languages and how they recuperate them. Paradis emphatically wrote in 2003 that "all the experimental studies of the past 25 years combined and the meta-analysis of their findings have not advanced knowledge of the lateralization of language in bilingual speakers."[26] A strong theory, which emerged after studying two hundred years of damaged multilingual brains, leads to what is called the "dual-language" or "overlap" theory, in which languages share some areas in the brain but not others. Bilingual patients are recorded as frequently losing one of their languages but not the other, implying that the two languages were found in distinct or overlapping areas of the brain. A recent study using brain imagining technology as opposed to autopsy showed that roughly 65 percent of bilingual stroke patients suffered a loss of both languages, while 20 percent lost just the second, and 15 percent lost just the first. Other researchers have documented how "selective impairment in one language after surgery demonstrates that each language has different anatomical representation."[27] A very interesting case showed how a trilingual recuperated his three languages at different stages over a six-week period post-stroke. He surprised his doctors by recovering his second language first, his third language second, and his native language last.

The idea that greater brain area is used by multilinguals is supported by other research as well. Studies based on handedness and language lateralization found that suggesting that spatial abilities are a "right brain" function is a gross overgeneralization because the opposite has been found to be the case (language in the right and spatial abilities on the left). That is, both language and spatial abilities have been found on the right or language and spatial abilities on the left. The study concluded that "all combinations of cerebral lateralization for language and attention may exist in the healthy brain."[28] Cases such as these appear to confirm earlier medical and linguistic suspicions that multiple languages in the brain may share some, but not all, physical areas, depending on different factors shaped by individuals' experiences. The bottom line is that although specific templates cannot be devised, general patterns of multilingualism in the brain can be found.

Multilingualism in the Brain

There is a common practice of mapping language areas in the brain prior to surgery to avoid further damage. The purpose of this procedure is to clearly delineate areas of the brain dealing with language in order not to remove them during surgery to take out tumors, blood clots, or other damaged areas. This procedure has led to unplanned discoveries about the brain. For example, while conducting normal pre-surgical mapping for languages on bilinguals, Panagiotis Simos and colleagues found "substantial differences in the receptive language maps."[29] Simos' observation indicates that being bilingual changes the perception patterns of language in the brain compared with monolinguals. This may indicate that bilinguals have language in a wider area than monolinguals, and process languages in slightly different areas of the brain. This finding means that if a person learns a second language alongside a first (bilingual from birth), the brain mechanisms are basically the same as a monolingual. However, if a person learns a second language after infancy, the actual brain mechanisms change.

What Factors Change the Multilingual Brain Most?

A group of researchers at the University of Basel have been trying to answer this question for years. Rita Franceschini, Daniela Zappatore, Georges Lüdi, Ernst-Wilhelm Radü, Elise Wattendorf, and Cordula Nitsch are lead researchers in Switzerland who have been managing *The Multilingual Brain Project* since 2000. They conduct brain imaging studies combined with interviews about participants' lives to try and piece together an answer as to whether languages are found in the brain in differing areas based on when the languages were learned, whether or not there was formal schooling involved, the age of the participants, and how similar the language typologies were. Their primary goal is to determine if "new neural networks [are] created when second and third languages are learned only in the early adult age [and if so] are different learning strategies used?"[30] The general findings to date point to no pattern for multilingualism. One explanation could be due to the fact that no two people have the same life experiences, and these experiences change the brain daily. That is, a Hungarian immigrant construction worker who arrives in Zurich, Switzerland, at the age of 15 is different from a 30-year-old immigrant doctor from Turkey, both of whom may have cemented their life experiences in such different ways as to actually use slightly distinct areas of the brain to manage their respective languages. This could be affected by the levels of education these individuals had or could be the result of whether these individuals formally studied their third languages in school or learned them informally. They could also differ depending on the combinations of languages learned. What we do know is that certain factors play larger roles than others in shaping both success and the physical structure of language areas in the brain.

Visible Language Factors within the Brain

"Current neuro-imaging and neurophysiologic techniques have substantially increased our possibilities to study processes related to various language functions in the intact human brain," writes linguistic researcher Johansson. His research identifies that "proficiency, age of acquisition, and amount of exposure can affect the cerebral representations of the languages,"[31] yet it is still not known how and to what extent language typologies (historical roots), the age of acquisition, and the length of time and proficiency in the second or subsequent language impacts the language's physical location in the brain. Let's consider each of these factors individually.

Age. Many people believe that the age that a person learns a language is the main factor that influences not only success but also language location in the brain. As we discussed previously, multiple languages learned from birth are all treated as "first" languages in the brain. For example, research by psychologists Wuillemin, Richardson, and Lynch at Monash University in Australia found that "age of acquisition proved to be a significant contributor to the laterality effects obtained."[32] Others dispute this finding, however. Does this mean that the age a person learns a language determines whether or not the language is located primarily in the right or left hemisphere? Such a generalization would be shortsighted and ignore other evidence that shows that other factors also contribute to which areas of the brain are changed by managing more than one language. As mentioned in the review of Ullman's declarative/procedural model, the maturation of memory systems in the brain may also cause changes in the physical structure of multilingual versus monolingual brains. Age may have an impact of first versus second and subsequent language location in the brain, but other factors may be equally influential.

Proficiency. Researchers Mira Goral, Erika Levy, Loraine Obler, and Eyal Cohen in New York and Boston studied a trilingual who suffered language loss due to a stroke. They compared the different ages at which she learned her languages, the frequency of language use, and the similarity of vocabulary in the languages to see where all this ended up in the brain. When they placed the influencing factors of age of language learning, degree of language recovery and use, and prevalence of shared lexical items on a hierarchical scale for influence, they concluded that "whereas age of language learning plays a role in language recovery following aphasia, the degrees of language use prior to the aphasia onset and of shared vocabulary determine the ease with which words are accessed."[33] In this patient's case, the ages at which she learned her different languages were not as important as the amount of use she gave each when it came to recuperating her three languages. The level of fluency (which can often relate to age in terms of the number of years of practice) is more important than age in determining if a language can be recalled easier. This makes sense in terms of basic learning principles in which rehearsal is key in solidifying information into long-term memory.

Regula Briellmann, Michael Saling, Allie Connell, Anthony Waites, David Abbott, and Graeme Jackson at the Brain Research Institute at the University of Melbourne in Australia conducted a study that seems to support the finding that use is more influential than age of acquisition. They studied people who spoke four languages by testing noun-verb generation. (For example, you see the word "dog" and decide if the correct verb that goes with it is "run" or "runs.") They repeated this exercise in all the languages that the participants knew. They then measured brain responses through functional magnetic resonance imaging (MRI), which showed how different languages triggered different intensity levels of the language areas in the brain. These researchers hypothesized that proficiency in each language was related to these areas and varied in intensity based on proficiency. Their work also showed that "activation did not appear to be dependent on the age at which the language was learnt,"[34] but rather on the fluency, which is similar to Goral and colleagues' findings.[35] It seems that language dominance and the location of languages in the multilingual brain are more dependent upon level of fluency and familiarity with the language than upon age. However, these studies are important not so much because of their ranking of "age" versus "fluency" but rather because they demonstrate that brain mechanisms change with proficiency. Other studies show additional changes based on different linguistic structures.

Language Typology. Different linguistic structures can cause languages to be found in different areas of the brain, such as those found in different writing systems, for example. Studies by Mei-chun Cheung, Agnes Chan, and Yu-leung Chan in Hong Kong show that English and Chinese written language processing is in different hemispheres[36] (English in the left and Chinese in the right). This is presumably because Chinese is in part based on pictographs, or images, though this is still open to debate. Studies of Japanese aphasics who were unable to read the pictograph symbol system but retained the ability to interpret the Romanji or Phoenician alphabet lend credibility to this claim, however. This could have implications for multilinguals who seek literacy skills in languages that have different writing systems. The most common written language families are Latin (Phoenician), which includes English. The second most common is the Cyrillic writing system (including Russian, Ukrainian, and Bulgarian), and the third is Arabic (Arabic, Punjabi, and Turkish). In terms of population, the Chinese writing system (which includes some elements of Japanese written language as well) is the largest. In addition, some writing systems are unique (Armenian, Greek, Thai, and Korean). In India, Chenhappa and colleagues found that orthographic differences between English and various Indian languages were distinct enough to be found in different parts of the brain, resulting in different levels of aphasia in each after a stroke. The differences between the symbols used can impact where the various languages are located in the brain, as well as the ease with which a learner gains literacy skills in different systems. This also means that when the bilingual's writing systems share a similar structure, reading problems in bilingual populations seem to mirror those found in monolingual populations. This finding has important implications for teaching in both diagnostic tools as well as classroom methodologies.

This information is very important to consider when we decide that multiliteracy skills are part of our language goals. It is probable that languages that share the same writing system are easier to learn than languages with different writing systems because they are located in similar areas of the brain. This information begs the question of the factors influencing exceptions to the rule in multilingual brains, to which we turn next.

"AVERAGE" VERSUS "SPECIAL" BRAINS

We said that there are no two brains alike; whereas the basic parts are common to all humans, no two brains are identical. Even identical twins have different brains from birth because the main change-agent for brain structure is experience, and no two people share the same experiences. Brain structures differ for a wide variety of reasons, including gender, handedness, frequency of language use, and genetic variations, which we will turn to now.

Gender

There are so many potential factors that can have an impact on foreign language acquisition that it is often difficult to filter out what is cause and what is effect. Take gender, for example. There is an extensive body of knowledge about how boys and girls (and later men and women) process language differently.[37] This may be related, in part, to how their physical memory structures also differ, and the differences in hormonal balances between the genders.[38] One of the interesting findings is that apparently women use far more parts of their brains to consider stimuli. Porter Coggins, Teresa Kennedy, and Terry Armstrong's research on male and female multilinguals showed that the corpus callosum, which joins the left and right hemispheres, is larger in bilinguals than in monolinguals "to accommodate multiple language capacity in bilingual individuals compared to monolingual individuals"[39] and also slightly larger in women than in men. Does this explain a general tendency for woman to "multi-task" better than men? Or can the multilingual's increased working memory be the cause of physical differences from monolingual brains? In comparative gender studies involving multilinguals, the brain is reported to work differently in men than in women. Is this because of gender, or because of bilinguality? There are simply not enough studies available to say with certainty, though it stands to reason that given other studies showing women's greater cross-hemisphere processing of first languages, they could use both hemispheres with their second languages as well. Men's and women's brains look different. Do these differences impact foreign language proficiency? Not at all. Men and women are equally capable of being multilingual. However, it should be recognized that these physical differences may manifest themselves in learning preferences, which we will consider in Chapter 7. Another way our brains are different is in their genetics.

Genetics

Some distinctions between brains may not be based on gender but rather connected to genetic factors. Neurologists have found that "genetic factors significantly influenced cortical structure in Broca's and Wernicke's language areas, as well as frontal brain regions,"[40] which could point to a genetic link for foreign language aptitude. Although such findings could lead to definitive answers about why some people learn foreign languages easier than others, far more research is needed to confirm such suggestions. Despite the fact that "these genetic brain maps reveal how genes determine individual differences, and may shed light on the heritability of cognitive and linguistic skills,"[41] there is just not enough data to definitively say. It has been noted by historical linguists that successful bilinguals tend to run in families, but it has remained questionable whether this is a result of social factors, such as the lifestyle of bilinguals—some of whom are diplomats or other expatriates who live abroad and value foreign language abilities—or a result of ability, as genetic studies suggest. Identifying a gene for foreign languages would lend credibility to this idea, but the evidence to date is still inconclusive.

Much of the information available about multilingual brains presumes an "average" brain. The research literature illustrates, however, that such generalizations should be read with caution because differences (such as the number of languages in a single brain, gender, and genetics) influence the exact location and use of certain brain areas for processing multiple languages. An additional area of study that concerns the definition of an "average" brain and has received increased attention as of late relates to hand use as a reflection of hemisphere dominancy in languages.

Hand Use as a Reflection of Cerebral Dominancy

Handedness is one of the lesser-known aspects of the human brain's hemisphere dominance for language. Human beings are predominantly right-handed, though a significant number of individuals, an estimated 7 to 11 percent of the world's population, are left-handed.[42] As we saw in the previous section, multilingualism may lead to a rearrangement of brain areas related to language, with greater reliance on the right hemisphere being noted in some cases. Handedness may reflect additional changes in language location. Ninety-five percent of right-handed people and 70 percent of left-handed people have their main language areas in the left frontal and parietal lobes, which is apparent in the physical asymmetries between the two hemispheres. For example, the 5 percent of right-handed people and 30 percent of left-handed people who do not have their main language areas in the left frontal and parietal lobes are split fairly evenly between those who have language in the right hemisphere and those who have language symmetrically divided between the hemispheres.[43] To complicate matters, up to half of all people born left-handed should really be right-handed but, because of over- or under-stimulation during gestation, become left-handed. (This occurs because the two hemispheres of the brain develop at different rates during gestation. Over- or under-stimulation, trauma, or other causes during certain times in pregnancy could cause a to-be righty to become a lefty.)[44] This may explain why some left-handed people have their language areas in the opposite (right) hemisphere while others do not. Brains with left-hemisphere dominance for languages look different from brains that are right-hemisphere dominant. However, the brain changes. For example, it was found that the left hemisphere in bilinguals was active during both first- and second-language tests but that "greater cognitive effort may be subserved by less well-tuned neural representations that require greater neuronal activity."[45] Narly Golestani from the Institute of Cognitive Neuroscience at the University College-London and colleagues in France offer evidence that initial second-language learning requires different parts of the brain than fluent use of the language, "suggesting a functional reorganisation of regions involved in syntactical production as a function of syntactical proficiency."[46] The physical changes in the brain that accompany experiences in the "average" brain are highlighted in "special" brains.

Other research related to handedness and language suggests that specific parts of the brain related to language[47] are symmetrically different in right- and left-handers and could be related to the development of language: "These findings demonstrate that important relationships exist between hand preference, and the anatomy of posterior cortical language areas."[48] How does this impact you and your foreign language quest? Well, in one way it makes us wonder if these "special" brains approach literacy acquisition in a different way. Although studies in this area are relatively scarce, some hypothesize that this could explain learning differences among children, and further research may yield a better understanding of cognitive preferences for language teaching methodologies.

In an interesting study of left- versus right-handed bilinguals, Hernandez, Camacho-Rosales, Nieto, and Barroso found a correlation between good and poor readers and handedness, suggesting a link between where language is learned in the brain and success at learning literacy in our traditionally formal education system. Reading is centrally located in the "average" brain in the left hemispheric fusiform cortex. Children found to be at a risk for developing reading problems at the end of kindergarten showed different activation of "normal" reading areas. Other researchers found that such children display markedly different activation profiles than children who have by this stage already mastered important pre-reading skills. This aberrant profile is characterized by the lack of engagement of areas normally involved in converting print into sound and an increase in activation in the corresponding right-hemisphere region.[49] Does this point to a "mis-wiring" of the brain for reading skills in children? Further research is needed, but parents and teachers should be vigilant. Handedness may reflect a different hemisphere dominance for language, which in turn may reflect cognitive preferences and a rejection of traditional reading methods. It is intriguing to consider that teachers may some day consider a child's hand preference (as a reflection of hemisphere dominance for language) before she determines the best teaching strategy for a child. This may be closer to occurring than one might first presume, because it is becoming increasingly easy to identify hemispheric dominance without specialized brain imaging tools. Though bordering on pseudo-science, take hair whorls and turning preference for example.

Curiosities: Can Your Hair Tell You Something About Your Brain?

A physically evident marker of hemisphere dominance for language is found, strangely enough, outside the brain in the hair. Jansen, Lohmann, Scharfe, Schlmeyer, Deppe, and Knecht found that "atypical anticlockwise hair-whorl direction has been related to an increased probability for non–right-handedness and atypical hemispheric language dominance."[50] Though far from obvious, but literally visible to the naked eye, the authors of the study found that "hair-whorl direction is a structural marker of lateralization and could provide a readily observable anatomical clue to functional brain lateralization."[51] Others in the field confirm an association between scalp hair-whorl direction and hemispheric language dominance[52] and base this on the fact that human handedness and scalp hair-whorl direction "develop from a common genetic mechanism."[53] Though probably not noted in most newborns' checkups, the *Journal of Advanced Pediatrics* notes that clockwise rotation (to the right) of hair whorls is in keeping with right-sided dominance in humans as in right-handedness, right-footedness, right ear preference, and right eye preference. It is notable that 80 percent of individuals have right "hairness." This is somewhat correlated to the 89 to 91 percent of right-handed people if we also factor in the 2–7 percent related to people who use both hemispheres for language. I confess that I share this

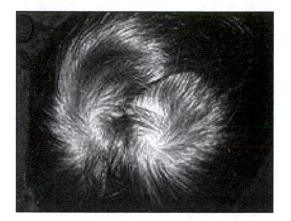

information in part because my three kids have three different combinations of total number and direction of hair whorls, which correlate with the suggested conclusions about language hemisphere dominance. Though anecdotal at best, this experience encourages my belief that the more we learn about the brain and languages the more we will find that many indicators are literally within plain sight. Sometimes the answers to complex questions are found right in front of our eyes.

Though initially sounding far-fetched, whether this finding means that we may soon create differentiated learning plans based, at least in part, on hair whorls is yet to be seen—but it is an intriguing thought. Other physical markers that can be measured without invasive tactics include turning preferences. It has been found that right-handers preferred left-sided turning and left-handers preferred right-sided turning. These same studies also point to a link between handedness, hemispheric dopamine asymmetries, and language. It is interesting to entertain the idea that by simply observing which direction a person turns his head when spontaneously asked to do so or observing a student's hair, teachers and parents may soon be able to determine language hemisphere dominance in their pupils and, in these cases, trace speech or reading differences. Far more studies need to be done in this area before conclusions can be reached, however, and these curiosities are shared with the reader only to illustrate new theories about influences on successful foreign language acquisition. We will now summarize what is known with certainty about the brain and languages.

CONCLUSIONS

Language is a complex system involving a mélange of neurological, psychological, sociological, pedagogical, and philosophical elements. We began by considering whether language was the key to intelligence and suggested that, at a minimum, it is the primary distinguishing feature of humans as compared with other animals. We then examined where language is found in the brain. We honed in on first-language acquisition and the main areas of the brain responsible for the language functions, as well as the pedagogical implications for these distinct language areas.

Memory is the key to learning. We considered how different memory systems (emotional, procedural, and declarative) play distinct roles in language acquisition. The physical parts of the brain related to memory vary for at least four reasons. First, different aspects of language (reading versus speaking, for example) are in different parts of the brain, as are their sub-skills. Second, there is a difference between languages learned early in life versus late in life, the brain treating all languages learned from birth as "first" languages. Third, individual experiences shape memory structures. Good and bad experiences have an impact on the ability of the brain to learn. This includes high-stress environments as well as those that use positive emotional links to languages. Fourth, the brain is an efficient taskmaster; as we get better at a task, we use less or different areas of our brain to process language. After tracing first-language acquisition processes, we turned to second, third, and subsequent languages and highlighted the similarities and differences between them.

The information about multilingual brains to date indicates four main findings. First, multilinguals use more areas of the brain than monolinguals.[54] Having said this, there is no confirmed pattern of brain changes, and in fact the studies to date point to "uninterpretable contradictory results."[55] However there is confirmation of greater brain use (as in the enlarged corpus callosum) as well as greater right hemisphere stimulation in multilinguals than in monolinguals.[56] Second, studies of multilingual brains mirror studies of monolingual brains in that they confirm that there are no two brains alike and that even where patterns are found, exceptions exist, which cautions us against overgeneralizations about results. Third, a myriad of factors, including gender, genetics, language typologies, age of acquisition, and length of time in the second or subsequent language, impact not only the degree of fluency but also the location in the brain. To highlight the complexities of the brain, we ended by discussing peculiarities of individuals who do not process language in the same areas of the brain as "average" people, people who are identified by their handedness, and the implications this has for teaching and learning foreign languages.

Knowledge about the human brain and language remains at a young stage of development. The little information we have about multilingual brains indicates greater overall use and increased complexity as compared with monolingual brains, though most other comparative aspects are a mystery. One thing recent brain studies do assure us of however, is that the human brain is designed for the multilingual challenge. How can we take advantage of this new knowledge about the brain? We turn to this as we consider the role of the family, community, and school in maximizing each person's potential with languages in the next chapter.

7

Putting It All Together: How This Information Shows Us How to Reach the Potential of Every Multilingual

SPHERES OF INFLUENCE

There are different spheres of influence in an individual's life. Some things can be changed or impacted by what we do or choose to give our time to; other things are more complex. For example, although global warming is a concern, worrying about melting ice caps can be frustrating, and this type of worry is not as helpful as thinking about what we can do personally, such as driving cars less, changing to lower energy consumption light bulbs, or producing less waste. In a similar vein, there are spheres of influence in language acquisition. By using our energy to make realistic changes we are not only more effective individually but also increase our collective impact. As parents, there are certain things we can do, and as teachers or school administrators there are others; as members of a community, there are still others. Recognizing these roles and how to maximize the potential of each gives us a better sense of control over our actions and makes living languages an easier process.

Individuals, parents, school, and community all play distinct roles in successful foreign language acquisition. This is true whether the learner is a newborn or a seventy-year-old. How individuals manage their experiences, the support they receive from family, the guidance they receive from prepared teachers, and the reaction from the community to their language abilities all influence the ultimate success they find with languages. In this chapter we will look at each of these individual roles so we can maximize the potential of all persons to reach their language goals. However, as *Raising Multilingual Children* was devoted to the role parents play in language acquisition. For this reason we will only briefly comment here on the family role in child language development, whereas we will take a more detailed look at the school and community.

It is easy to see how having the right recipe of factors increases our chances of being successful multilinguals. When individuals have the right balance of motivation, strategy, consistency, and opportunity, they will be able to piece together a winning combination for language learning, especially if they can take advantage of the similarities between them or unique opportunities they have for use. For example, a student may use siblings for increased practice in languages. This implies that success lies at least partially in finding each person's source of motivation, designing and maintaining a consistent strategy, and creating opportunities for language use. Some experts have determined that of these factors, motivation and interaction with the target language are two of the most volatile, because a person's family, friends, school, and community can easily influence them. Human beings spend time in social contexts. Language quality and success are deeply influenced by the people that surround the learner. The team made up of parents, community, and teachers is the foundation upon which a child's language support system rests. The balance and quality of this input is important in being successful with languages. Each family situation forges different relationships within the community and the school.

For example, a new Vietnamese immigrant in Los Angeles who sends his children to the local English public school will probably form a different role for himself within his neighborhood and within the school community than will a newly arrived French diplomat who arrives in Peru and sends his children to the international school. The role of parents and the family's place in the community in both cases are extremely important as they relate to the outcome of their children's language experience. Some essential elements of language, such as metalinguistic skills, depend on the individual alone. However, other people in the learner's life influence most other elements to some degree. In children's cases, parents and caregivers are the architects of their children's successful language structure.

FAMILY MEMBER INFLUENCE ON LANGUAGE DEVELOPMENT

Student achievement is influenced by parental involvement. That is, the more time and energy mom and dad show related to their child's schooling, the better the child performs. In fact, Edith Harding-Esch, co-author of the classic book *The Bilingual Family Handbook*, points out that bilingual parents who are most successful are those who simply pay more attention to good parenting skills in general.[1] It seems that when parents start families knowing they will be adding on the challenge of additional languages, they also start to pay more attention to other aspects of parenting. For example, when dad agrees to use his native language with his children, even though it's different from the community language and the language he speaks with his wife, he has to be very conscious of his communication skills. This in turn makes him more conscious of other aspects of his relationship with his children. He thinks more not only about how he uses language with his children but also about when and in what contexts. Perhaps he becomes more concerned about doing different activities with the children as he realizes he typically only talks about soccer and homework, and he knows that as he broadens his language use with the children they will benefit not only linguistically but also as social beings.

Many authors in recent literature have emphasized the importance of the child's native language. If a child has a good vocabulary, proper syntax, and good grammatical expression in the first language, then there is a strong possibility of doing well in second and subsequent languages. Success in languages can be deeply influenced by a child's home surroundings and the interest parents take in guiding the child in the early years. Challenging children to use ever more sophisticated words as they express themselves, insisting on dinnertime conversations instead of passive television watching, and subtle corrections about proper language use are all appropriate parental roles. However, children also spend a great deal of time outside of the home. Although parents are their child's first teachers, this slowly gives way to the time children spend in the community and within school. The role of other family members can also be determining factors in language success.

British researchers Williams and Gregory determined that siblings and grandparents could also be used to bridge literacy gaps in multilingual contexts. These researchers found that in multilingual London communities, language development, including reading activities, was stimulated through interactions with family members other than parents. For example, when observing how multilingual siblings play, they found "older siblings reflect[ed] the values of both community and school as they blended practices from each domain in their play with their younger brothers and sisters."[2] This means that school and community values are learned by the immigrant family's older child and brought home, thus easing the younger sibling's entrance into school in the community language. These same researchers also noted how multigenerational immigrant families help maintain native language fluency and support emergent literacy skills in school by strengthening the home language. Non-immigrant multilingual families, such as expatriate workers, diplomats, missionaries, or military families, can also benefit from similar support.

For example, let's assume Ana's Norwegian family is moved overseas to Senegal to work with her petroleum company. This is a huge career move for Ana and her two daughters, ages eight and ten years old. All three family members are excited but also have concerns related to school and their new community. The two girls attended a regular public school in Norway, which teaches English starting in fifth grade, and the oldest just started English this year. When they move to Senegal, the kids will enroll in the Dakar International School, which follows an enriched American curriculum and teaches French starting in middle school. French will be a new language for Ana's children. Ana is a single mom and will be bringing a Norwegian nanny with her as she often works long hours, and the company pays for this service. Ana is concerned about the children integrating well and worries that her youngest only speaks Norwegian. Although this case sounds different from the immigrant families in London described previously, this family can apply many of the same strategies. For example, the nanny could be instructed to maintain the native Norwegian in the home and give support in English to the girls as they do their homework. This would serve two purposes, both giving the girls academic support in their school language and allowing the children to reintegrate into the Norwegian school system upon their return. (To be consistent, however, it is important that, if the nanny will be using both Norwegian and English, there is a strategy for use; that is, English is only used during homework time, or Norwegian is restricted to storytime, etc.) The older child's experiences starting French can create a support system for the younger sibling, easing the younger child's move into an abrupt third language structure, while also giving the older sister confidence in her own emerging French skills. Ana can be supportive of both her daughters by inviting new friends to the house to play in either English or French to create a larger number of opportunities for practice as well as for social integration. All members of the family have a role to play. A benefit that Ana will enjoy is that she is arriving as an expat worker, highly educated herself and a speaker of two high-status languages, English and Norwegian. Other families may not be so lucky, however.

One reason that parent-teacher and parent-community relations are fragile is that power relationships vary depending on the status afforded the language. People who have high-status languages (such as the French diplomat in the Peruvian community or the Norwegian expat worker in Senegal) are received differently by the school community than those who speak low status languages (such as the Vietnamese immigrant in the American community). There are a variety of reasons for this, including the expectations that schools have of parents and the availability of resources. According to Lopez, Scribner, and Mahitivanichacha, there are multiple and systematic barriers to minority language parental involvement, which include immigrant moms and dads working more than one job to meet family needs, limited communication skills in the school language, and lack of resources to fund extracurricular activities to extend school experiences beyond the classroom. Additionally, parents with poor school language skills (such as the immigrant Vietnamese mother who knows little or no English), who may also have only a few years of basic education themselves, may find it very difficult to manage basic communication, let alone help their children with their homework. "The perception that parents are either unwilling or unable to support their children's educational achievement is particularly strong when there are unequal peer relationships between teachers and staff on the one hand and minority students and their parents on the other."[3] All of this contributes to problems with the parents' ability to support their child's education, including their multilingualism. Solutions to this dilemma can be found either through parent initiatives or through the school attempts at integration. Parents who accept that they are expected to become involved often approach the school when they are concerned or need extra help. However, this is a typically Western approach to education, and many other cultures feel that parents who take initiative in the school context are either rude or crossing the boundaries in terms of responsibilities. This means that some parents often wait for the schools to take the initiative and invite their participation. Many schools fail to consider this cultural difference, and as a result of unclear expectations, the school sees uninvolved parents, and the parents see the school as uninviting. There are schools, however, that manage this situation successfully. Recent research has documented just why some schools with high minority language populations find success where others fail.

THE SCHOOL COMMUNITY

Our children's schools are instrumental in aiding their success in multiple languages. In this section we will talk about children's education on four levels, from at the "top" to "down" in the trenches: policy decisions, the curriculum design, teacher training, and specific classroom activities.

In 2006, the National Literacy Panel on Language Minority Children and Youth offered general policy suggestions on multilingualism. We will review these general recommendations and then turn to some specific curriculum recommendations. We will follow with information about successful teacher training programs in multilingual schools, and finish up with some ideas about specific tools teachers can use in their classrooms to help their students reach their full potential as multilinguals.

Educational Policies on Multilingualism

In 2006, August and Shananhan were charged to assess the state of education for minority-language students and to make recommendations for U.S. public schools.[4] The six major findings of their report are listed here with my own interpretation of their implications for policy and teaching:

1. *The components of reading, covered in the U.S. National Reading Panel recommendations (2000), are also helpful to second-language learners.* The components of phonemic awareness, phonics, fluency, vocabulary, and text comprehension should be priorities for language minorities as well as monolinguals.
2. *Although emphasis on reading is good and necessary, more emphasis should be placed on oral skills, which are, at this*

time, overlooked. Good oral skills have a greater impact on self-esteem and social acceptability than previously believed. Explicit instruction in oral skills needs to be improved in English language learners. When a child has low self-esteem in the target language, this can lead to a negative impact on the development of sophisticated language skills, such as reading and writing.

3. *Oral proficiency in English and oral and written skills in the native language are crucial to second-language success.* Parents should be encouraged to strengthen their home language skills; this is the primary building block upon which a second language can be constructed. Although mother-tongue proficiency is stressed at home, schools should create activities that require a high level of oral English skills.

4. *Individual differences contribute significantly to English language literacy development.* Differentiated teaching methods are the key to supporting children from minority language backgrounds. Not all Latinos have the same language challenges, for example, just as generalizations about other minority language groups can be misleading. There is no single one-size-fits-all solution to foreign language methodology. Teachers need to know their students well if they are to meet their needs.

5. *Most assessment tools used today are inefficient in gauging learner deficiencies/strengths and weaknesses.* Because teachers do not often understand their students' weaknesses, they are inefficient in devising activities that respond to true learner needs. Teachers need to learn to apply different types of assessments to different students at different stages of their language development.

6. *There is surprisingly little research on how home environments impact literacy, though what is available points to the importance of the school-home alliance in helping emerging readers.* When a child learns a new language in the school setting, the child's family and community play a key role in securing the success of that endeavor. Schools must take the initiative of getting parents to participate constructively in their child's education.

These six general recommendations are reflective of conceptual frameworks of differentiated learning, best practice in multilingual classrooms, assessment tools, curriculum and syllabi structures, recommended methodologies, teaching and learning strategies, classroom activities, and the roles of teachers, families, and communities in foreign language learning. We will now explore each of these important pieces of the puzzle of foreign language learning.

Multilingual Curriculum Structures That Work

After visiting schools in Europe and watching first-grade French children move effortlessly in and out of French, English, and Spanish, Elizabeth Clayton, an American teacher, came back with a determination to improve the quality of foreign language instruction in the United States. After collecting data from 19 different countries around the world, including Clayton's observations, the Center for Applied Linguistics determined that successful language programs shared several common factors. First, successful multilingual programs start foreign language instruction early, normally in elementary school. Second, successful multilingual programs teach through coherent, well-articulated frameworks and are careful to scaffold their learning in a developmental style. Third, the successful multilingual schools typically enjoy strong leadership and have enthusiastic backing from key stakeholders. Fourth, successful multilingual programs teach languages as core subjects (unlike the American tendency to make foreign languages electives). Fifth, successful multilingual school teachers receive rigorous preparation and are trained to manage students from different language backgrounds. They also make language a priority, giving it equal status with prestigious courses such as math, physics, and core language. Sixth, good multilingual programs creatively use technology in the classroom to increase interaction with native language speakers. Seventh, successful multilingual schools offered support for heritage language, or the child's mother tongue. The importance of these observations is that they are based on a wide variety of school systems around the world. Such international recommendations could help shape a new U.S. multilingual policy.

In the U.S. context, other excellent observations come from Collier and Thomas, who note that the successful multilingual program design includes many different elements, some of which echo the National Literacy Panel report. Thirteen of Collier and Thomas' recommendations are noted in italics and elaborated upon as follows.

1. Successful multilingual programs provide *ongoing assessment using multiple measures*. Not all students can or should be

evaluated on the same scale. Carol Ann Tomlinson, author of *The Differentiated Classroom: Responding to the Needs of all Learners*, notes that this is true in any differentiated classroom and especially so for limited language proficient (LLP) students. When evaluation methods are differentiated, teachers are more likely to pinpoint problems with more precision. There is nothing more frustrating in a student's life than to be told they are poor at math, for example, when they are really challenged by math in *English* (or Spanish or German or any other language). By using a variety of measures, teachers can confirm their assessments.

2. In successful multilingual programs, there is *integrated schooling* (*all language learners together*). Thomas and Collier's research has determined that students are more successful when they are in the mainstream classroom and not pulled out for instruction. Keeping all learners together prevents language-deficient students from missing out on classroom content, encourages learning from peers, and speeds up the mainstreaming process. Although others disagree with this approach and staunchly defend pullout ESL programs, Thomas and Collier's research is compelling and some of the most convincing in the field.

3. Successful multilingual programs have *high expectations by teachers of their students*. Students are known to rise to the occasion, as well as bend to it. For example, Proctor found that when students were told the teacher believed in them and their abilities, they achieved higher than when the teacher told them they were probably not going to do well in class. Teachers must realize that their perceived beliefs about students impact their learning. No matter what the students come into the classroom believing their teachers think about them, teacher expectations alter student levels of self-esteem and motivation for the course material.

4. Successful multilingual programs have *equal status of languages*. Schools that demonstrate a value for all the cultural heritages represented by their student body place all their respective languages on equal ground. By celebrating the ethnic diversity in the school setting and eliminating the perception of "high" and "low" status languages, the learning environment is more healthy, democratic, and accepting.

5. Successful multilingual programs have *healthy parent involvement*. By bringing parents into the school in positive

ways (through celebrations, festivals, open house invitations, and opportunities to come into the classroom and share), schools can manage healthy parent involvement. This curtails problems of miscommunication, encourages positive family support, and stems any negative flair-ups.

6. Successful multilingual programs offer *continuous staff development*. Teacher training is invaluable in "helping teachers and staff to utilize the home languages and cultures of the students as resources," say researchers Rachel Grant and Shelly Wong. It also provides a space for seasoned teachers to share and for new teachers to learn about modern pedagogical methods related to limited language proficient students. Like all branches of pedagogy, the field of language teaching and learning has changed significantly over the past years, and teaching methodologies need to keep pace.

7. In successful language programs, *foreign languages are taught through academic content*. Programs that use the target language as a medium for regular subject instruction are more successful because they create authentic learning experiences, give context to vocabulary, and model correct use of concepts.

8. Successful multilingual programs ensure *critical thinking across the language program*. Critical thinking activities give students opportunities to interpret, analyze, evaluate, infer, explain, and self-regulate their learning activities, all of which enhance understanding and true learning.

9. Successful multilingual programs *activate students' prior knowledge*. One of the best ways to get information into our memories is by linking new information to something we already know. For example, when new concepts can be connected to a student's past experiences, then the new learning is easier to recall in the future.

10. Successful multilingual programs show *respect for students' home language and culture*. Demonstrating respect for the home language and culture go a long way in elevating the status of all languages to the same level. This values mother-tongue proficiency, which increases the probability of success with additional languages, brings families into the learning environment fold, and gives students pride in their heritages. "Teachers and educators can do a great deal to help children develop pride in their heritage—and in themselves—and to help them learn quickly and fully. . . . In bilingual education, culture is reinforced as a valuable asset."[5]

11. Successful multilingual programs utilize *cooperative learning*. Classroom environments that encourage peers to assist one another are not only conducting best practice in teaching methodologies, they are also creating opportunities for authentic language use. The best way to learn anything is to teach it, says learning specialist and brain expert David Sousa. It is also well known that in imbalanced pairs (in which one student has a lot of knowledge and the other very little), even though both students gain, the student who actually gains the most out of such a peer teaching experience is the better-prepared student. As the more prepared student is teaching, he or she is also consolidating prior knowledge.

12. Successful multilingual programs encourage *interactive and discovery learning*. "Uncoverage" is a term coined by curriculum experts Grant Wiggins and Jay McTighe. They say that students have to experience in order to discover information on their own. Students do not learn by memorizing lists of words, but rather they learn by creating their own knowledge. Languages need to be experienced, not memorized.

13. Successful multilingual classrooms have *intense and meaningful cognitive/academic development*. The thirteen "best practice" elements of successful learning experiences noted by authors Zemelman, Daniels, and Hyde are those that are student-centered, experiential, holistic, authentic, expressive, reflective, social, collaborative, democratic, cognitive, developmental, constructivist, and challenging. When teachers ensure that their in-class activities employ several or all of these elements, they are devising intense and meaningful experiences that lead to both personal as well as academic growth.

In the United States it has come to light that English-only settings are not as successful as bilingual programs that allow limited and guided use of non-English languages in school (where students are allowed to translate for one another). However, neither bilingual nor English-only schools are as good as dual-immersion programs when it comes to learning English in the U.S. school system. This is especially evident when it comes to native-language instruction in reading, which has an edge over using English-only methods. Dual immersion programs create a curriculum structure in which all parties—both minority as well as majority language learners—participate in a language learning process. Although some studies have shown inconclusive results, the majority agrees that dual-immersion, or two-way

bilingual programs, are more effective than ESL pullout, ESL shel-
tered, or total immersion programs. Several experts in the field
(including Christian, Montone, Lindholm, and Carranza; Cloud,
Genesee, and Hamayan; White Soltero; and Nieto) argue in favor of
dual-language programs. Others, including heavyweights Cummins,
and Thomas and Collier, have documented dual immersion's increasing popularity in the United States. This rides on the tail of new findings that show second language study in the United States has
generally not promoted high levels of proficiency. Traditional ESL
programs that stress a rapid transition into English-only classrooms
"have proven to be detrimental and ineffective for their academic
and linguistic attainment."[6] Dual immersion has proven to be the
most effective structure because all learners are second language
learners, mutual respect of the learning process is cultivated, a high
level of acceptance for cultural differences is encouraged, and the
time devoted to the language learning process is optimized. In light
of these benefits, let's look closer at the dual-immersion structure.

Dual-Immersion Programs

In the United States, four decades of less-than-adequate education
utilizing pure bilingual education, in-class and pullout, and early and
late exit have not offered a track record worthy of a great nation of
immigrants. If closing the achievement gap between minority language users and the dominant community is the goal, and if we hope
to encourage all our students to learn a second language to increase
their life prospects, transitional bilingual programs and English-only
programs should give way to dual-immersion programs. Dual immersion is accelerated instruction in two languages, which works when
education is conducted in meaningful contexts, at an age-appropriate
level. "Of course, this approach can work only with competent,
inventive teachers in schools with strong leadership, and it ordinarily
should start in the early grades."[7] This means that although it may be
the best program available, it is not an option for all schools because
of the make-up of their student bodies.

In their research of the Houston Independent School District,
Thomas and Collier found that lower-income English learners who
received five years of dual-language schooling reached the fifty-first
percentile on a nationally normed test in English. This method was
compared with students in a bilingual program, who scored in just
the thirty-fourth percentile after the same amount of time. Further

research in twenty-three school districts in fifteen states, and an analysis of over two million student records, "show that dual-language programs can close the achievement gap for English learners and provide a superior education for native English speakers."[8] Dual immersion is a win-win situation. Such a program not only ensures "that language-minority children interact from the start of their schooling with classmates who are proficient in English, but it gives middle-class parents with a strong orientation to education a good reason to have their children in a school with immigrant children— a school they might otherwise avoid."[9]

Dual immersion also responds to the tragedy of "tongue-tied" Americans who are denied the right to speak their own language daily. Otto Santa Ana wrote *Tongue-Tied* in 2004 to draw attention to "the unspoken issue that silences Americans" and draws attention to the potential vulnerability of multilingual children if teachers do not take the time to treat them as individuals. A negative consequence of failing to differentiate, argues Santa Ana, is that minority language learners may sense "rage, regret, and resistance" toward their communities, resulting in higher drop-out rates, a loss of cultural identity, and a disassociation with the majority culture. Santa Ana stresses that it is every educator's responsibility to try to break the silence of these minority-language speakers. Dual immersion could be an answer. Barlow reports that "each day millions of Americans are denied their right to speak in their own words. Social institutions and empowered individuals coolly go about their day proscribing a large portion of our society from speaking their mind."[10] Benefits of dual immersion are seen across the board. In their Houston study in 2000, Thomas and Collier found reciprocal benefits as well. English learners benefit, and "English speakers, including African American students, not only scored higher than their monolingually educated peers, but they also acquired a second language for their lifelong use."[11]

The successful characteristics of dual-immersion programs, according to Thomas and Collier, include criteria often hard to comply with, however. They write that a minimum of six years of bilingual instruction; a focus on the core academic curriculum rather than a watered-down version; high quality language arts instructions in both languages integrated into thematic units; separation of the two languages for instruction (no translation and no repeated lessons in the other language); use of the non-English language for at least 50 percent of the instructional time and as much as 90 percent in the early grades; an additive (that is, adding a new language) bilingual environment that has full support of school administrators, teachers, and parents; promotion of positive interdependence among peers and between teachers and students; high quality instruction personnel, proficiency in the language of instruction; and active parent-school partnerships, are necessary for such a program to work.[12]

Dual-immersion programs mean that there is a great deal of peer tutoring going on which increase the interest that students have for the curriculum. There is also evidence that two-way bilingual education programs may help at-risk students. Maria Lopez and Abbas Tashakkori note, "Children with limited English proficiency are known to be at higher risk of school failure than their peers. Risk starts early, and the achievement lag of these children often widens with age and progression in the educational system."[13] Their study showed that early kindergarten intervention with at-risk students through two-way bilingual programs closed the achievement gap and that at the end of first grade, "no statistically significant differences were found" between the regular English competence students: "Thus, the two-way bilingual program [dual immersion] seems to have broken the aforementioned pattern of academic failure" typical of at-risk students.[14] Whether your school has dual immersion or another structure, there are other non-curriculum decisions that also impact foreign language learning, to which we now turn.

Administrative Decisions

This section will look at some choices by school administrators that shape multilingual communities. Rachel Grant and Shelly Wong offer seven core recommendations for administrators in multilingual schools,[15] which are in italics and are elaborated upon here.

Conduct linguistic and ethnic audits of children and parents. Schools that take the time to understand which languages are present in their school can make great headway in curtailing problems. Understanding students' ethnic backgrounds also helps teachers perceive family needs with more accuracy and prepares teachers in a way that develops the school community to its fullest potential. When administrators know which languages are present, they can, if desired, hire support staff in the target languages. If budget restraints are a problem, then hiring non-teaching staff, such as secretaries and grounds staff, who can serve a double role as translators on call can be of great help.

Hire with priority given to the most commonly spoken languages. While controversial and in some states illegal, Grant and Wong are adamant that enhancing the linguistic balance in favor of language minority students will change the school environment. This means that when hiring for any position, efforts are made to contract minority language speakers who are representative of the school make-up.

Recruit parent liaisons. Parent liaisons with minority language skills can help translate for minority language students and their families, which will help integrate them into the school fabric.

Conduct professional development to examine notably culture-deficient models. Some schools are guilty of assimilationist, English-only attitudes. Reminders of the benefits of multilingualism through professional development sessions can help teachers be conscious of every student's potential to succeed in the system. This leadership move is meant to place all languages on the same level, though it is the most philosophical of the recommendations.

Translate all official letters. While this is time consuming and costly, most schools will realize that this helps ensure that communication with all parents is clear. Is the cost–benefit ratio favorable? Each school will have to gauge this for itself.

Purchase multilingual materials for the library, such as CDs, DVDs, audiotapes, videos, reference materials, and textbooks in the languages children speak. Investing in multilingual media shows respect for children's native languages and provides them with mother-tongue support.

Establish a "triage" plan and other frameworks that allow teachers to efficiently identify the problems that typically face multilingual schools working with minority language students and parents. By planning definitive "if-then" scenarios, teachers can respond to challenging situations with confidence.

These seven recommendations are good food for thought, though each school may choose to apply them to different degrees. "Leadership from the top must promote linguistic diversity,"[16] and it requires a good recruiting plan in which minority languages are represented in the staff make-up. Schools that are successful in involving positive parent involvement in multilingual communities are those that demonstrate "an unwavering commitment to meeting the multiple needs of the migrant families on a daily and ongoing basis," and create culturally sensitive models of school structures.[17] Successful administrators envision this as "integrating all school staff (teachers, office personnel, cafeteria and maintenance support) within the school and across the school system and the community to work with language minority students and their parents to support student success."[18] Ongoing training is also seen as an integral part of cultivating respect and use of languages in the school setting.

The role of school should be examined on two different levels for clarity. First, school administration decisions should include how schools design the curriculum to integrate languages into their system. Second, hiring and training of teachers is probably the single greatest influencing factor in learning a foreign language in school settings. Other recommendations are also worth considering, though all may not be possible due to financial or calendar constraints. For example, supplemental classes to strengthen mother-tongue proficiency create links to the home culture, demonstrate cultural respect, and encourage faster integration into regular classroom structures. I witnessed a very successful, low-cost initiative in the Collège du Léman in Geneva recently, for example. The school is close to the United Nations in Geneva and, as a result, enrolls students from dozens of language backgrounds. The administration was concerned that many families appeared to want their children to integrate quickly and discouraged home language use as a result, forcing their children into full-immersion French–English bilingual education. For example, a child from Kuwait was encouraged *not* to use Arabic by his parents because they thought he should spend all of his time in French or English in order to "fit in" faster. This attitude often leaves the home language without any support. Parents began to acknowledge that children were losing their home language in favor of English and French. The administration was concerned about finding a way to encourage mother-tongue fluency because they recognized this was the building block upon which their students would be able to build new language structures in the school languages. In a creative solution, the parents organized themselves and offered before- and after-school reading time in various native languages (Arabic, Spanish, Chinese, etc.). The school provided the parents with the physical setting, and teachers helped spread the word of the service. Parents simply volunteered to read to children once or twice weekly in their native language. This initiative celebrated the ethnic diversity of the student body, showed a value and respect for the various community languages, united a very diverse group of people under a single cause, and met the primary goal of stimulating better academic achievement through mother-tongue solidification.

Another proactive measure that school administrators can take is organizing or expanding teacher-training sessions. Research shows undeniable benefits for student learning when schools can count on knowledgeable teachers who understand the students' home environments. Teachers can gain this through group workshop sessions as well as through peer guidance. For example, teachers can be instructed of the typical pitfalls native speakers of certain languages will encounter in English. If teachers know that their native-Spanish-speaking students will be challenged by the English gerund form (-*ing*), they can be better prepared to both recognize the problem and to remedy it. The key to successful in-service sessions, however, lies in identifying teacher needs. I have often seen schools contract outside workshop facilitators simply to fill in the "in-service" day blank without really taking into consideration what the teachers themselves needed to work in multilingual environments. By auditing teachers on their own perceived pedagogical needs, administrators can be better prepared to organize sessions that will truly fill voids in teaching skills sets. For example, a group of teachers may feel they are lacking ideas about classroom activities that take advantage of peer teaching structures. Others may not be so advanced in their preparation and unable to understand why everyone just can't speak English and get on with schooling, calling for a more basic workshop on the challenges that face foreign-language learners. Still others may believe that they would be better served by learning more about how to distinguish special needs for normal foreign-language acquisition blocks. Each of these topics is legitimate and is generated by the end-users themselves (the teachers in this case), which means the information will most likely not only be learned but also used. We will now take a look at the most effective ways teacher formation occurs in multilingual environments.

TEACHER TRAINING IN MULTILINGUAL ENVIRONMENTS

One of the most influential books about the general concepts of learning came from the U.S. National Research Council Committee on Learning Research and Educational Practice, and was written by John Bransford, Ann Brown, and Rodney Cocking. *How*

People Learn highlights three keys to effective learning, which excellent teachers execute almost as if by instinct, and which average teachers can be taught. Although these concepts are useful in teaching all subjects, we will review them as they apply to teaching languages.

First, people learn best when new information is related to what is already known. By engaging prior knowledge and understanding, people can link new ideas to those that are already known and accepted. This implies that it is easier for me to teach you how to subtract if you already know how to add. As a teacher, if I know how to help link the two concepts in your mind then I have accessed your prior knowledge, which facilitates your learning. For example, teachers who know that a Spanish speaker who begins to learn French can use already existing basic grammatical understanding and transfer this to the new language are more successful than teachers who are unaware of this. Teachers who know how to access a student's prior knowledge are more efficient.

Second, people need to integrate conceptual frameworks with factual knowledge in order to learn efficiently. It is far more effective to get people to use language to create a meaningful dialogue than to memorize lists of verbs, for example. This is a huge argument in favor of teaching language through content subjects. By learning new vocabulary and literary concepts in a literature class (or biological concepts in biology or art concepts in art class), children are far more likely to understand the conceptual frameworks of the topic and to use to the new language in the correct way.

Third, people like to feel in control of their learning experiences. A certain level of autonomy or choice spurs on successful learning encounters. For example, asking second grade children if they would like to read the left side of the page or the right (or sit quietly and let the teacher read) lets children exercise autonomy. Telling middle school students they can go to the library and pick any book in a certain genre gives them a level of freedom and forces an understanding about the genre that they would not gain if the professor assigned a book. Likewise, telling high school students they can choose any five of the twenty questions about the chapter they want to answer instead of telling them exactly which ones demands a greater analysis of the problem set. Similarly, letting students choose whether they turn in a handwritten draft of their short stories on Monday or a typed draft by Friday also gives them a level of control over their work and encourages them to weigh options. By setting clear but flexible parameters to assignments, teachers help students "own" their work by distinguishing it in certain ways from the kid next door. This also means giving students some level of control over what, how, or when they learn certain skills. By using these three basic concepts in daily encounters, teachers in multilingual classrooms can be assured that they are creating authentic learning experiences significant for their students. This leads to the personalized nature of teaching.

Who Is Responsible for Student Learning?

Making students feel good about themselves and how they approach their learning tasks is one of the most challenging and controversial aspects of multilingual teaching. Some teachers believe that it is their job to deliver information—period. If the student chooses to learn, fine, but it is not the teacher's responsibility. In the end, learning is the student's job. This view is being challenged by modern pedagogy. How teachers perceive themselves, how students perceive the teacher, and how students feel about themselves as a result all impact student learning in the end. With this in mind, teachers need to be aware that every interaction, good or bad, impacts the quality of student learning.

Emotions play a large role in how long it takes an individual to become fluent in a new language. As we saw in Chapter 4, good learning environments can speed up the learning process and improve the quality of the experience. This is of vital importance when the learner may not have a choice of what language he or she is expected to learn. We cannot control whether that language is similar or different structurally from the learner's native language, but we can impact the emotional environment within which the language is learned. In schools, teachers also have a great deal of influence over the emotions attached to languages. In the United States, "by welcoming a student's home language into the classroom, schools actively engage English language learners in literacy."[19] A teacher who celebrates a class's diversity rather than shunning it is more apt to meet with success. Feeling safe is the first step in developing sufficient confidence to explore new knowledge, and it is the teacher's role to structure this secure learning environment. Unfortunately, many teachers are unaware of how much this influences students' learning. For example, a negative learning environment is one in which participants sense anger, fear, sadness, or disgust. These feelings can be triggered by a myriad of sources— subject difficulty level, peer relationships, home problems, and especially perceptions of the teacher's feelings towards the students— and it is the teacher's job to monitor the pulse of the class. Teachers need to keep their sights on creating optimal positive learning environments in which the participants sense joy, pleasant surprise, curiosity, and acceptance.

The role of qualified teachers is the single greatest factor influencing language-learning success, say educational researchers Marzano and colleagues. Great teachers produce great students. However, not all teachers are born great; some work hard to get that way. Students who don't believe their teachers are competent do not believe they will learn from them. Teachers must remember that when they doubt their own abilities, they also lose the confidence of their students. This reminds me of a great line in the movie, *Mona Lisa Smile*, in which a new teacher is coached by an experienced one. The veteran tells the new teacher something to the effect that "students smell fear." This can put teachers at a great disadvantage when they are meant to be the authority figure. When this happens, teachers need the support of good administrators to get the right training. To reinforce this point, let me mention a study. Author Malcolm Gladwell reports a correlation between what students think of their new teacher just minutes after they begin a course and their formal evaluations of the same teacher after an entire semester together. It takes only a few minutes for an opinion to be formed about a teacher's own self-confidence in his or her abilities. Luckily, opinions can change when student perceptions of teacher preparedness change. Several researchers have clearly documented that what teachers think about their own skills affects the learning of their students.[20] Additionally, what students *think* their teachers think about them also impacts their learning. That is, a student who thinks his or her teacher believes he or she is a "loser" or an "idiot" will never produce brilliant work, just as a mediocre student who senses the teacher's confidence and high expectations will rise to the occasion. This does not mean teachers should tell all their students they believe they are "A" material (unless they mean it), but it does give us reason to promise them all they have the potential to grow and learn. Such perceptions directly impact a student's motivation level about school.

What Motivates Students to Learn?

Studies show that several things influence students' motivation to attend class, most of all teachers' own enthusiasm for the subject matter. Ann Barnes of the University of Warwick in the United Kingdom says one of the best indicators of new teachers who will find success are those who have an innate motivation and passion for their work.[21] According to Edmund Sass, the eight most influential factors that motivate students and that are controlled by the teacher are the following:[22]

1. Teacher enthusiasm
2. Relevance of the subject
3. Organization of course
4. Appropriate difficulty level
5. Active participation by student
6. Variety of activities and methodology
7. Personal link between teacher and student
8. Use of appropriate, concrete, and clear examples

Language teachers who adhere to these guides are more successful. Some skeptics might say that only "natural" teachers or those born to be educators can do all of this, but I disagree. Knowing that these eight things motivate students gives any teacher the start-up tools to improve. For example, any teacher can release enthusiasm for his or her subject area, show how the subject relates to students' lives, organize class time well, create active and appropriately difficult and varied activities, give good examples, and believe in each student's ability to succeed. These factors make any teacher better whether born or trained. Knowledge of what influences students is already a start toward affecting them.

Traits of Great Teachers in Multilingual Classrooms

Best practice in multilingual classrooms reflects overall teaching and learning best practice of languages in general. Steven Zemelmann, Harvey Daniels, and Arthur Hyde's groundbreaking book *Best Practice* (1998) highlights thirteen characteristics of excellent teaching, which, if applied consistently, have been shown to enhance student learning. Although any of the thirteen characteristics can be applied on its own, creating language activities that involve several of these characteristics together are most effective.

Imagine a classroom in which students are taught through activities that are the following:

1. Student-centered
2. Experiential
3. Holistic
4. Authentic
5. Expressive
6. Reflective
7. Social
8. Collaborative
9. Democratic
10. Cognitive
11. Developmental
12. Constructivist
13. Challenging

Some clever teachers in Switzerland who I worked with recently insisted that this list be expanded to include a fourteenth element: fun. They found that successful activities are also normally entertaining. For example, an activity that meets nearly all of these criteria is debate. Debates have been shown to be extremely effective teaching tools, and they can be used with minority-language classrooms. A debate is student centered, experiential, authentic, expressive, social, collaborative, democratic, cognitive, constructivist, challenging, and normally fun, which epitomizes best practice. Teachers can ask their mixed-language ability English levels to debate controversial themes to help stimulate responses from students. Debates function well primarily because they are emotional experiences. For example, a debate on school uniforms, parental monitoring of the Internet, legalizing marijuana, or same-sex marriages forces students to clearly express their opinions and use language creatively. Such an activity is demonstrative of the types of engagement that teachers can create among students.

Characteristics of Good Teachers in Multilingual Settings

In the multilingual classroom each of these pieces of advice plays a significant role in maximizing the potential of all students. Many of the best authorities in the foreign-language instruction field note that teachers with high qualifications have at least six key traits. First, great teachers are versed in appropriate teaching methods (we will explore many of these later). Second, they understand the students' native language structure or, in the best case, know how to speak it. Knowledge of other languages makes teachers more adept at identifying problem areas. Third, they understand different types of learning styles and know how to bring out the best in students by using a variety of activities, which lend themselves to teaching toward all types of cognitive preferences. Fourth, they have a good toolbox of optional teaching methods to reach all students on their own level. Fifth, they know how to use appropriate evaluation methods and manage different types of feedback mechanisms. Sixth, good teachers in multilingual schools demonstrate respect for other cultures. As we consider other aspects of the multilingual learning environment we will give examples of each of these points in more detail. Let's turn now to aspects of a good learning environment.

Aspects of a Good Multilingual Teaching Environment

Multilingual classroom teachers are called on to know more than the normal core pedagogical teachings, and teachers around the globe are faced with growing multilingual populations. Skill sets once required only by ESL specialists are now needed by many public school teachers. This means that every teacher is a language teacher—not only those specifically teaching language courses. Training all teachers in specific content areas, such as how languages are actually learned, is only part of the solution, however. Other pieces to this puzzle rely on good organization and the cultivation of a good learning environment.

Whitmore and Crowell conducted a longitudinal study on classroom environments and their impact on student learning. They showed that classrooms that catered to high-risk students in the United States, many with low economic status and who came from Spanish-speaking neighborhoods, were able to thrive in a bilingual school setting that harbored four key elements:

1. Teachers had a high level of intellectual expectations for their students.
2. Teachers allowed students' questions to guide authentic learning.
3. Additive, not subtractive bilingualism and biliteracy, which embraces the value of the home language, was applied.
4. The school appreciated bicultural values and celebrated minority as well as mainstream languages.[23]

Their study implies that by raising the bar for students, we give them permission to be all they can be. It also means that what students bring into the classroom is potential material for new learning. Whitmore and Crowell are careful to stipulate that the goal of learning a new language is to add it to the individual's other characteristics, not to replace a home language. These authors also believe that this means cultivating a mutual respect between learners, the teacher, and the family to create a positive learning environment for the child. Their work is very reflective of other best practice literature that documents successful teacher practices.

There are also things that administrators and teachers can do together to create a better learning environment. For example, good multilingual school environments often have a space in which regular, informal meetings allow for more exchange between experienced teachers and novices. This can be enhanced by more formal peer observations and formative evaluations by coordinators of teachers just beginning to teach in a multilingual environment. Ongoing feedback to and from new teachers opens the door for an exchange between experience and new theories. New teachers gain from experienced teachers, and experienced ones can hear about new methodologies from the newer teachers.[24] To keep a finger on the pulse of the school environment, many schools I have worked with around the world query their teachers and students on a regular basis about newly implemented changes (e.g., "What do you think about the new policy of allowing students to check out only two books at a time from the library?" or "What do you think of the 'Italian-only' rule during recess?"). This allows for the identification and containment of problem areas and gives a continuous voice to both the students as well as the teachers, who are often better at recognizing festering conflicts than are administrators, who are not on the front lines.

Teaching Practices—What *Not* to Do

Sometimes it's easier to note what should not occur as opposed to giving endless advice about what should exist in the ideal world. Ramirez, Yuen, Ramey, and Pasta made some very specific recommendations after observing classes for English language learners in the United States. Some of the most striking observations are that in over half of the interactions that teachers have with students, students do not produce any language at all; they only listen or respond with non-verbal gestures or actions. They also noted that when students do respond to teacher prompts, they typically provide simple information recall statements rather than full sentences or thought-provoking ideas. Additionally, students were asked to provide simple discrete close-ended or patterned responses rather than being provided with the opportunity to generate original statements. Ramirez and colleagues recommend that to optimize student learning, teachers should make classes student centered and try to limit their own speaking time. This could be achieved by allowing students to initiate the majority of the exchanges by asking questions of one another. They noted that poor language teachers make about twice as many utterances as do the students in classroom situations. Additionally it was typical that students produce language only when they are working directly with a teacher, and even then only in response to teacher initiations. These authors also noted that asking "Does anyone have a question?" is inviting silence. They recommend teachers call on students individually by name instead and approach them personally to offer support and answer questions. Finally, they recommend that teachers should not only modify their own speech in response to students' requests (verbal or non-verbal), they should also request modifications of the students' speech. Correcting students is not enough, the students need to then practice the correct structure. This allows the students to self-correct errors. Although modeling is excellent, it is not as effective as practice. This leads to other recommendations that teachers should seek out "sustained negotiation" in which teachers and students verbally resolve incomplete or inaccurate messages through prolonged discussion (as opposed to one question, one answer).[25] I like to call this "ping-pong." Are teachers skilled enough to volley the questions back and forth? Painfully familiar as these scenes may be, they are helpful reminders of traps teachers easily fall into when they rush through material and lose sight of the real objective of the class which is long-term student learning. Other challenges facing teachers relate to the ability to assess student needs accurately.

TEACHER MULTITASKING

Teachers these days play several roles: caregivers, models, and more recently, learning specialists. The challenges for modern classroom teachers in multilingual settings include proper diagnosis of language difficulties. Knowing how to evaluate student progress is a key element in gauging the qualifications of a good teacher. Given common school staff cuts, this means teachers are often called upon not only to teach but also to play a diagnostic role in multilingual school environments. Teachers in multilingual environments need to be aware that when a child presents a communication challenge or learning disability in one language, it is not automatically due to the "weight" of the additional language in the brain, but rather because some language systems in the brain are not be wired right, affecting all child's languages. For example, if a child is suspected of having dyslexia, then teachers in a multilingual environment should be aware that the child should be tested for this learning disability in all languages. Although it is true that some children are, indeed, overwhelmed by the effort, energy, and demands of a new language, this cannot be blamed on an overtaxing of the brain. Teachers need to be able to recognize the potential problems of children in their multilingual classrooms and the steps they can take to support them in the best way possible.[26]

Knowing the Rules

Language is a complex mental task, and problems can occur. Sometimes there are rules that were missed at the beginning of the learning experience that come back to haunt multilinguals, as in missed points of grammar that become fossilized errors. Such errors are akin to telling yourself a lie so long that you eventually accept it as a truth. For example, a child using "got" instead of "have" ("I don't got any more money") over and over may fail to realize its incorrectness. Relearning the correct use of fossilized words is often more difficult that learning an entirely new language structure. In other cases, one piece of language gets lost and is no longer in play, as when a person learns a second language at the expense of the mother tongue. Filtering out problems that are part of normal language development from those that are special to second or subsequent languages is a challenge. "In bilingual and multilingual settings one is constantly challenged by the difficulty of teasing apart phenomena associated with normal second language (L2) reading acquisition from authentic warning signs of reading failure," say experts. Language problems are not limited to language classes, however. Teachers are often challenged in multilingual classrooms even when teaching "language neutral" subjects they thought free of language biases—such as math—only to find that different cultures approach formulas and processes differently. For example, division in the United States differs from division in German or division in Spanish in how the numbers are laid out, which numbers are "carried," and where carried numbers are placed. The way we read and write math varies from language to language just as much as the way we read newspapers.

Knowing the Students

Other problems that can occur are not neurologically based but rather are the result of poor preparation in early schooling. Several studies indicate how children who come from lower socioeconomic status backgrounds tend to have less access to early language stimulation from parents. This also includes less material supports, such as books. The only way to really learn what root causes of problems may affect a child is to know the child and his or her family. Talking to children, interviewing during parent-teacher conferences, and reviewing student records are all ways teachers can better understand what social variables impact the student's in-class performance.

Knowing the Typical Problems

Other common challenges related to language development include poor summarizing skills. Even though this is a normal developmental stage of language proficiency, this often makes students candidates for being placed in special education classes. Research in this area has found that teachers who know how to teach summarization as a reading strategy help students in a number of ways. Summary skills explicitly help students acquire and use information better, comprehend concepts more thoroughly, and when combined with other vocabulary building activities, "enhanced the students' ability to apply information to discussions, laboratory reports, and projects."[27]

Knowing Teacher Limitations

Acevedo and colleagues found that many teachers at present are unable to assess in any other language than English, rendering them unable to identify many problems that may face their students. This is echoed by findings in the field that cite problems of cross-cultural analysis in which they found that overgeneralizations about language disabilities led to poor diagnosis and treatments. But what tools do teachers actually have to do this? Gregory and Chapman offer an example of a curriculum structure that applies differentiated instructional and assessment methods based on individual differences. Their method begins by designing a climate for learning, getting to know the learner, assessing the learner, and providing constant feedback. This sounds simple, but they note that these four steps are often not achieved in the multilingual classroom. These authors also show how teachers can adjust the curriculum, compact concepts, and group ideas for better learning. They emphasize the importance of getting to know students more individually when they first join the class (ESL or otherwise) in order to build up confidence and create affinity with the new language. They suggest activities for integrating new students, making them feel safe and secure, which is most important, to create a sense of belonging. Teachers need to appreciate how cultural differences affect teaching and learning. This means that the teacher has a role in recognizing and appreciating the cultural "baggage" students bring with them to the class. Good teaching begins with a good assessment.

ASSESSMENT

Assessment of students learning should include a diagnosis of where they begin, a tracking of their progress, and an evaluation of their achievement of the objectives. Teacher knowledge of different types of evaluation methods that ensure "instructually embedded assessment"[28] is vital in the teaching-learning exchange. I am convinced that the primary purpose of evaluation should be to serve as a teaching tool. Gone are the days where individuals are measured against a single number or final product and the worth of a student is reflected in a test grade. This, however, is not always easy to achieve.

Guidelines for assessing bilingual and trilingual children can be complex. Some excellent advice on general guidelines for doing this come from McLaughlin, Blanchard, and Osani, who believe that assessment must be both developmentally as well as culturally appropriate.[29] Though some traditional methods of evaluation are successful in monolingual classrooms, they may not work as well in multilingual classes. For example, relying on oral presentations in front of the class may be an unfamiliar practice to students from some cultures. Scoring those students lower for not looking their audience members in the eye, for example, would be an unfair assessment as well as a cultural affront in many non-Western societies. Several Asian cultures believe it is disrespectful to look at authority figures, such as teachers, in the eyes. A non-fluent speaker's final product may not be as telling of a child's development as an understanding of his or her progress, or the process he or she has undergone to reach the present stage of development. Teachers are advised to consider product, process, and progress simultaneously.

Product is understood to be "performance-based learning objective," or what is achieved in the end (the final "score"). Process asks how the student arrived at the product. What steps were taken on the way to reaching the product? Progress queries how much the student gained in terms of new learning. Did the student start from zero and learn a great deal, or did the student already know a lot and learn nothing? McLaughlin and colleagues also recognize that "bilingualism is a complex concept and includes individuals with a broad range of speaking, reading, writing, and comprehending abilities in each language. Furthermore, these abilities are constantly in flux," meaning that it is unfair to evaluate students' language abilities by using just one of these measures at any one time. They feel that "the goal must be to assess the child's language or languages without standardizing performance, allowing children to demonstrate what they can do in their own unique ways," and evaluate the use of language in proper contextualized situations. Currently there is a move toward standards in education. Meeting standards while differentiating teaching is a challenging task. To do this, teachers must be well versed in a variety of ways of evaluating students.

Assessment Tools

Assessments are, in part, based on cultural distinctions: language is a cultural system and as such it plays a role in the schools to form communities. Teachers need to know where their students are coming from in order to ensure they get where they need to go. Some methods of multilingual assessment include narrative reporting, observations of language development, and sampling the child's language abilities. Good assessment also includes accepting additional perspectives, including parents, family members, the students themselves, or other teachers, who should be asked for their input about the student's progress. Parent views can often provide a more detailed account of the actual state of the child's languages than classroom performance, according to other researchers, such as Nissani. Such interviews help others in the child's life understand their roles in creating the best learning environment possible. According to Nissani, this means understanding "the extent to which significant others—adults or children—provide language assistance by modeling, expanding, restating, repeating, questioning, prompting, negotiating meaning, cueing, pausing, praising, and providing visual and other supports." Such out-of-school assessment information may be hard to gather, even though it may be the best way of truly taking into account the child's context. If teachers can achieve this quality of assessment, they will help every player understand his or her role in helping the child advance as quickly and as naturally as possible into his or her additional languages. When interviewing possibilities are limited, other tools can help teachers achieve fair assessment.

There are many ways to approach evaluation in the multilingual context. One of the most creative I have seen comes from Langdon and colleagues. They devised an assessment tool that they believe is more effective than traditional methods for evaluating limited English proficient (LEP) students. According to the authors, "following this model prevents false diagnoses of language learning disabilities in LEP students and delineates some helpful strategies for intervention."[30] Their "teaching-learning wheel" applies a three-pronged approach that should be applied in the home as well as the school. Similar to other recommendations but graphically represented, this wheel describes three steps to ongoing assessment. First, to understand where children are when they begin their journey, a good diagnosis of their starting abilities is necessary. To do this, they recommend observations and ethnographic interviewing at the start of a child's career in the school. Second, they suggest formal analysis of oral and written performance, which can be done in a variety of ways, including formal testing situations using rubric scoring with clear point systems. This helps establish a benchmark performance from which the child should grow. Third, they suggest dynamic or formative assessment. The goal of the assessment tool is to analyze the cultural and linguistic biases that a student enters the classroom with in order to use that information to create better teaching activities. By sharing this information with the students, they too can mark their own progress toward clearly established goals.

Tools that can support teacher efforts in multilingual classrooms come from a variety of sources, and we will review a few of them here.

For example, the use of graphic organizers or portfolios serves assessment as well as self-esteem purposes. Many teachers use portfolios to track development by keeping student work in a simple chronological binder. This allows the student to look back over the vast progress made, especially in times of difficulty when feeling frustrated and as if in a rut. Other teachers use portfolios to maintain initial writings, subsequent drafts, and then final products of the same assignment. Yet other teachers use the portfolios to bind by time or theme. I have seen creative teachers move portfolios to the virtual realm as well. For example, the introduction of electronic portfolios has been experimented with in Taiwan to teach and assess English as a foreign language. This gives important work a permanent, albeit virtual, home, and also allows it to be transported for other people's viewing or critique. Portfolios are dynamic and can be both evaluative and formative tools, depending on the teaching objective. They not only structure documented progress but can also enhance student self-esteem.

TEACHING TOOLS

Hundreds of books have been written on classroom activities that enhance achievement. We will mention a few of the most imaginative activities to give readers a taste of the variety of low- or no-cost additions that can be used. I encourage a deeper reading of the material in this area for further inspiration.

Think-Aloud Activities

For example, "think-aloud activities," which encourage children to talk about how they solve problems, are excellent ways of getting children to recognize their own errors. This process helps the other students in the class self-correct similar errors in small group situations and guides teachers in their understanding of which points need reinforcement. When this happens and the children receive proper, explicit feedback on their work, their growing awareness about their use of language leads to enhanced learning. Think-aloud activities are the basis for developing metalinguistic skills.

Games and Imaginary Play

Another exciting way for children to get introduced to a new language is through games. Everyone likes to play games, and for children, this is the primary vehicle toward learning. It has been commented that children can learn more language through playground interaction than through formal classroom teaching. "Traditional transmission of morphology and syntax by way of rules, and practicing such rules via written exercises, does not lead to spoken language, for with this type of practice the retrieval of learned material is too slow and often incomplete to enable successful speech," says Macedonia.[31] By creating spaces for the integration of play into learning contexts, parents and teachers can ensure more authentic learning. Games, from imaginary play to the most structured of board games, are efficient means of bringing languages to life in small children's lives. Take imaginary play, for example. When children are observed playing house or school they are testing language assumptions as well as social norms.

> Susana: *"Ok, let's say you say you're the teacher and you tell me 'Margaret, please don't spill the paint on the table,' and I'll say, 'It wasn't my fault, Juan pushed me,' and then you say, 'Juan, did you push Margaret?' and then José, you be Juan, and you say, 'No, she spillded it by herself.'"*
>
> José: *"No, spilled it by herself."*
>
> Susana: *"Yeah, ok, spilled it by herself."*

In this way, children correct each other through scaffolded structures. One child generally always knows slightly more than another, and through play, they find subtle and natural ways of making corrections. Games in early childhood are often related to these imaginary situations in which social themes are developed and explored. In formal schooling, thematic learning is of vital importance. Some specific ideas follow to help parents and teachers begin to think of their own thematic approach to language.

Writing Mini-Books

Professionals feel some activities particularly help younger students integrate in the multilingual classroom and feel part of a community, such as orientation activities, the creation of mini-books or the designing of games, and thematic activities around shared concepts ("At school," "All about me," "Colors and shapes," "Food," "Time and date").[32] Other teachers encourage a thoughtful reflection about how reading material is chosen for children, especially when they are just beginning on their literacy journey. Barnitz argues that teachers and parents should make linguistically conscientious decisions about their choices for reading material and writing assignments. She feels that if we "make linguistically informed decisions about curriculum and instruction, children can learn to read and write English in the context of linguistically diverse classrooms and communities."[33] She argues that caregivers who make more informed choices about materials are better able to engage diverse populations in the multiliteracy venture. In a similar vein, Clachar believes choosing appropriate topics that have an emotional link to them help students learn second language writing more authentically. In her studies she found that "results indicated that the emotional topic motivated students to focus on the lower, lexicomorphosyntactic level of discourse processing during planning and composing, but led them to attend to the higher pragmatic and textual levels during revision."[34] Using emotionally charged reading materials or writing topics will encourage greater experimentation with the language and yield higher quality output. This has been found to be true in average foreign language courses as well as with slower learners.

Identity Texts

Other powerful learning tools are identity texts. Identity texts were pioneered by Thornwood Public School in Toronto, Canada, and documented by Patricia Chow and Jim Cummins in 2003. This school system has over forty different home languages in their K-5 structure, and Patricia Chow's first and second grade classes were the first experimental grounds for this powerful tool. Its simple structure makes it all the more attractive. Initially, students write drafts in whatever language they choose, usually the stronger one, which gives them a portal toward their feelings and gives them the space to share their ideas. They refine these stories, and then translate them into English. If the teacher does not have the same language skills as the child, the school looks to the community for help with the translation. Often other school workers (cleaning staff for example) or older students from the high school become informal tutors, so "consequently, dual language texts have become a catalyst for fruitful forms of school-community engagement"[35] as well as language learning. Identity texts create links to home language and culture and are a powerful way of engaging all students: "English language learners' cultural knowledge and language abilities in their home language are important resources in enabling academic engagement; and English language learners will engage academically to the extent that instruction affirms their identities and enables them to invest their identities in learning," say Cummins and Chow.[36] Identity texts showcase the individual students creativity and celebrate their cultural backgrounds while improving English language skills. "These products, which can be written, spoken, visual, musical, dramatic, or multimodal combinations, are positive statements that students make about themselves," say the authors.[37] The beauty of this tool is that identity text assignments value the background of the students and teach language skills at the same time.

Technology in the Classroom

Other electronic tools are also worth mentioning. Janet Bremer and Lyn McGeehan offer several examples of how they bring technology and foreign language together. These two Ohio schoolteachers designed a myriad of activities to help students learn both foreign language as well as computer class skills. A few of their ideas included having students make a form of "Jeopardy" using PowerPoint®, create a translation program with Microsoft® Visual Basic®, and design a travel brochure with Photoshop® and InDesign®. These student also used Microsoft Word® to write a Spanish newspaper and Microsoft Excel® to make a spreadsheet for a trip they would like to take to a foreign country, including costs. They also used Macromedia® Flash® MX® to create vocabulary games with pictures and the correct pronunciation, and they used digital cameras to photograph local scenes, which students then had to describe in Spanish. These teachers gave students choices, resulting in individual products. Some students opted for creating a music video in Spanish, whereas others participated by doing the editing and correcting the lyrics for grammar. These activities are a brilliant testimony to creative teaching skills. Other tools are also readily available to these students who have Internet access at home or in school.

Digital Libraries

The development of the International Children's Digital Library is an excellent tool for multilingual communities. This is an online library of children's literature and is aimed at multilingual, multicultural, and multigenerational audiences. Web sites that offer stories in two languages are relatively common. However, this Web site is one of the first attempts at developing a freely accessible, child-friendly library in many languages. "The mission of the International Children's Digital Library Foundation is to excite and inspire the world's children to become members of the global community— children who understand the value of tolerance and respect for diverse cultures, languages and ideas—by making the best in children's literature available online." The easy-to-maneuver site has books divided by age, size, genre, and format, as well as a section for award-winning books and recent additions. This is an extremely economical way to bring the richness of literature into every multilingual community. The International Children's Library can be a great tool, especially for children whose parents have not yet encouraged much reading in the home. Gregory and Chapman write that literacy traditions in different cultures have different impacts on student performance in the classroom. Some cultures have a long tradition of valuing books, whereas others do not, and teachers should be aware of this in order to nurture a love of reading if it is found to be absent. Steven Krashen points out that finding strategies to excite children about reading through authentic texts is not only the key to biliteracy but also the door to academic success.[38] This leads us to the last tool for enhancing language learning, multimedia options.

Multimedia

Media, such as television and movies, can promote language learning. Although parents have more control over this than teachers, schools can offer guidance as to what they consider beneficial multimedia elements for reinforcing school learning. If children are small (zero to eight years old), for example, early learning programs such as *Sesame Street* can be the key to unlocking the basics of language. *Sesame Street* is currently seen in some seventy countries and generally focuses on the local life of the Muppets in a certain community. The local beliefs are expressed through well-planned modules that reinforce community values such as citizenry, respect, and responsibility while promoting the proper use of language as well as preliteracy and prenumeracy skills. Other educational television productions such as *Arthur*, *Barney*, the *Berenstain Bears*, and *Reading Rainbow* have also proved successful, though none has the forty-year history of success that *Sesame Workshop* enjoys. All of these programs also have computer versions to support early language development.

Older children who are beginning a new language can benefit both socially as well as linguistically by learning more about the local television programming, including popular sitcoms, for-television movies, and educational programming. However, parents and teachers should be aware than nothing replaces a human when it comes to language development. Television and computers, when used conscientiously, can provide additional language stimulation, but they are passive tools. True learning comes with use, and use related to language implies practice with others. With this in mind, we will now summarize the main points of this chapter.

PUTTING IT ALL TOGETHER—THE COMMUNITY'S ROLE

Back to the key players—we began this chapter talking about how different players in a multilingual's life have different roles and responsibilities. Parents and other family members as well as teachers have stellar roles in this process. To put this into context, let's see one last example from Rachel Grant and Shelly Wong's work.

"Customizing for multilingualism" is a concept used by Rachel Grant and Shelley Wong in which they present six keys to building a successful community. The six keys are parenting, communicating, volunteering, learning at home, decision-making, and collaborating with community. Society can help to promote the value of speaking other languages by getting opinion leaders to articulate their importance to the communities; the value of multilingualism is underacknowledged in many societies, and especially in the United States. It is evident that "when a child builds on his home language, he learns more quickly and feels better about himself and his heritage. Teachers and educators can do a great deal to help children develop pride in their heritage—and in themselves—and to help them learn quickly and fully."[39] Although merely semantic, a good example is the move from the "ESL" (English as a second language) to the "ELL" (English language learner) to the "LEP" (limited English proficiency) label in U.S. public schools. This small change does two powerful things: First it recognizes that the student is probably proficient in a language other than English already—elevating his "knowledge" status; and second, it acknowledges that a large percentage of Americans have cultural roots elsewhere and that this is something to proud of. Perhaps I am reading too much into the letters, but "bilingual" and ESL were dirty words when I was a kid because it meant you were slower, probably not in the right grade for your age, and not really part of the same social fabric as everyone else. Things have changes drastically, as we saw in Chapter 2; bilinguals and their multilingual counterparts are now more prized globally than ever before.

Changes toward a multilingual society must be well planned and clearly articulated as well as executed. Community leaders need to be clear about the value of being multilingual, articulate to this to their constituents, and then act properly. Examples in other countries, such as South Africa, document that "lack of coherence between a language policy and the implementation plan for that policy can potentially reduce both the policy and the implementation plan to symbolic acts of no tangible benefit to students, teachers, or communities."[40] It is crucial that educators provide a socioculturally supportive school environment that allows natural language, academic, and cognitive development to flourish. Community or regional social patterns such as prejudice and discrimination expressed toward groups or individuals in personal and professional contexts can influence students' achievement in school. These views can also influence societal patterns, such as the subordinate status of a minority group or acculturation versus assimilation forces at work. These factors can strongly influence a student's response to a new language, affecting the process positively only when the student is in a socioculturally supportive environment.

Though it is evident that many school administrators feel that their hands are tied and there is no room, money, or other resources to fund programs that benefit language-minority students, I feel confident that creative school leaders will take many of these recommendations to heart. Some believe that dual immersion is too costly to fund and too complex to convert to, often without even understanding the simplicity of the system. Others point to the No Child Left Behind legislation, which channels resources away from foreign language classes while simultaneously asking all students to pass rigorous English language exams within short periods of time. I believe that every challenge is an opportunity, however: "Educators, individually and collectively always have choices. They can choose to go beyond curricular guidelines and mandates"[41] and maximize the learning potential of all of their students through innovative activities and parent support. Creative administrators and teachers find ways of helping even the most disadvantaged children achieve. The examples of the initiatives in this section are a testimony to the possibilities.

Clear family language goals, which respect the role of mother-tongue fluency, are a responsibility fundamental to multilingual success. Although some researchers have found a positive link from simply hearing a target language in childhood to a later ability to speak it, others point to the need for explicit instruction for true proficiency to occur, especially if the goal is multiliteracy. The importance of forging multilingual and multicultural communities to instill a sense of pride in new language learners is also prominent in the literature, as is the primary role of the families as being keepers of the native language. Williams and Gregory found that reciprocity of beliefs could be an encouraging way to undertake community language values. By finding like-minded school systems, schools undertaking multilingual curriculums can be supported in their quest for excellence in teaching. Schools with similar multilingual goals should work closely to share ideas and encourage each other's development. Such sharing is seen through international school organizations such as the European Council of International Schools (ECIS) and the East Asian Regional Council of Overseas Schools (EARCOS), but it is not done with enough frequency in the U.S.

SUMMARY

Successful multilingual schools ensure that language basics, including phonemic awareness, phonic fluency, age appropriate vocabulary, text comprehension, and grammar are taught explicitly. They emphasize good oral skills and encourage active, authentic language use by students. Successful multilingual schools integrate the student's family in a positive way. They use a variety of assessment tools and consider the product, the process, and the progress of the student. Some of the most successful schools use thematic syllabi and work within dual-immersion structures in which all students take pride in their home language while learning a second or third. The most successful schools conduct linguistic and ethnic audits and know their clients (students) well. When possible, they hire staff who speak the home languages of the families they serve and make every effort to keep clear channels of communication. Successful schools conduct regular teacher training to ensure that teachers keep an up-to-date toolbox of activities handy. They also have high expectations of their students. The best multilingual schools allow a portion of their budget to be invested in multilingual materials and media. Successful multilingual schools do their best to create significant learning experiences that relate new information to prior knowledge and give students a certain level of control and choice.

Successful teacher training programs in multilingual schools emphasize ongoing assessment of student learning and progress. These programs also ensure that all language learners are taught under similar circumstances in the multilingual classroom and with equal status. These teachers teach foreign languages through academic content and ensure a high level of critical thinking throughout.

The best teachers in multilingual environments know and respect their role and responsibility in motivating learners and demonstrate their enthusiasm for their topic. Great teachers in multilingual schools understand that good learning environments are made, not found. They also appreciate that students learn in different ways and that distinct learning styles and cognitive preferences impact overall learning levels. These teachers know that cooperative learning activities are great for creating peer-teaching situations that enhance learning.

Children need to receive a consistent message from all of the people in their lives when it comes to learning a new language. Each person in a multilingual's life has a role to play in maximizing potential. Teachers, parents, and learners themselves have areas of influence in this endeavor and should exercise their roles with responsibility, consistency, and creativity. Those who feel supported in their endeavors to learn a second or subsequent language by their families as well as the communities, or who feel this skill is valued in their communities, are more likely to find success in the progress. If parents do not show value and respect for the target language, children will be hard-pressed to do so on their own, especially if the family language goals include literacy skills. In the final chapter we turn to a documentation of my own family's multilingual adventure, which puts many of these challenges into perspective.

8
Our Story

This chapter recounts our family story, which consists of five countries, four languages, three children, two nationalities, and one home. I want to begin by talking about the countries we have lived in and the impact this has had on our languages. Next we'll look at the combination of our family languages and just how that has impacted the learning patterns of my children. Then I want to share some anecdotes about my own children's upbringing, and we'll look at how being binational has impacted our language experiences. We will finish this section with a look at our multilingual family and how each person has influenced the other in our success with languages. The goal of this final chapter is to put a human face on all of the data, studies, hypotheses, and literature presented here. Our story is by no means perfect, but it is encouraging. I hope as a closing chapter it gives parents and teachers the right push toward a multilingual lifestyle, if that is their choice.

FIVE COUNTRIES

Japan

After we married, my husband's role as a diplomat took us to Tokyo, Japan, where we lived for three years. I worked in an international school that enrolled students from eighty-nine different countries. This was a wonderful multilingual experience that opened my eyes to a culturally rich world of experiences and, as a newly-wed, gave me many aspirations for the formation of our own family. I watched wonderfully successful students make their way through school as adolescents. Some were half Japanese and half German, others were from Sri Lanka but had lived half their lives in Japan, and still others were from mixed French, Philippine, and Korean marriages; and there were many other exotic combinations from all around the globe. I openly admired their unguarded approach to new cultures and the languages that accompanied it. For the most part, these were highly successful students who also appeared balanced emotionally, had a strong sense of civic duty, and were very open-minded and optimistic about their futures. However, I also saw some students who failed in this environment. Seeing some students do so well, whereas others barely made it through the year in one piece, raised my curiosity as well as concern. As the senior class homeroom teacher, I grew to know and love these students and learned what separated the successful ones from the failures. Something became eminently clear to me after learning more about my students, and that was how important the students' families were to their success. For example, a student at the school who had moved thirteen times in fourteen years was nonetheless one of the most stable kids I knew. She was able to move into our school system with ease and made friends quickly, and when her family moved to their next posting, she had her going-away party, smiled, and left feeling fulfilled with her experience. On the other hand, there was another student who was half Thai, half Japanese. The move to Tokyo was her first time abroad, and she was an emotional mess. Her father would come and go and she never knew if he would be there in the morning when she woke up. Sometimes he would be gone for months at a time. Other times he would stay at home for months on end, but she never knew when to expect him to be around. There were as many stories as students, and I was fortunate to receive excellent in-service training at that school, which gave me tools with which to help these types of students, as well as to plan for my own family.

The late David Pollock was one of the pioneer researchers on "third culture kids," children who are raised for a significant part of their young lives outside their home culture. In the case mentioned previously, the student was Thai and Japanese by passport and was attending an international school system with British leadership. Pollock says that after forty years of studying third culture kids, he found that only one variable truly influences whether children are successful with this lifestyle or not—the stability of the nuclear family. He found that it does not matter if the child moves one time or one hundred times, which countries are home, what combination of languages is necessary, or the family's level of economic status. What seems to influence the emotional stability and academic success of these children more than any other factor is whether they know their place within the family ("I am the older sister"; "I am the first boy"), who their mom and dad are ("My dad is a gardener/ CEO/teacher"; "My mother is the ambassador/marketing specialist/ translator"), and, most importantly, what they can count on their parents to do for them ("Mom is always there after school to help me with my homework"; "Dad spends every weekend with me"). It turns out that it doesn't really matter if a child's mother will be there every day after school or if she'll be there every six months; what matters is that the child knows what to count on. This was a powerful lesson to learn before my husband and I started having children of our own.

Tokyo was a very special place for me personally because I am half Japanese. The country was a wonderful eye-opener for me in terms of personal insights. Although I had visited there as both a high school and university exchange student, actually living and working there (going to the local markets and large department stores, getting my hair cut, taking the subway, riding my bike back and forth to work, etc.), and most especially experimenting with the language, was personally rewarding. My husband had spent the year prior to our marriage on scholarship from the Japanese government learning about Japanese language and culture. It was ironic that although I had more Japanese in my blood, he seemed more entrenched in the cultural history and norms than I.

I learned a very important lesson about the concept of language during those years. Although Japanese is considered one of the more challenging of languages in the world, as we saw in Chapter 4, how one approaches language learning makes all the difference in the world in terms of eventual fluency. This means that my personal level of emotional investment made me ignore the belief that this was a hard language, and instead I clung to the thought that each new word I learned might be a link to my own heritage; it was exciting to think each new *kanji* had a piece of history in it. This experience made me a firm believer that some factors can have a greater influence on success with languages than others depending on the individual. In this particular case, my personal motivation and the opportunity to practice every day in authentic contexts helped me learn survival Japanese. On the other hand, my husband took advantage of his natural aptitude for languages. All of the factors are important and all can be equally influential, depending on the person and the situation. Likewise, different factors can be influential in the same person in different situations. For example, when we left Japan, we went to Ecuador, which posed a very different language challenge. We went to Japan as newlyweds, but we left as parents-to-be.

Ecuador

Natalie, my daughter, was "made in Japan." I was five months pregnant when we arrived in Ecuador, my husband's home country. By this time I was determined to raise a child who knew English and Spanish, but my Japanese teaching experience showed me the importance of smoothly integrating students into other cultures and valuing what those cultures could add to children's formation. I knew we would be sent abroad again because of the nature of my husband's job, so we spoke about the need to keep all schooling options open. We decided that I would speak English, and my husband would speak his native Spanish. I worked throughout my pregnancy at the American School in Quito advising their curriculum shift from a standard American to an International Baccalaureate program. When Natalie was born, she came with me to work strapped to a kangaroo pouch on my front, looking out at the world. She was googled and goggled at by the students and teachers alike; she would oooooh and ahhhhh back at them, trying to imitate their Spanish sounds. I would spend hours talking with her in English to balance the input. At this time, we also began traveling.

Switzerland

We went to Geneva, Switzerland, when Natalie was just one year old and stayed for a five-month course my husband was taking. I spent our afternoons walking in the Parc de Genève, where she would waddle on her unstable baby legs and play in the sand next to the other children, "speaking" baby French. These were very formative months for her, and I firmly believe her exposure to French at this time, along with my English and her father's Spanish, was influential in her future linguistic success. Though this was only a five-month period, we were able to take advantage of every moment, for I had the luxury of being a new mother dedicating her time and energies solely to my daughter. The amount of attention I was able to give my daughter allowed me to provide her both high-quantity and high-quality input in her language formation.

Ecuador

When we came back to Ecuador, my second child, Gabriel, was born. He was a very expressive kid and laughed easily, but he also screamed and cried easily. Natalie, his older sister, catered to him constantly, bringing him toys she thought he would want to play with, singing to him, and keeping up a constant chatter in her developing English. Though he was very expressive facially, he used no real words. He would scream, and she would rush to him with a fallen toy. He would throw his spoon on the floor and delight at how quickly she would pick up it for him. His first year of life was active, and he accompanied me back and forth to Natalie's day care and on class trips (I would strap him, too, into the kangaroo pouch as I served as the unofficial photographer for Natalie's field trips). He was a part of several play groups and attended early stimulation programs with me. Though everyone around us spoke Spanish, I spoke to my children in English. When Gabriel turned thirteen months old we moved to Massachusetts for a year of study. At that time his language skills were low compared to what his sister's had been at the same developmental stage. At the time I presumed that was because of difference between girls and boys, but I soon changed my opinion.

United States of America

In Cambridge, my husband and I worked out alternating schedules so he could do his degree program and I could take classes in the evening and begin researching my new passion for foreign languages. Up to this point, I had spoken solely in English with the children, and my husband spoke in Spanish. But we thought, at the time, that Spanish would be lost when we went to Cambridge, because my husband was the sole source of the language and he would be away most of the day. We decided to change our family language strategy, making our home a Spanish domain and leaving English to the rest of the community. As my research progressed that year, however, I realized the mistake we were committing. Whereas my daughter's language skills had been forming in a normal developmental pattern for the past three years, and she had just enrolled in the Peabody Terrace School, where she was in a wonderful learning community, my son was just beginning to speak and find patterns in his world, patterns that we were changing by switching languages on him at this stage. Children form self-conceptions about themselves based on their identities with others, their relationships with the world, and the concepts they form about all of these. Words play a huge part in forming understandings about the world. By changing languages on Gabriel before he had an understanding of language relationships (that is, mom and dad speak English and Spanish and can switch at will), we threw his developing mind for a loop. Of course I didn't know this at the time; only after a year of progressive research did we realize our mistake. This incident was probably my strongest motivation for writing *Raising Multilingual Children* the following year. I hoped our mistaken choices would help others avoid the same problem in the future. My son had a small vocabulary when we arrived in Cambridge, and when we changed languages on him he stopped speaking altogether for several months. He would continue to gurgle and smile and be generally happy, but he did not use real words. When I spoke to him in Spanish he would look at me with entertained eyes as if I was very confused and would then continue on in his silent world. The more I learned about foreign language acquisition and children, the more I realized our decision to change languages on Gabriel at this time was a mistake. He had not yet established a firm grounding in his first languages, meaning that any clues he could get from his surroundings were vital to his development. We removed one of the biggest clues, his face-to-language crutch. Whereas before he could always count on my face speaking English and his father's face speaking Spanish, all of a sudden it was reversed. When I slowly came to the realization that we were creating a less-than-optimal environment for Gabriel to maintain his languages, Natalie began to mix her English and Spanish and started to have an accent in Spanish. I realized that I had been less than loyal to my commitment to speak in Spanish while at home—it didn't feel natural at times. I also found that my American accent (though not as pronounced as some I have heard) had evident flaws, which were also rubbing off on her in Spanish. All the while, in a slightly comical-philosophical way, Gabriel was quiet, presumably waiting for all of us to straighten ourselves out. At the same time all of this was occurring, we were beginning to think about schools for Natalie. Our stay in the United States was coming to an end, and we had some decisions to make.

One night friends from Quito, Ecuador, called to say that Natalie needed to come back immediately for kindergarten interviews. They said if we didn't come back "we would never get her into any of the good schools." There is an interesting panic of preschool parents— we all believe that we make or break our children's future by the first school we put them in. Although there may be some truth to this, we did not make the trip back for the kindergarten interview; instead, we accepted that we had two options: the American School, where I had taught, or the German School, from where my husband had graduated.

During this time, in between research and studying, Mateo, our youngest, was conceived. He was born in Boston, and, because of a health problem, our family stayed in the United States until he was three months old. He was hospitalized with meningitis caused by a congenital kidney problem, which required an operation, meaning that his first few months, which coincided with Cristian's final exams at Harvard, were a rough time for the whole family. Both my mother and sister came in to help us celebrate Gabriel's second birthday that year and were real lifesavers during those difficult times. But Mateo came through, healthy, loud, and clear. It was when he was a robust, noisy three-month-old that I sensed he had a particularly high aptitude for languages. Was this because we overstimulated him as a sick infant? Did we talk to him in such an exaggerated way that he became particularly perceptive about language? Or was he born with a naturally high aptitude for languages that our stimulations simply kicked into gear? We will probably never know. He loves sounds to this day, however—music, talk, animal noises, trains passing, the wind, any noise, really. It was at that time that we found out we would be going back to Geneva, Switzerland.

Switzerland

We went back to Ecuador for nine weeks before moving to Geneva, Switzerland. This was the beginning of a wonderful time which saw all of our children begin their formal schooling. Natalie was officially enrolled in the German school system, guaranteeing her a place when we got to Geneva, though we still had the option of the international schools and the local Swiss school. My husband gave a good argument in favor of starting the children's schooling at the German school: We could always begin in the German system, he said, and if it didn't work out it, we could move into the international, American, or Spanish-speaking systems, but we couldn't do it the other way around. The German school system only accepts students in kindergarten or in fifth grade, but, once children have been in the system, they are always accepted anywhere in the world. This was appealing, because all German schools were said to all be on the same page of math on the same day in all third grade classes around the world, and all were generally of high quality. (While this turned out to be a slight exaggeration, the consistency of the system was attractive nonetheless.) In contrast, depending on which country one was in, different international schools could have levels of learning that varied notably, and didn't all follow the same base system (some were American, others were British; some were International Baccalaureate, others were Advanced Placement). So we decided to give the German school a shot.

The first day of school for Natalie was traumatic—but for me, not her. She was very excited and ready to go. I entered the building with her, and as I heard the excited German and French chatter of the parents and children all greeting one another, I began to wonder what on earth we were doing. I could barely piece together a sentence in either the school language (German) or the community language (French); how would I ever make friends? Worse, how would my daughter survive in this Babel until I picked her up at noon? A heavyset Swiss-German woman welcomed me with a not-unfriendly face and then proceeded to make it clear to me that my daughter was "an exception," for neither my husband nor I spoke German to Natalie at home. She told me she hoped I was planning on learning German, because parents should speak to their children in their school language. About this time I was beginning to write *Raising Multilingual Children*. I had done significant research and grounded many of my ideas about children and languages in hundreds of texts and well-documented studies. I felt strongly about what I knew to be true about languages, and this experienced teacher was giving me advice I knew I could never accept. I told her, politely, that I would continue to speak in English with my children, my husband would be speaking in Spanish, and we were looking for someone, a babysitter, perhaps, who would stay with the children a few hours per week and speak to them in German to offer extra school language support. Natalie's teacher looked at me, startled, for a moment and then shook her head as if I just didn't get what she was saying. Then she pronounced, "You can go. Leave her to me."

That was the first of December. By December twentieth, when the school held its annual Christmas play, the teacher rushed over to me excitedly and said, "Did you see? She is singing, oh my God, she is singing!" I didn't want to burst her bubble by telling her that a parrot can sing; it does not mean that the child has any idea about what the words mean at all. It was enough, however, to get this teacher to begin to believe that a nonnative speaker could enter the German system and not only quickly integrate but also learn and use the language.

Gabriel was another story. We returned to the one-parent, one-language strategy once in Switzerland, and I remained faithful to speaking only English once we left the United States. It was a relief to speak with him in my own voice again, and I think he sensed that as well. He kept me company for the first six months until he had his third birthday and could start school. When he started at the German school, he was given a more open reception. His sister had blazed a trail into the classroom for him, and his teacher was a younger, more progressive woman who had raised four children herself in multilingual environments. She believed in the gift of languages and worked very hard to ensure that everyone in her prekindergarten group thrived. When I told her I was working on a book about children and foreign language acquisition, she was quick to apply what I suggested in her classroom, and we critiqued her results together. For example, in Gabriel's class there were three children who spoke French at home as their primary language, two children who spoke English (Gabriel among them), and one child who spoke Hungarian. Everyone else spoke German. The teacher began her first school day by welcoming the children, first in German, then French, and then English. She then set them out to do a project. She asked all the children in German to please stand up and get the scissors out of their boxes. Most of the children jumped to their feet to get the scissors, but the non-German native speakers remained. She then repeated this command in French. *Voilà!* All of the francophones jumped up to get the scissors. Then she repeated her request in English, so that the only person left sitting was the Hungarian girl, who figured out the request based on the actions of the other students. She, too, jumped up to get her scissors. This same ritual happened for weeks until the teacher and I had an informal conversation outside of the classroom after school one day. I asked which of the non-native German speakers had progressed the most the past semester. She said that had to be Orsyla, the Hungarian girl. "Hmmmm. And why do you think that is?" I asked innocently. After a brief reflection she said, "Well, I suppose it's because I can't speak Hungarian," and her eyes lit up. Could it be that "helping" the children in their native language was not helpful at all? When the next semester began, the teacher welcomed all of the children into the classroom with big bear hugs and a German-only policy in her classroom. What had she learned? This teacher wanted to create a positive, welcoming learning environment and thought that one of the best ways to put children at ease was by using their native language. What she later learned was that she could create this same warmth through actions alone and leave the words in German, thus speeding up the German-learning process.

When Mateo began school he entered as if he owned the place. His semi-spoiled, youngest-child attitude got him into loads of trouble, but his charming smile and arched, flirtatious eyebrows, which seemed to hint at a secret, always got him off clean because he usually said he was sorry and meant it. Mateo went to Switzerland when he was just shy of seven months old, and he lived there until he was five-and-a-half. He grew up from the start with his mother speaking English, his father speaking Spanish, his schoolteachers speaking German, and his playground friends speaking French. He had no consistency problems; he knew what to expect from each player and they delivered, in high quality language. This is in stark contrast to the inconsistencies in Gabriel's life. Because the German school system in Geneva starts when children reach three years of age, Mateo had some time in the French system. He began in the crèche when he was almost two and stayed until he started the German school at three. The crèche was only a few hours a day, but it put him into contact with the language on a daily basis at an age-appropriate level. The most wonderful thing about the crèche, however, was his loving teacher, Lucy. Her school was nothing fancy, but it was full of props, wooden blocks, and art supplies. She was patient and loving and gave Mateo a deep affection for the language. He was lucky enough to enjoy the same warmth from the German school teachers the following year, and he listened to his brother and sister play with friends in German on play dates or as we stood waiting to pick them up in the schoolyard. He seemed to fit right in and joined with the greatest of mischief-makers in the class, independent of their language. One friend, Tim, was German; another, Alex, was Swiss (French speaking); and another, Kai, was half German, half British. Together they reigned during more than a few days of terror over the kids playing house, kings of the jungle gym. These children's parents ended up being some of the best friends anyone could have asked for. They encouraged the children's multilingual play and celebrated Mateo's growing German and French skills as their own children learned some English from him. This shared community value of languages in Switzerland sends a powerful message to children about the importance of being multilingual.

Being in Switzerland was an eye-opener for us as far as multilingualism was concerned. The Swiss have four national languages, and students know them all. They are extremely proud and sovereign and are privileged to be in the middle of Europe, locked in by Germany, Italy, and France. While we lived there, we traveled together on family trips to dozens, if not hundreds, of towns and cities that included Paris, Rome, Berlin, and Barcelona. Being in Geneva, we would go food shopping across the border in France. The value of language is immense in this region of the world. The discussion of the emerging European Union was the main topic while we lived there, and we celebrated the coming of the Euro in 2000 on New Year's, in Rome. We stayed there until 2003, when we went back to Ecuador to my husband's new post.

Ecuador

When we arrived, it was terrible at first. I think that, between us, we cried at least once a day for the first three months, missing everyone we had grown to know and love during those nearly six years in Geneva. But there was a lot going for us as we returned to one of our homes, especially the built-in family and friends, on whom we heavily relied in our readjustment. Cousins, aunts, uncles, and a paternal grandmother helped ease our way back into Ecuador. To top it off, Natalie's original play group, which we joined when she was one year old, before we went to Boston, was still meeting. These friends called us within a few days of our arrival to ask us, "Well, are you coming to the *Spielgruppe* on Friday?" (Two of these friends and the originators of the group are from German origins, and thus named it in German.) "What?" I asked, surprised. "But the kids are all big now. Do you guys still really meet every week?" "Of course! But the rules have changed," they explained eagerly. "Now, we still rotate houses, but when it's your turn you have to prepare a great meal and provide wine, and it actually doesn't matter if the kids come along." Despite the new flexibility, most of the children still came along. I was surprised but relieved. This gave my three children an instant group of friends who loved them unconditionally and had known them since birth. Friends like these create positive emotional links to the culture as well as the language and eased our reintegration tremendously. I cannot emphasize how much importance I place on these types of support systems. "Play groups" may sound juvenile and focused on the children, but they also actually serve a huge support system role for parents.

We got additional help adjusting back into Ecuadorian life from the German School of Quito, which had a warm and welcoming administration and good teachers. Mateo's teachers in kindergarten introduced him on the first day as "Mateo, from Switzerland," and he played the charade, telling everyone he was Swiss. Gabriel settled in with a small group of friends who were quiet but smart and creative. Natalie had a harder time, because she was older and most of the kids in her class had been together since kindergarten, making it hard for her to break into groups. Eventually, however, advice to "be herself" and let whoever was "lucky enough" appreciate her proved itself good counsel, and she made a solid core of friends as well, to our relief, with whom she is still close to today. Sometimes there is nothing more anguishing for a parent to worry about than how well your children will fit into a new school, neighborhood, or language. Schools can and should aid in this orienting process; when they do this, they help their students focus on the task of learning. It was a burden off our minds to see the kids fit back in, despite the initial months of social bumps and emotional bruises.

My husband had a busy job, which meant he often worked very long hours and traveled, but he was sure to be home every weekend. He made special efforts to be at school events, which meant the world to the kids. I remember he even postponed his arrival to a summit by half a day to be at the inauguration of the Sports Day at school—the kids and I were so pleased his priorities stayed in place throughout all the pressure he experienced at work. I appreciate how lucky we are; many families I counsel have troubles with their multilingual lifestyle precisely because one of the parents works such long hours that they have very little time with the children, thus resulting in less language, not to mention other aspects of parenting. I began working at a university, but tried to limit my teaching hours to the mornings when the kids were in school. The children's overall language experience was Spanish in the community, English at home, and German in the school environment. The main drawback of relying on the school for German, however, was a phenomenon that is growing around the world in the entire system. The make-up of the student body at the German school was heavily Ecuadorian, not German. Barely 3 percent of the families are German-German make up, with both parents and the child coming from Germany for a temporary stay in Ecuador. Though the German school system around the world was originally established after World War II as a gesture of goodwill and to cater to the many Germans living outside of the country, now it serves people interested in a German education and descendents of German immigrants. The majority of students at the German school in Quito are Ecuadorians who are second- or third-generation Germans whose parents speak Spanish at home. This makes maintaining a quality German environment very difficult within the school walls. The "playground language" is overwhelmingly Spanish. Even newly arrived German children are co-opted into playing all recess games in Spanish. In effect, the only German the children have is in the classrooms with their professors. The quality of German was getting harder to maintain at an appropriate age level because there were fewer Germans. To complicate matters, German was getting harder as the kids grew older and their textbooks more complicated—so much so that we asked the children if they wanted to change to the National Section, in which they could have their instruction in Spanish. They reminded us that, technically, none of them had ever been schooled in Spanish before arriving in Quito. Additionally, they stubbornly defended their place in the German group and felt very close to the German culture as well. So we decided to hire a tutor to support the children's developing German skills, a former German school teacher who knew the system well and understood the challenges facing the kids. He came once or twice weekly and helped with whatever homework was pressing, corrected old tests, and basically got the kids to use the language in meaningful ways. There were many times when we first returned to Ecuador when we discussed, especially with Natalie, whether we should continue with the German system— mainly because the level was getting beyond what my husband and I could help with easily. We nearly dropped German completely at this stage, prompted by the increasing difficulty level and some school officials' advice. But we stuck with it and, with the help of the tutor, made our way through Natalie's fifth and sixth grade, two extremely challenging grades that added several new academic subjects. We were very fortunate to be able to afford this type of support. I am not sure if we would have continued if we hadn't had the resources to hire someone with language knowledge that we lacked. I realize this is a limitation many families face, and we were fortunate.

But I have seen other less costly solutions, too. For example, I know of schools that provide after-school homework help in the target language. I have also seen many a family do what we did in Switzerland and organize play dates with native speakers in order to use the language in meaningful contexts, as well as to strengthen growing friendships. Other solutions can be found through language exchange dates as well, where there is an agreement to use one language at one person's house and then another when the visit is repaid. I have seen excursions arranged around languages in which children bring friends to the movies shown in the target language. And I have also watched parents learn the language alongside their child, keeping up with them grade after grade. This shows a deep interest in the child's schoolwork but also requires much devotion on the parent's part. I also watched our own children's language skills evolve to the point where Natalie began to be her brothers' best tutor. By the time she entered the seventh grade she was a better academic support to her brothers than any paid tutor could have been. All of these solutions work, depending on the family situations. We were in Quito for three years, and the children were nine, eleven, and twelve when we moved again—this time to Lima, Peru.

Peru

We moved to Lima in 2006, and the children joined the Humboldt German School there. They remained in the German section of the school, as opposed to the Spanish section, meaning that all subjects, except for Spanish, English, French, and Peruvian History are taught in German. I admit that I was worried about how the kids would take the change, but they were great and made us so proud of their adaptability. Granted, the cultural change was mild moving from Quito to Lima in comparison to the change from Geneva; but, though no one can say change is ever entirely seamless, they managed to make it look easy. They jumped right into the middle of school year, because Lima is in the southern hemisphere and August is midterm, meaning that Natalie and Gabriel skipped into the next grades (eighth and sixth) and Mateo finished up third grade with shining colors.

I was able to take a two-year sabbatical from my university job and completed my doctorate during this time. This meant I was able to work at home and be available whenever my kids were. This might sound like I was perched in the perfect position to be a good mom, but I found that even when parents try to be abreast of everything that goes on in school and with their kids, things go amiss. Even when I was the parent rep for Mateo's class I realized that so much goes on between kids and different teachers that even if you make parenting a full-time job, you never meet your own expectations of being able to look into the crystal ball of your kids' minds. Luckily our family's communication channels are good. We try to have as many meals together as possible during the week, and we normally keep weekends to ourselves so the five of us have time to be together at once. While in Peru, we were lucky enough to live close to my husband's job, and he was often able to join us for lunch when he wasn't traveling. Again we asked the kids if they wanted to change to the Spanish section or attend an international school, and again they refused. Natalie was most articulate about her reasons, and she made it clear that she felt more comfortable within the German group than with the Peruvians, because she had been schooled with Germans her whole life but was meeting the Peruvians for the first time. The majority of her classmates were Peruvians, ironically, but were second- or third-generation Germans—similar to our situation in Quito.

In Lima, the linguistic situation remains as it was in Quito—English in the home with me, Spanish with their father and the community, and German, Spanish, and English at school. Natalie also started French again, as is the custom of German Schools around the world in the ninth grade. We have been able to take trips with the children, enjoy the museums and theater, and see some things that might not have been possible in Ecuador. Having said that, I am sure that when this stay comes to an end and we return to Ecuador once again, there will be mixed feelings, as always. Each time we change countries, however, I see an amazing maturation in the kids—in particular—and in our family as a whole. We have talked about ceasing the traveling now that the kids are older. Ironically, they are the ones who tell us we "shouldn't close any doors" on work options. Natalie says she would "go out" again, but only to a big city, such as Berlin, Paris, or Washington, D.C. Gabriel says he'll do what we all want to do, being by far the most easygoing of the three. Mateo says he would only go if it was to Boston (where he was born, but of which he has no memory) or Geneva (to play with his friends again). Only time will tell if we move again after we leave Peru, but it's great to know the option is there.

FOUR LANGUAGES

The four languages in my children's lives have varied in the intensity of their presence, with the exception of English, which has remained relatively the same since my original debacle in Boston. When we were in the United States the children learned English and Spanish, with Spanish receiving far less quality input than English, which was also the community language. In Switzerland, I used English, which was a constant because I was home with the children more than my husband was at the time. Spanish was also a constant but was less frequently used. French was the community language, and the children had classes at school as the "second language." German was the school language and was used for roughly five hours a day. In Ecuador this shifted, and, although English use remained constant, Spanish increased dramatically and became the community language. French all but disappeared except through the videos we brought back and the friendships that were kept up. German remained the school language, but the quality and quantity were reduced in the new school population. In Peru, English use remained constant, and the strength of Spanish remained as well. French returned in force for Natalie as part of the German school curriculum beginning in the ninth grade. German remained the school language and was strengthened relatively simply because the number of native German speakers was slightly greater than it had been in Ecuador. As a result of the academic training in German and Spanish over the years, as well as the home and school support of English, I am very pleased to say that my children have learned to read and write with considerable accuracy in these three languages. Natalie is beginning to launch into literacy skills in French now, and although it is not as easy for her as speaking French, she is doing well.

Before the children began their schooling, we knew that they would be learning to read and write in German. However, we decided as a family that learning to read and write in English and Spanish were also priorities, and so we devised a literacy plan that, I now realize, was the perfect answer to our situation. We realized that the German school does not teach children to read or write until they enter first grade, when they are about six. Based on this, we decided to teach them to read in English at home before they would do so in German. I created an early reading program at a local center and we taught four- and five-year-olds to read and write in English before the French and German systems begin teaching them at age six or seven. We had many excited parents join the program who said that they had thought of doing this on their own but did not know how to do so successfully. Often they doubted their own expertise in being able to support their children in learning to read or write. Little did they know that enthusiam and some simple tools, like good workbooks, go a long way. We held workshops with parents, gave them a space to share their concerns, talked about the importance and value of learning to read in English, and also talked about the necessity of "letting it go" when the children began to formally learn to read and write in the school language. Why? My gut feeling was related to the conflict in authority. What happens when mommy says to write the letter "f" one way, and the teacher says to do it another? What happens when the child learns that "R" is pronounced one way by mom, and a different way by the teacher? One reason to restrain from pushing multiliteracy skills simultaneously is that there can be a conflict psychologically. There can also be one linguistically. Learning two similar things, such as languages that share the same alphabet, is harder than learning two distinct things, such as learning two languages with distinct writing systems. This is why it is harder for someone to learn to play the flute and the oboe (two wind instruments) simultaneously than to learn to play the flute and the guitar (a wind instrument and a string instrument) simultaneously. In our case, by teaching the children to read in their home language prior to school literacy instruction in the second or third language, we assured them of a strong literacy base when it came to metalinguistic understandings about print, as well as assured a firm foundation upon which to build future skills.

One day, out of the blue, when Natalie was in ninth grade she said she wouldn't mind going abroad again, but she thought that going someplace with a completely new language would be harder to adapt to. When I asked her to explain, she said, "Well, like, Italy would be okay, because Italian is just so easy, like Spanish and French. Or Brazil or Portugal, because that's also the same. But Japanese; now that would be hard, because it's just so unlike anything I know." When I told her that sometimes learning things that are really different is actually easier, she didn't respond immediately. Then I told her she had one of the highest aptitudes for foreign language I had ever seen in a person, and no matter what new language she faced, she would succeed. She was a little flustered, and said, "Yeah, I know. I mean I *know* I could do it, but it would just be *harder*." I hope that this youthful self-confidence never abandons my children, because I honestly believe that understanding you can do something is half the battle.

THREE CHILDREN

I should preface this section by saying that I am the mother of a teen and two preadolescents, meaning that anything I say can and will be held against me at some point in my future as a mother, so I will exercise a bit of caution in my normally overzealous descriptions of my nearly perfect kids and how they live their multilingual lives.

Natalie invited two girlfriends over for lunch after school one day. The three just-fourteen-year-olds walked in the door jabbering away in German about the music teacher who had "done his best" to "humiliate" the girls by asking them to sing solos in class. Pink-flushed faces grinning broadly in a purely adolescent mixture of pride and embarrassment, they related how awkward it was to sing the Beatles (in *this* day and age), and be corrected about their English pronunciation by the German teacher. In perfect English they switched to an exchange about what George and Ringo would have thought of the idea. Upon seeing my husband come in the door they changed to Spanish and conversed throughout lunch in that language only. Mateo, my nine-year-old, said he did something new in music as well and promptly burst into *We Wish You a Merry Christmas* in four languages between mouthfuls of *chaufa*, a Peruvian version of fried rice. He began in English, then Italian, then Spanish, and finally German. His only error was that in Spanish instead of saying "*prospero año*" (which means "prosperous New Year"), he said "*peruano*" (which means "Peruvian"), and we all cracked up. Gabriel, eleven, took this light moment to tell me he had detention the next day for forgetting his English homework, again. "But, Ma! It's just present perfect and plain past and that's *boring*!" (I don't recall being able to label verb tenses until high school, and that was when I learned Spanish.)

When the girls left the table they went into Natalie's room and returned to German as they tackled their homework. Gabriel and Mateo played in English with Spanish on the TV in the background.

I recently asked nine-year old Mateo which of his three languages he knew best. "I don't know," he said.

"Well, which do you speak best?" I said, trying to pry an answer from him.

"English," he said definitively.

"Which do you read best?"

"Spanish," he said without a blink.

"Which do you write best?" I asked curiously.

"German," he said, reminding me he wrote a ten "chapter" book over the vacation in German.

"So what's your best language?" I persisted.

"English, I guess," he said thoughtfully.

"Why do you say that?" I asked.

"Because you speak more than you read or write." The logic of a nine-year-old—excellent!

When I asked Gabriel, my eleven-year-old, which language he knew best he showed less definitive responses. "What's your best language?"

"English," he said immediately, looking at me for confirmation.

"English?" I asked again.

"Well, yeah," he responded, unsure this time.

"What language do you think in most?"

"English. Except when I think about numbers. When I count, they mix together."

"What do you mean?" I pressed, fascinated.

"Like I start off with *ichi, ni, san, shi* . . "

"In *Japanese*?" I asked in disbelief.

"Yes, but then I find myself thinking '*five, six, seven* . . .,' then '*ocho, nueve, diez,*' then '*elf, swelf* . . . .," he explained thoughtfully.

"Why do you think that is?" I pressed.

"Well, maybe because numbers are more important in Japanese," he said logically.

"What do you mean 'more important'?" I asked, now perplexed.

"Well, if I count wrong in judo, the *sensei* hits me with the belt," he said as he looked up to the left, smiling mischievously, recalling past situations.

"Hmm, so you always start in Japanese, just in case?" I said with a grin.

"I guess so," he replied, smiling, realizing that what he just said is a bit curious.

"But you just finished doing all that math in German," I said, pointing out his homework notebook.

"But those were *word* problems in math, not real numbers," he clarified. I am struck by his distinction and metalinguistic awareness. He knows that math can be either in words or in numbers.

"I see. What language do you write the most?" I asked, turning the subject slightly.

"English. Sometimes German. Other times Spanish," he responded matter-of-factly.

"What language do you *read* in the most?" I asked, trying to get a more definitive answer.

"English," he said without a second thought, but then he added, "for fun. But German for school. Sometimes Spanish for fun and school, though." It seems we will not be able to nail this down either.

"So English, or German, or Spanish?"

"All three. It depends," he said, looking at me like I just don't get it. I give up prying for the answer—for now.

I asked my fourteen-year-old a similar question, but I prefaced it with some information about languages. "You know, I am reading something that says it's really rare to find a person who is a perfectly balanced bilingual, meaning that they can use their languages with equal fluency. What do you think your best language is?"

"Well, if you don't count French, I am a perfectly balanced multilingual. French is behind German, English, and Spanish."

"Do you really think you manage all those languages equally?"

"Well, maybe I'm a better writer in German because I write more in German, but if I wanted to, I guess I could be just as good a writer in Spanish. Or English. But listening, all three are the same; French [listening] is almost the same, but a little behind."

I was fascinated with her understanding that fluency is related to the amount of time spent in the language. She recognized that she writes better in German primarily because she spend more time doing so, not because German is any easier than the other languages. These three children have grown up with the same parents, but their life experiences have greatly colored their success with their languages. Languages are just a piece of their being, however, it does not define them.

Natalie is great in physics, does well in biology and chemistry, and gets decent grades in history/culture, math, German, French, Spanish and English, but if you ask her, she'll probably say she prefers her theater elective over any academic class. Gabriel is a walking Guinness Book of World Records. He has a great mind for his culture/history/society class and enjoys biology. He is famous within the family for memorizing wildly useless statistics and facts, and for being a wonderful artist. He has invented a new series of comic strip figures, rewritten several Greek myths, and made a couple of videos with his Lego figures. Mateo, on the other hand, is the math king of the family. He thinks in numbers. If you ask him what the weather is like, it is probable that he will tell you, "It's nineteen degrees, and since it's the twelfth of May, there are just thirty-nine more days until June twenty-first, which is when summer starts in the north and winter starts in the south, so here in Lima, it'll probably be colder tomorrow." But if you ask, he'll say his favorite class is sports. He is a very physical kid and loves soccer and swimming, as well as judo, and he is more active than the other four of us combined.

These three children have very different gifts and are wonderful in three different ways. Most parents, I'm sure, understand the irony of working so hard to be consistent parents only to find results so different. Each chapter in life adds a bit more understanding to this puzzle of parenthood. Again, ironically, we don't master this until the kids are nearly grown.

TWO NATIONALITIES

My husband is Ecuadorian, and we all carry Ecuadorian diplomatic passports as a result. The children and I are also American and, as such, carry U.S. passports. We are some of the 20 percent of Americans who own passports, and part of a much smaller number with dual nationality. Why do we have two nationalities? Convenience is the primary reason. It is much faster entering and leaving the United States as an American these days because of the Homeland Security Act. But you might ask if they know we're also Ecuadorian? Sure, they do. The world's computer bases are all linked. The minute I flash my U.S. passport, they also see my Ecuadorian information; but this doesn't matter so much these days. Hundreds of thousands of families are exactly like our own, and we are also the families most likely to travel, making our passport identities uninteresting to immigration authorities. The larger question is not which documents you carry, but how they make you feel.

Is it possible to divvy up loyalties between nationalities? Doesn't this make us patriotically schizophrenic on some level? I think it's important to talk about our nationalities because I think many sense that it is like having a space for language in the brain; if you divide it, you can never be fully competent in one or the other. Whereas we now know that this is ridiculous (it is indeed possible to be multilingual as well as proficient), the answer to single versus multiple nationalities is a political one and involves more people. Personally, my second nationality is similar to my married last name, which is added on to my maiden name (Tokuhama-Espinosa). One does not replace the other but is an addition to my whole.

I have never been asked to split my loyalties between Ecuador and the United States. I became Ecuadorian because Ecuadorian law obliged me to do so, which was recognized by the U.S. government, as it is in thousands of cases per year. My children, on the other hand, were given the two nationalities upon birth. If you were to ask them where they come from, I think you will find that all three have different answers. Mateo is sure he is from Boston, although he only physically lived there from birth to three months. Natalie and Gabriel, who were born in Quito, quickly respond that they are both, dual nationality being as legitimate as single. Their view reminded me of a thesis work David Pollock told me he was supervising concerning a woman who made the case that "international" qualified as its own culture. That is, being from the American culture and the Ecuadorian culture could legitimately be replaced by being from the international culture. I found this fascinating. Pollock believes that these are signs of the times. It is getting more and more difficult to pigeonhole children who have been brought up around the world. They do not commit to either their birthplace or their passport country; they are citizens of the world. As I reflect on this I remember that when Gabriel was seven, he had a week in which he claimed four different origins. On Monday, he made an oral presentation about Japan, because he is Japanese. On Tuesday, he was Ecuadorian, because we had a charity drive for homeless children in Quito, and he brought pictures from his birth country. On Wednesday, he was American, because the Boy Scout group met and sang cowboy camp songs in the forest. On Sunday, he was American Indian, because the church was organizing Thanksgiving and he identified with his great-great grandfather, Charlie Hawk, my mother's mother's father, an Indian. Did he feel schizophrenic because of these identities? On the contrary—I never saw him so proud to be able to claim such rich heritage as his own. Pollock writes that with third culture kids, it ultimately boils down to a single reflection: Home is not necessarily where you were born, which passport you carry, or the country you spent the most time in. Home is where your family is.

ONE HOME

I grew up in Berkeley, California, and attended public schools all my life. After high school, I picked the point furthest on the map for college simply because I wanted to see more of the country. I went to Boston University, where I met Cristian, who would become my husband. Cristian grew up in Quito, Ecuador, and attended the German School of Quito his entire life. After high school, he went to Washington, D.C., to brush up on his English for a semester, and then he came to Boston. Our married life has carried us to five different countries: Japan, Ecuador, the United States, Switzerland, and Peru. We have raised our three dual-nationality children in four languages: English, Spanish, German, and French. Contrary to where my unhidden passions lie, languages do not define our family; our family defines its languages. As with any other family, life has offered us many choices, some of which have been very painful, such as leaving friends and family for better jobs. This comes with the job description and life we have chosen. Adopting to a new country and culture for years on end, making friends who you know you will leave, choosing to integrate without assimilating are all part of it. As I read over these words I realize how truly lucky we have been as a family. Though many of the moves we have made were bumpy at the start, they all resulted in growth—both together, as a family, and toward each other. I see my kids as being each other's best friends. They are a solid crew. But I also realize how fragile this all is.

In the diplomatic corps, the rate of divorce is probably double that of the average population. Asking families to pull up and ship out because the head of the household has just been assigned somewhere is a great sacrifice. The military, businesses, and missionary corps are subject to the same kind of uprooting. As the world becomes more globalized, being sent to Hong Kong is becoming as common as being sent to New York. The nature of political relations also means the United States has more troops abroad these days than ever before in our history; in many cases, for every person assigned to a new unit, two to four more follow along as family members. Whereas many of these families stay centralized and a faux American lifestyle can be maintained on the base, the move away from friends at home, and the need to invest in new ones abroad remain challenges. Companies are beginning to recognize

the cost of poorly planned moves as well. In a study I reported in
The Multilingual Mind it was noted that for every failed transfer,
thousands of dollars are lost. This means choosing the right person
for the job is not enough anymore; companies have to ensure that
the entire family is on board with the change. Instead of waiting for
multinationals, the military, the church, and the foreign service to
catch up, however, each family can its own steps.

This book is about languages, and languages are about communication. The single most important element of my own family's ability to use our country upheavals to our advantage has been
communication. Why do you want to go? Why do you want to stay?
What would be best for the children? How can we make this work?
I recall that when my husband was first posted in Peru, we had many
a "discussion" about what would be best for the children. It was
December and we had just finished building our house in Quito and
planned on moving in January. Cristian was to begin his new job, if
he took it, in February. I recalled that when we moved the children
from Geneva in March and put them into school in April, it was one
of the worst decisions we had ever made. There was no chance for
real closure; the kids joined the school with three months left in the
school year—a time when the local kids were consolidating all their
friendships and uninterested in new ones. I promised myself we
would not do that to the children again. To complicate things, Peru
is in the southern hemisphere, meaning that the school year actually
starts in March and ends in December. Should we move the kids
when their northern hemisphere year ends (in July) or when their
new southern hemisphere school ends (in December)? We decided
to move in August, which was when the Lima school had their half-
year break, and which gave the children enough time to end the
school year with proper closure. We knew that they would also be
near a summer boredom stage and would probably welcome the
change. The point is that this decision was long, laborious, and
painful. It was discussed, shouted about, and explored with teachers,
schools, friends, family, and—especially—the kids themselves. Even
though my husband could have insisted that we all go together in
February, he didn't. Instead, he chose to commute every weekend
for five months until the kids and I moved. That is, instead of asking
four members of the family to sacrifice and move when we weren't
ready, he sacrificed for all of us. This is a flexibility I have not seen
in some families I know. I have a girlfriend from El Salvador who
married a German. At the time they both worked for the same phar-

maceutical company, but when they married, one had to quit because company policy didn't allow in-company relations, so my girlfriend stepped down from her post. They lived for years in Ecuador on one of his postings and had just built a house when one afternoon she announced to us that they would be leaving in ninety days for company headquarters in Germany. She looked shocked by the whole thing but explained, "What can you do? We have to follow him wherever he goes." She was resigned to make the most of her change, and I admired her loyalty to her husband. But at the same time I couldn't help but feel the inequality in their relationship. That is not the home I want to make, I decided then and there, and luckily, my partner in this adventure agrees. It would be easy to say, "This is where the work is," and follow it. But the truth of the matter is that building a home is more than the sum of careers.

I will close by writing that I know it is rare to find a spouse who believes in this kind of a partnership, but hopefully it is becoming more common in today's world. It is also rare to be blessed with the choices we have been able to have about which schools to place our children in, whether to pay for a tutor or not, and the luxury of being able to maintain home visits and ties to our cultures in the ways we do. It is also rare to have three wonderfully diverse children who work so well together and who love one another.

What is not rare is the search for all of the above. Wanting something is not the same as being willing or able to work for it. I have seen hundreds of families with far fewer resources be equally or even more successful than we have been at building a multilingual family. What they lacked in resources, they made up with love and perseverance. Paul and Marge, for example, were not lucky enough to have ever met their father, who left their mother for another woman when they were infants. Their mother, however, got back up on her feet and used her tenacity of spirit and devotion to her children to create opportunities for them that could have easily been lost by someone with less love for her children. She fought to make her house a home and succeeded. Originally from Rwanda, she spoke French and English and had learned German. She used those language skills to begin work at the United Nations and was quickly promoted to areas of more responsibilities. Her children attended the subsidized German school (as their father was a national), where they also learned German, French, and English. She used this platform to find an even more attractive job and moved to the Netherlands, where the children added Dutch to their repertoire. This woman and I share very different stories, but we have fortunately both reaped the successes of forming homes that are launching pads for our children. Maria is another example. Also a single mother, her two children were abandoned by their father when they were just four and six. Perhaps this is even harder than the earlier case, because these children knew their father, but from one day to the next he was gone. Maria placed the children in a bilingual school for low-income families in California, and this experienced changed their lives. By strengthening their Spanish while learning English, these two children also gained confidence in other subject areas and have become good students. The children stay extended hours at the school because Maria has a full-time job and needs the income, but she is careful to supervise their homework after she returns from work each evening. Maria could have given up and abandoned her dreams, but she chose to make this problem an opportunity. She sought out resources in her area, and she realized the importance of bilingualism in the workforce; after all it had helped her get her job at the hospital. She understood that the key out of this cycle of poverty was by getting her children the best possible education, which she knows includes languages.

My family has been lucky, but we have also worked hard. Independent of what you start with, resources are out there to be found and used. I have also seen hundreds of families with all the resources in the world who failed miserably at their attempts to build multilingual homes; money doesn't buy happiness, which is where we close. Languages are a gift, which can open the doors to economic opportunity, to cultural sensitivity, and to self-knowledge. They are tools for living, but they are not life itself. Having all the ingredients does not make the delicacy; knowing how to mix the ingredients in the right balance is where good cooking and good parenting come into play. Living languages is an ongoing, dynamic process. Families can change, and the roles we play within them shift. The languages we invest in are a part of our home design, and they should be thought about carefully and always used to their maximum potential.

Notes

CHAPTER 1

1. A. Clark, *Being There: Putting Brain, Body, and World Together Again* (Cambridge, MA: MIT Press, 1997), 218.

2. See David G. Mandelbaum, ed., *Selected Writings of Edward Sapir in Language, Culture, and Personality* (Berkeley, CA: University of California Press, 1963), and John B. Carroll, ed., *Language, Thought, and Reality: Selected Writings of Benjamin Lee Whorf* (Cambridge, MA: MIT Press, 1956).

3. Raymond Cohen, "Language and Conflict Resolution: The Limits of English," *International Studies Association* (2001):26.

4. Ibid.

5. Ibid.

CHAPTER 2

1. M. Marshall, "Lack of Languages Could Damage UK Business in the Single Market," *Education* 174 (April 15, 2005):1.

2. Araceli Ortiz de Urbiana, "In Praise of Multilingualism," *UNESCO Courier* 53, no. 4 (2000):29.

3. Thane Peterson, "The Importance of Being Multilingual," *Business Week Online* (2002).

4. Karen Jenkins, "Recognizing the Values of Foreign Language Skills," *Diverse Issues in Higher Education* 22, no. 26 (2006):36.

5. Thane Peterson, "The Importance of Being Multilingual," *Business Week Online* (2002).

6. William Frey, "Multilingual America," *American Demographics* (July/August 2002):20–23.

7. Janette K. Klinger and Alfredo J. Artiles, "English Language Learners Struggling to Learn to Read: Emergent Scholarship on Linguistic Differences and Learning Disabilities," *Journal of Learning Disabilities* 39(5) (2006):386–389.

8. Karen Jenkins, "Recognizing the Values of Foreign Language Skills," *Diverse Issues in Higher Education* 22, no. 26 (2006):35.

9. Beth Potier (May 6, 2004), "Two Is Better Than One" Harvard News Office. *Harvard University Gazette*. Retrieved from http://www.hno. harvard.edu/gazette/2004/05.06/12-bilingual.html.

10. Abstracts from this meeting can be found on the Georgetown University Web site: http://cbbc.georgetown.edu/workshops/2006L2.html.

11. William Frey, "Multilingual America," *American Demographics* (July/August 2002):20–23.

12. M. Zehr, "Foreign Languages," *Education Week* 25, no. 24 (2006):16.

13. Greg Toppo, "Is Bilingual Education Report Being Downplayed?" *USA Today*, (n/d); "U.S. Department of Education Declines to Publish Report on Literacy Education of Bilingual Children," *Reading Today* (August 29, 2005). Retrieved from www.reading.org.

14. Thane Peterson, "The Importance of Being Multilingual," *Business Week Online* (2002).

CHAPTER 3

1. Brian Mac Whinney, "The Emergence of a Second Language," presented at the Center for the Brain Basis of Cognition, The Neurocognition of Second Language Workshop, Georgetown University, 2006. Retrieved from http://cbbc.georgetown.edu/workshops/2006L2.html.

2. Ellen Bialystok and Kenji Hakuta, *In Other Words: The Science and Psychology of Second-language Acquisition* (New York: Basic Books, 1996), 75.

3. Joy Hirsch, "Distinct Cortical Areas Associated with Native and Second Languages," *Nature* 388 (July 10, 1997):171.

4. For a more lengthy discussion about early and late bilinguals, I suggest a look at the following articles: B. Harley and D. Hart, "The Effects of Early Bilingual Schooling on First Language Skills," *Applied Psycholinguistics* 7, no. 4 (1986):295–322; J. Navarra, N. Sebastián-Gallés, and S. Soto-Faraco, "The Perception of Second Language Sounds in Early Bilinguals:

New Evidence from an Implicit Measure," *Journal of Experimental Psychology/Human Perception & Performance* 31 no. 5 (2005):912–918; J. D. Ramirez, S. D. Yuen, and D. R. Ramey, *Longitudinal Study of Structured English Immersion Strategy, Early-exit and Late-exit Transitional Bilingual Education Programs for Language-minority Children. Final Report to the U.S. Department of Education. Executive Summary and Vols. I and II* (San Mateo, CA: Aguirre International, 1991); L. Wei, "Dimensions of Bilingualism," in *The Bilingualism Reader*, ed. L. Wei (London: Routledge, 2000); Ellen Bialystok, ed., *Language Processing in Bilingual Children* (Cambridge: Cambridge University Press, 2000).

5. J. Navarra, N. Sebastián-Gallés, and S. Soto-Faraco, "The Perception of Second Language Sounds in Early Bilinguals: New Evidence from an Implicit Measure," *Journal of Experimental Psychology/Human Perception & Performance* 31, no. 5 (2005):912.

6. Ellen Bialystok and Kenji Hakuta, *In Other Words: The Science and Psychology of Second-language Acquisition* (New York: Basic Books, 1996), 93–94.

7. Ibid.

8. Ibid.

9. For a wonderfully detailed view of how children gain conceptual understanding of the world, see Vittorio Gallese and George Lakoff, "The Brain's Concepts: The Role of the Sensory-Motor System in Conceptual Knowledge," *Cognitive Neuropsychology* 22, nos. 3–4 (2005):455–479.

10. Ibid.

11. G. Dehaene-Lambertz, S. Dehaene, and L. Hertz-Pannier, "Functional Neuroimaging of Speech Perception in Infants," *Science* 298, no. 5600 (2002):2013.

12. Patricia Kuhl, "Early Language Acquisition: Cracking the Speech Code," *Nature Reviews Neuroscience* 5, no. 11 (2004):831.

13. Ibid.

14. Barbara T. Conboy and Debra L. Mills, "Two Languages, One Developing Brain: Event-Related Potentials to Words in Bilingual Toddlers," *Developmental Science* 9, no. 1 (2006): F1.

15. Philip Lieberman, "The Evolution of Human Speech: Its Anatomical and Neural Bases," *Current Anthropology* 48, no. 1 (2007):39.

16. Ellen Bialystok and Kenji Hakuta, *In Other Words: The Science and Psychology of Second-language Acquisition* (New York: Basic Books, 1996), 28.

17. James Fledge, "A Critical Period for Learning to Pronounce Foreign Languages?" *Applied Linguistics* 8 (1987):162–177.

18. Istvàn Winkler, T. Kujala, H. Titinen, P. Sivonen, P. Alku, A. Lehtokoski, I. Czigler, V. Csepe, R.J. lmoniemi, and R. Naathanen, "Brain

Responses Reveal the Learning of Foreign Language Phonemes," *Psychophysiology* 36, no. 5 (1999):638–642.

19. Salim Abu-Rabia and Simona Kehat, "The Critical Period for Second Language Pronunciation: Is There Such a Thing? Ten Case Studies of Late Starters Who Attained a Native-like Hebrew Accent," *Educational Psychology* 24, no. 1 (2004):77–98.

20. Kathryne McGrath, Deborah Taylor, and Ruth Kamen, "Storytelling: Enhancing Language Acquisition in Young Children," *Education* 125, no. 1 (2004):3.

21. William H. Calvin, "The Emergence of Intelligence," *Scientific American Presents* 9, no. 4 (November 1998):44–51. Retrieved from http://www.williamcalvin.com/1990s/1998SciAmer.htm.

22. Ibid.

23. Ibid.

24. Lies Sercu, "Implementing Intercultural Foreign Language Education: Belgian, Danish and British Teachers' Professional Self-concepts and Teaching Practices Compared," *Evaluation and Research in Education* 16, no. 3 (2002):150.

25. Paloma Castro, Lies Sercu, and Maria del Carmen Méndez García, "Integrating Language-and-Culture Teaching: An Investigation of Spanish Teachers' Perceptions of the Objectives of Foreign Language Education," *International Education* 15, no. 1 (March 2004):91.

26. For more about this concept see David Sousa's book, *How the Brain Learns* (Thousand Oaks, CA: Corwin Press Inc., 2000).

27. Patricia Heasley, "Reading and Language Arts Worksheets Don't Grow Dendrites: 20 Literacy Strategies That Engage the Brain," *Library Media Connection* 24, no. 6 (2006):87.

28. Alison Taylor, Elizabeth Lazarus, and Ruth Cole, "Putting Languages on the (Drop Down) Menu: Innovative Writing Frames in Modern Foreign Language Teaching," *Educational Review* 57, no. 4 (2005):435.

29. Ibid.

30. Ibid., p. 175.

31. Ibid.

32. Sara Simonson, "What If and Why? Literacy Invitations for Multilingual Classrooms," *Illinois Reading Council Journal* 34, no. 3 (2006):56–57.

33. D. Brinton, M.A. Snow, and M.B. Wesche, *Content-Based Second Language Instruction* (Boston: Heinle & Heinle Publishers, 1989), 5.

34. University of Minnesota, "Content-Based Learning Second Language Instruction. What Is It?" Retrieved February 15, 2007, from http://www.carla.umn.edu/cobaltt/cbi.html.

35. B. Miller, "At Play: Teaching Teenagers Theater," *Library Journal* 131, no. 10 (2006):120.

36. A. P. Nilsen and D. L. F. Nilsen, "Working Under Lucky Stars: Language Lessons for Multilingual Classrooms," *Voices from the Middle* 11, no. 4 (2004):27.

37. Shiro Ojima, Hiro Nakata, and Ryusuke Kakigi, "An ERP Study of Second Language Learning after Childhood: Effects of Proficiency," *Journal of Cognitive Neuroscience* 17, no. 8 (2005):1212.

38. Michael Ullman cites others in the field who have shown reason to believe that there can be proficient L2 learning after childhood. These include Doughty and Long, 2003; and Ullman, 2001b, 2005.

CHAPTER 4

1. Wayne P. Thomas and Virginia P. Collier, "The Multiple Benefits of Dual Language," *Educational Leadership* (October 2003):63.

2. John Archibald, Sylvie Roy, Sandra Harmel, and Karen Jesney, *A Review of the Literature on Second Language Learning*. Prepared by The Language Research Center (LRC) of the University of Calgary (Alberta, Canada: Minister of Learning, 2004).

3. Virginia P. Collier, *Promising Practices in Public Schools* (paper presented at annual meeting, Teachers of English to Speakers of Other Languages, Baltimore, MD, 1994).

4. S. Murphy, *Second Language Transfer During Third Language Acquisition* (New York: Teachers College, Columbia University, 2002).

5. Antonio Damasio, *The Feeling of What Happens* (New York: Harcourt, 1999), 19–20.

6. William Henry James, *Principles of Psychology* (New York: Holt, 1890), 670. Excerpts retrieved from *Classics in the History of Psychology*. Retrieved on March 13, 2007, from http://psychclassics.yorku.ca/James/Principles/index.htm.

7. R. Plutchik, *The Psychology and Biology of Emotion* (New York: HarperCollins, 1994).

8. Christian Balkenius and Jan Morén, "Emotional Learning: A Computational Model of the Amygdala," *Cybernetics and Systems* 32, no. 6 (2001):611.

9. Personal communication with Edith Harding Esch, March 22, 2007.

10. Patricia Wolfe's references were made to some of the brightest minds in the field, including Amaral and Soltesz, 1997; Damasio, 2005; Gazzaniga, Ivry, and Mangun, 1998; Gazzaniga, 1998; LeDoux, 1996; Ornstein, 1998; Squire and Kandel, 2000; and Sylwester, 1995. See Patricia

Wolfe, *Brain Matters: Translating Research* (Alexandria, VA: Association for Supervision and Curriculum Development, 2001).

11. Patricia Wolfe, *Brain Matters: Translating Research into Classroom Practice* (Alexandria, VA: Association for Supervision and Curriculum Development, 2001).

CHAPTER 5

1. Bernard Comie, *The World's Major Languages* (New York: Oxford University Press, 1990).

2. *Education Today Newsletter*, United Nations, July–September 2003.

3. S. Flynn, C. Foley, and I. Vinnitskaya, "The Cumulative-Enhancement Model for Language Acquisition: Comparing Adults' and Children's Patterns of Development in First, Second and Third Language Acquisition of Relative Clauses," *The International Journal of Multilingualism* 1, no. 1 (2004):3–16.

4. See Lena A. Ricciardelli, "Creativity and Bilingualism," *Journal of Creative Behaviour* 26, no. 4, (1992):242–254.

5. No significant effect on reading ability was observed. For more information, see Kenji Hakuta, Y. G. Butler, and D. Witt, *How Long Does It Take English Learners to Attain Proficiency?* (University of California, Linguistic Minority Research Institute, 2000).

6. David G. Mandelbaum, ed., *Selected Writings of Edward Sapir in Language, Culture, and Personality* (Berkeley: University of California Press, 1963), and John B. Carroll, ed., *Language, Thought, and Reality: Selected Writings of Benjamin Lee Whorf* (Cambridge, MA: MIT Press, 1956).

7. Cristina Sanz, "Novice vs. Experiences Language Learners: Age, Cognitive Capacity and Type of Input," presented at the Center for the Brain Basis of Cognition, The Neurocognition of Second Language Workshop, Georgetown University, 2006. Retrieved from http://cbbc. georgetown.edu/workshops/2006L2.html.

8. Jasone Cenoz, Britta Hufeisen, and Ulrike Jessner, eds., *The Multilingual Lexicon* (Dordrecht, The Netherlands: Kluwer Academic Publishers, 2003).

9. Ibid.

10. See Reza Talebinejad for discussion on "Vocabulary Acquisition in the Third Language: English, German, Persian." Also, Jasone Cenoz, Britta Hufeisen, and Ulrike Jessner, eds., *The Multilingual Lexicon* (Dordrecht, The Netherlands: Kluwer Academic Publishers, 2003).

11. Michel Paradis, "Implicit Competence and Explicit Knowledge in Second Language Acquisition and Learning," presentation made at the Center for the Brain Basis of Cognition, The Neurocognition of Second

Language Workshop, Georgetown University, 2006). Retrieved from http://cbbc.georgetown.edu/workshops/2006L2.html.

12. S. Murphy, *Second Language Transfer during Third Language Acquisition.* (New York: Teachers College, Columbia University, 2002).

13. W. P. Rivers, "Self-Directed Language Learning and Third Language Learner," paper presented at the Annual Meeting of the American Council on the Teaching of Foreign Languages, Philadelphia, PA, November 22–24, 1996.

14. John Archibald, Sylvie Roy, Sandra Harmel, and Karen Jesney, *A Review of the Literature on Second Language* (Alberta, Canada: Minister of Learning, March 2004).

15. J. Dewaele, "Activation or Inhibition? The Interaction of L1, L2 and L3 on the Language Mode Continuum," in J. Cenoz, B. Hufeisen, and U. Jessner, eds., *Cross-Linguistic Influence on Third Language Acquisition: Psycholinguistic Perspectives,* 69–89 (Clevedon, UK: Multilingual Matters, 2001); J. Cromdal, "Childhood Bilingualism and Metalinguistic Skills: Analysis and Control in Young Swedish-English Bilinguals," *Applied Psycholinguistics* 20, no. 1 (1999):1–20.

16. Deborah D. K. Ruuskanen, *Bilingual and Multilingual Children: Can My New Baby Learn Two or More Languages at Home? Ask a Linguist* (Vaasa, Finland: University of Vaasa, n/d).

17. Joshua Fishman, *Reversing Language Shift: Theoretical and Empirical Foundations of Assistance to Threatened Languages* (Clevedon, UK: Multilingual Matters, 1991).

18. Catherine Elizabeth Snow, W. S. Barnes, J. Chandler, I. F. Goodman, and L. Hemphill, *Unfulfilled Expectations: Home and School Influences on Literacy* (Cambridge, MA: Harvard University Press, 1991).

19. JoAnn Canales and J.A. Ruiz-Escalante, "A Pedagogical Framework for Bilingual Education Teacher Preparation Programs," Proceedings of the Third National Research Symposium on Limited English Proficient Student Issues: Focus on Middle and High School Issues (Washington, D.C.: United States Department of Education Office of Bilingual Education and Minority Languages Affairs: 1992). Retrieved on September 14, 2007, from http://www.ncela.gwu.edu/pubs/symposia/third/canales.htm.

20. Oxford Cambridge Research Achievement (2007). Retrieved on May 3, 2007 from http://www.ocr.org.uk/Data/publications/scheme_books_and_cars_cumulative_assessment_records/Unit_3-12_60471.pdf.

21. Brita Hufeisen, "A European Perspective: Tertiary Languages with a Focus on German as L3," in J. Rosenthal, ed., *Handbook of Undergraduate Second Language Education,* 209–229 (Mahwah, NJ: Lawrence Erlbaum, 2000).

CHAPTER 6

1. Michael Gazzaniga, ed., *The Cognitive Neuroscience, III* (Cambridge, MA: MIT Press, 2005); Steven Pinker, *The Language Instinct* (New York: Morrow, 1994).

2. Barbaro B. Johansson, "Cultural and Linguistic Influence on Brain Organization for Language and Possible Consequences for Dyslexia: A Review," *Annals of Dyslexia* 56, no. 1 (2006):13–50.

3. Michael T. Ullman, "A Cognitive Neuroscience Perspective on Second Language Acquisition: The Declarative/Procedural Model," in C. Sanz, ed., *Mind and Context in Adult Second Language Acquisition: Methods, Theory and Practice*, 141 (Washington, DC: Georgetown University Press, 2005).

4. The left perisylvian cortical regions.

5. V. Marian, M. Spivey, and Joy Hirsch, "Shared and Separate Systems in Bilingual Language Processing: Converging Evidence from Eyetracking and Brain Imaging," *Brain & Language* 86, no. 1 (2003):70.

6. Joy Hirsch, "Distinct Cortical Areas Associated with Native and Second Languages," *Nature* 388 (July 1997):171.

7. Marlene Gullenberg and Peter Indefrey, eds., *The Cognitive Neuroscience of Second Language Acquisition* (Malden, MA: Blackwell Publishing, 2006), 316.

8. D. A. Fitzgerald, M. Angstadt, L. M. Jelsone, P. J. Nathan, and K. L. Phan, "Beyond Threat: Amygdala Reactivity across Multiple Expressions of Facial Affect," *NeuroImage* 30, no. 4 (2006):1441–1448.

9. Marc R. Rosenzweig, S. Marc Breedlove, and Neil W. Watson, *Biological Psychology: An Introduction to Behavioral and Cognitive Neuroscience*, 4th ed. (Sunderland, MA: Sinauer Associates, 2005), 535.

10. J. Bachevalier and L. Málková, "The Amygdala and Development of Social Cognition: Theoretical Comment on Bauman, Toscano, Mason, Lavenex, and Amaral," *Behavioral Neuroscience* 120, no. 4 (2006):989.

11. From David Sousa's *How the Brain Learns*, 2000.

12. See S. Comeau, "Stress, Memory and Social Support," *McGill Reporter* 35, no. 2 (2007); A. Vyas, S. Jadhav, and S. Chattarji, "Prolonged Behavioral Stress Enhances Synaptic Connectivity in the Basolateral Amygdala," *Neuroscience* 143, no. 2 (2006):387–393.

13. For an excellent review of this topic, see John H. Schumann, *The Neurobiology of Affect in Language* (Malden, MA: Blackwell Publishers, 1997); John H. Schumann, "Summing Up: Some Themes in the Cognitive Neuroscience of Second Language Acquisition," *Language Learning* 56, supplement 1 (2006):313–319.

14. John D. Bransford, Ann L. Brown, and Rodney R. Cocking, eds., *How People Learn: Brain, Mind, Experience, and School* (Washington, D.C.: National Academy Press, 2003), 93.

15. Michael T. Ullman. "A Neurocognitive Perspective on Language: The Declarative/Procedural Model," *Nature Reviews Neuroscience* 2 (2001):717–726.

16. John D. Bransford, Ann L. Brown, and Rodney R. Cocking, eds., *How People Learn: Brain, Mind, Experience, and School* (Washington, D.C.: National Academy Press, 2003), 93.

17. Michael T. Ullman, "A Cognitive Neuroscience Perspective on Second Language Acquisition: The Declarative/Procedural Model," in C. Sanz ed., *Mind and Context in Adult Second Language Acquisition: Methods, Theory and Practice*, 148 (Washington, DC: Georgetown University Press, 2005).

18. Michael T. Ullman, "Contributions of Memory Brain Systems to First and Second Language," Center for the Brain Basis of Cognition, The Neurocognition of Second Language Workshop, Georgetown University, 2006, http://cbbc.georgetown.edu/workshops/2006L2.html.

19. Ibid.

20. Michael T. Ullman, "A Neurocognitive Perspective on Language: The Declarative/Procedural Model," *Nature Reviews Neuroscience* 2 (2001):717.

21. Michael T. Ullman, "A Cognitive Neuroscience Perspective on Second Language Acquisition: The Declarative/Procedural Model," in C. Sanz ed., *Mind and Context in Adult Second Language Acquisition: Methods, Theory and Practice*, 152 (Washington, DC: Georgetown University Press, 2005).

22. N. Golestani, F. X. Alario, S. Meriaux, D. LeBihan, S. Dehaene, and C. Pallier, "Syntax Production in Bilinguals," *Neuropsychologia* 44, no. 7 (2006):1029.

23. Brian Mac Whinney, "The Emergence of a Second Language," presented at the Center for the Brain Basis of Cognition, The Neurocognition of Second Language Workshop, Georgetown University, 2006, http://cbbc.georgetown.edu/workshops/2006L2.html.

24. E. M. Vikingstad, Y. Cao, A. J. Thomas, A. F. Johnson, G. M. Malik, and K. M. Welch, "Language Hemispheric Dominance in Patients with Congenital Lesions of Eloquent Brain," *Neurosurgery* 47, no. 3 (2000):562.

25. J. Pearce, "A Note on Aphasia in Bilingual Patients: Pitres' and Ribot's Laws," *European Neurology* 54, no. 3 (2005):127–131.

26. Michel Paradis, "The Bilingual Loch Ness Monster Raises Its Non-Asymmetric Head Again—Or, Why Bother with Such Cumbersome Notions as Validity and Reliability? Comments on Evans et al. (2002)," *Brain and Language* 87 (2003):441.

27. E. Gomeztortosa, E. M. Martin, M. Gaviria, F. Charbel, and J. I. Ausman, "Selective Deficit of One Language in a Bilingual Patient Following Surgery in the Left Perisylvian Area," *Brain & Language* 48, no. 3 (1995):320.

28. Ibid., 269.

29. Panagiotis G. Simos, E. M. Castillo, J. M. Fletcher, D. J. Francis, F. Maestu, J. I. Breier, W. W. Maggio, and A. C. Papanicolaou, "Mapping of Receptive Language Cortex in Bilingual Volunteers by Using Magnetic Source Imaging," *Journal of Neurosurgery* 95, no. 1 (2001):76.

30. Cordula Nitsch, Rila Franceschini, Georges Lüdi, and Ernst-Wilhlelm Radü, *Basel Neuroscience Program*, retrieved on May 25, 2007, from http://www.biozentrum.unibas.ch/neuro/html/members/nitsch.html.

31. Ibid.

32. D. Wuillemin, B. Richardson, and J. Lynch, "Right Hemisphere Involvement in Processing Later-Learned Languages in Multilinguals," *Brain and Language* 46, no. 4 (1994):620.

33. Mira Goral, Erika Levy, Loraine Obler, and Eyan Cohen, "Cross-Language Lexical Connections in the Mental Lexicon: Evidence from a Case of Trilingual Aphasia," *Brain and Language* 98, no. 2 (2006):235.

34. Ibid., 531.

35. K. E. Elston-Güttler, S. Paulmann, and S. A. Kotz, "Who's in Control? Proficiency and L1 Influence on L2 Processing," *Journal of Cognitive Neuroscience* 17, no. 10 (2005):1593–1610. Further evidence supporting the general view that language dominancy in the brain is based more on experience than age or other factors comes from Kerrie Elston-Güttler, Silke Paulmann, and Sonja Kotz of the Max Planck Institute for Human Cognitive & Brain Sciences, who studied German-English bilinguals. The results of their tests showed that being able to translate is based on two things—second language proficiency and sentence context—"as it helps high-proficiency learners control L1 activation."

36. Mei-chun Cheung, Agnes Chan, and Yu-leung Chan, "Language Lateralization of Chinese-English Bilingual Patients with Temporal Lobe Epilepsy: A Functional MRI Study," *Neuropsychology* 20, no. 5 (2006):589–597.

37. D. Kimura, *Sex and Cognition* (Cambridge, MA: MIT Press, 1999).

38. Michael T. Ullman, "A Cognitive Neuroscience Perspective on Second Language Acquisition: The Declarative/Procedural Model" in C. Sanz ed., *Mind and Context in Adult Second Language Acquisition: Methods, Theory and Practice*, 141–178 (Washington, DC: Georgetown University Press, 2005); L. R. Squire and B. J. Knowlton, "The Medial Temporal Lobe, the Hippocampus, and the Memory Systems of the Brain," in M.S. Gazzaniga, ed., *The New Cognitive Neurosciences*, 765–780 (Cambridge, MA: MIT Press, 2000).

39. Porter E. Coggins, Teresa J. Kennedy, and Terry A. Armstrong, "Bilingual Corpus Callosum Variability," *Brain & Language* 89, no. 1 (2004):69–75.

40. P. M. Thompson, T. D. Cannon, K. L. Narr, and T. van Erp, "Genetic Influences on Brain Structure," *Nature Neuroscience* 4, no. 12 (2001):1253.

41. Ibid.

42. C. McManus, *Right Hand, Left Hand: The Origins of Asymmetry in brains, Bodies, Atoms and Cultures* (Cambridge, MA: Harvard University Press, 2004).

43. Ibid.

44. Allen D. Bragdon and David Gamon, *Brains That Work a Little Bit Differently: Recent Discoveries about Common Mental Diversities* (Cape Cod, MA: The Brainworks Center, 2000).

45. N. Golestani, F. X. Alario, S. Meriaux, D. LeBihan, S. Dehaene, and C. Pallier, "Syntax Production in Bilinguals," *Neuropsychologia* 44, no. 7 (2006):1029.

46. Ibid.

47. The planum temporale and posterior ascending ramus.

48. A. L. Foundas, C. M. Leonard, and B. Hanna-Pladdy, "Variability in the Anatomy of the Planum Temporale and Posterior Ascending Ramus: Do Right- and Left-Handers Differ?" *Brain & Language* 83, no. 3 (2002):403.

49. The left-hemisphere superior temporal region.

50. A. Jansen, H. Lohmann, S. Scharfe, C. Sehlmeyer, M. Deppe, and S. Knecht, "The Association between Scalp Hair-Whorl Direction, Handedness and Hemispheric Language Dominance: Is There a Common Genetic Basis of Lateralization?" *NeuroImage* (December 29, 2006).

51. Ibid.

52. Bernard Weber, Christian Hoppe, Jennifer Faber, Nikolai Axmacher, Klaus Fließbach, Florian Mormann, Susanne Weis, Jürgen Ruhlmann, Christian E. Elger, and Guillén Fernández, *Association between Scalp Hair-Whorl Direction and Hemispheric Language Dominance* (Neuroimage, retrieved online November 10, 2005, from http://www.sciencedirect.com/science?_ob=ArticleURL&_udi=B6WNP-4HHWW701&_user=10&_cover Date=04%2F01%2F2006&_rdoc=1&_fmt=&_orig=search&_sort=d&view =c&_acct=C000050221&_version=1&_urlVersion=0&_userid=10&md5= ce0ea2162d186975ec74460c9aac43ec).

53. Amar J. S. Klara, "Human Handedness and Scalp Hair-Whorl Direction Develop from a Common Genetic Mechanism," *Genetics* 165 (September 2003):269–276.

54. Rita Franceschini, D. Zappatore, Georges Lüdi, Ernst-Wilhelm Radü, Elise Wattendorf, and Cordula Nitsch, "Learner Acquisition Strategies (LAS) in the Course of Life: A Language Biographic Approach," in *Interactive CD-ROM L3-Conference, Second International Conference on Third Language Acquisition and Trilingualism* (Ljouwert/Leeuwarden, The Netherlands:

Fryske Akademy, 2002); Michael Gazzaniga, ed., *The Cognitive Neuroscience, III* (Cambridge, MA: MIT Press, 2005); D. Wuillemin, B. Richardson, and J. Lynch, "Right Hemisphere Involvement in Processing Later-Learned Languages in Multilinguals," *Brain and Language* 46, no. 4 (1994):620–636.

55. Michel Paradis, "The Bilingual Loch Ness Monster Raises Its Non-Asymmetric Head Again—Or, Why Bother with Such Cumbersome Notions as Validity and Reliability? Comments on Evans et al. (2002)," *Brain and Language* 87 (2003):441.

56. Rita Franceschini, D. Zappatore, Georges Lüdi, Ernst-Wilhelm Radü, Elise Wattendorf, and C. Nitsch, "Learner Acquisition Strategies (LAS) in the Course of Life: A Language Biographic Approach," in *Interactive CD-ROM L3-Conference, Second International Conference on Third Language Acquisition and Trilingualism* (Ljouwert/Leeuwarden, The Netherlands: Fryske Akademy, 2002); Michael Gazzaniga, ed., *The Cognitive Neuroscience, III* (Cambridge, MA: MIT Press, 2005); D. Wuillemin, B. Richardson, and J. Lynch, "Right Hemisphere Involvement in Processing Later-Learned Languages in Multilinguals," *Brain and Language* 46, no. 4 (1994):620–636.

CHAPTER 7

1. Edith Harding-Esch and Philip Riley, *The Bilingual Family Handbook* (Cambridge, UK: Cambridge University Press, 1986).

2. A. Williams and E. Gregory, "Siblings Bridging Illiteracies in Multilingual Contexts," *Journal of Research in Reading* 24, no. 3 (2001):248; E. Gregory and A. Williams, *City Literacies: Learning to Read Across Generations and Cultures* (London: Routledge, 2000).

3. Rachel Grant and Shelley Wong, "Forging Multilingual Communities: School-based Strategies," *Multicultural Perspectives* 6, no. 3 (2004):21.

4. D. August and T. Sanan, eds., *Developing Literacy in Second-Language Learners: Report of the National Literacy Panel on Language-Minority Children and Youth* (Mahwah, NJ: Lawrence Erlbaum Associates, 2006).

5. Rebeca María Barrera, "A Case for Bilingual Education," *Scholastic Parent & Children* (November/December 2004):72.

6. Sonia White Soltero, *Dual Language: Teaching and Learning in Two Languages* (Boston: Pearson Educational, 2004), and D. August and Kenji Hakuta, *Improving Schooling for Language Minority Children* (Washington, DC: National Academy Press, 1998) are great resources in this area.

7. Charles L. Glenn, "Two-Way Bilingual Education," *Education Digest* 68, no. 5 (January 2003):45.

8. Wayne P. Thomas and Virginia P. Collier, "The Multiple Benefits of Dual Language," *Educational Leadership* (October 2003):63; Jim Cummins, *Negotiating Identities: Education for Empowerment in a Diverse Society*, (Ontario, CA: California Association for Bilingual Education, 1996).

9. Charles L. Glenn, "Two-Way Bilingual Education," *Education Digest* 68, no. 5 (January 2003):42–45.

10. D. Barlow, "Review of Tongue-Tied: The Lives of Multilingual Children in Public Education," *Education Digest* 70, no. 4 (2004):77–78: "Each day millions of Americans are denied their right to speak in their own words. Remarkably, civil rights advocates do not roundly condemn this silencing. The formal rules and prevalent norms of U.S. society are rarely questioned, much less disputed. Social institutions and empowered individuals coolly go about their day proscribing a large portion of our society from speaking their mind."

11. Wayne P. Thomas and Virginia P. Collier, "The Multiple Benefits of Dual Language," *Educational Leadership* (October 2003):63; Jim Cummins, *Negotiating Identities: Education for Empowerment in a Diverse Society* (Ontario, CA: California Association for Bilingual Education, 1996).

12. E. R. Howard and D. Christian, *Two-Way Immersion 101: Designing and Implementing a Two-Way Immersion Education Program at the Elementary Level* (Santa Cruz, CA: Center for Research on Education, Diversity, and Excellence, University of California-Santa Cruz, 2002); K. J. Lindholm Leary, *Dual-Language Education* (Clevedon, UK: Multilingual Matters, 2001); Wayne P. Thomas and Virginia P. Collier, *A National Study of School Effectiveness for Language Minority Students' Long-Term Academic Achievement* (Santa Cruz, CA: Center for Research in Education, Diversity, and Excellence, University of California-Santa Cruz, 2002), retrieved November 28, 2005, from www.crede.ucsc.edu/research/llaa/a.a_final.html.

13. Maria G. Lopez and Abbas Taskakkori, "Narrowing the Gap: Effects of a Two-Way Bilingual Education Program on the Literacy Development of At-Risk Primary Students," *Journal of Education for Students Placed at Risk* 9, no. 4 (2004):325–326.

14. Ibid., 334.

15. Ibid., 22.

16. Rachel Grant and Shelley Wong, "Forging Multilingual Communities: School-Based Strategies," *Multicultural Perspectives* 6, no. 3 (2004):21.

17. Ibid., 19.

18. Ibid., 20.

19. Jim Cummins, Vicki Bismilla, Patricia Chow, Sarah Cohen, Frances Giampapa, Lisa Leoni, Perminder Sandhu, and Padma Sastri, "Affirming Identity in Multilingual Classrooms," *Educational Leadership* (September 2005):38–43.

20. Lies Sercu, "Implementing Intercultural Foreign Language Education: Belgian, Danish and British Teachers' Professional Self-concepts and Teaching Practices Compared," *Evaluation and Research in Education* 16, no. 3 (2002):150; A. A. Yeung and E. K. P. Wong, "Domain Specificity of Trilingual Teachers' Verbal Self Concepts," *Journal of Educational Psychology* 96, no. 2 (2004):360–368.

21. Ann Barnes, "A Passion for Languages: Motivation and Preparation to Teach Modern Foreign Languages in Eight Cohorts of Beginning Teachers," *Research Papers in Education* 20, no. 4 (2005):349–369.

22. Edmund James Sass, "Motivation in the College Classroom: What Students Tell Us," *Teaching of Psychology* 16, no. 2 (1989):86–88.

23. Kathryn F. Whitmore and Carril G. Crowell, "Bilingual Education Students Reflect on Their Language Education: Reinventing a Classroom 10 Years Later," *Journal of Adolescent & Adult Literacy* 49 (December 2005/January 2006):4.

24. For a great resource, see Tara Goldstein, *Teaching and Learning in a Multilingual School: Choices, Risks, and Dilemmas* (Mahwah, NJ: Lawrence Erlbaum Associates, 2003); Sue Pearson and Gary Chambers, "A Successful Recipe? Aspects of the Initial Training of Secondary Teachers of Foreign Languages," *Support for Learning* 20, no. 3 (2005):115–22.

25. D. Musumeci, "Teacher-Learner Negotiation in Content-Based Instruction: Communication at Cross-Purposes," *Applied Linguistics* 17, no. 3 (1996):286–324.

26. Ellen Bialystok's *Language Processing in Bilingual Children* (Cambridge, UK: Cambridge University Press, 2000); Patricia McAleer Hamaguchi, *Childhood Speech, Language & Listening Problems: What Every Parent Should Know* (New York: John Wiley and Sons, 2001).

27. A. Honnert and S. Bozan, "Summary Frames: Language Acquisition for Special Education and ELL Students," *Science Activities* 42, no. 2 (2005):19–29.

28. Barry McLaughlin, A. G. Blanchard, and Y. Osanai, "Assessing Language Development in Bilingual Preschool Children," *NCB Program Information Guide Series* 22 (Summer 1995).

29. Ibid.

30. Ibid., 3.

31. Manuela Macedonia, "Games and Foreign Language Teaching," *Support for Learning* 20, no. 3 (2005):135.

32. K. Einhorn, *ESL Activities and Mini-Books for Every Classroom: Terrific Tips, Games, Mini-Books and More to Help New Students from Every Nation Build Basic English Vocabulary and Feel Welcome!* (New York: Scholastic, Inc., 2001).

33. Ibid.

34. A. Clachar, "It's Not Just Cognition: The Effect of Emotion on Multiple-Level Discourse Processing in Second-Language Writing," *Language Sciences* 21, no. 1 (1999):360.

35. Jim Cummins, Vicki Bismilla, Patricia Chow, Sarah Cohen, Frances Giampapa, Lisa Leoni, Perminder Sandhu, and Padma Sastri, "Affirming Identity in Multilingual Classrooms," *Educational Leadership* (September 2005):41.

36. Ibid., 40.

37. Ibid.

38. Stephen Krashen, *The Power of Reading* (Westport, CT: Libraries Unlimited, 2003).

39. Rebeca Barrera, "A Case for Bilingual Education," *Scholastic Parent and Child* 12, no. 3 (November/December 2004):72–73.

40. Solange G. Taylor, "Multilingual Societies and Planned Linguistic Change: New Language-in-Education Programs in Estonia and South Africa," *Comparative Education Review* 46, no. 3 (2002):313.

41. Jim Cummins, Vicki Bismilla, Patricia Chow, Sarah Cohen, Frances Giampapa, Lisa Leoni, Perminder Sandhu, and Padma Sastri, "Affirming Identity in Multilingual Classrooms," *Educational Leadership* (September 2005):42.

References

Aarts, R., and L. Verrhoeven. "Literacy Attained in a Second Language Submersion Context." *Applied Psycholinguistics* 20, no. 3 (1999):377–394.

Abdelrazak, M. *Towards More Effective Supplementary and Mother-Tongue Schools*. London: Resource Unit, 2001.

Abedi, J. "Standardized Achievement Tests and English Language Learners." *Psychometric Issues Educational Assessment* 8 (2002):231–257.

Abramson, S., L. Seda, and C. Johnson. "Literacy Development in a Multilingual Kindergarten Classroom." *Childhood Education* 67 (1990): 68–72.

Abunuwara, E. "The Structure of the Trilingual Lexicon." *European Journal of Cognitive Psychology* 4, no. 4 (1992):311–322.

Abu-Rabia, S., and S. Kehat. "The Critical Period For Second Language Pronunciation: Is There Such A Thing? Ten Case Studies Of Late Starters Who Attained A Native-Like Hebrew Accent." *Educational Psychology* 24, no. 1 (2004):77–98.

Acevedo, M. C., C. J. Reyes, A. Robert, and E. M. López. "Assessing Language Competence: Guidelines for Assessing Persons with Limited English Proficiency in Research and Clinical Settings." *Journal of Multicultural Counseling and Development* 31, no. 3 (2003):192–204.

Adamson, P., B. Adamson, N. Clausen-Grace, A. Eames, C. Einarson, J. Goff, M. J. Kelley, R. L. Olness, A. L. Sandmann, E. Swaggerty, and D. A. Wooten. "Reading, Writing, Thinking: Proceedings of the 13th European Conference on Reading." *School Library Journal, Supplement* 52 (2003):81.

Adler, Jill. *Teaching Mathematics in Multilingual Classrooms*. Dordrecht, Netherlands: Kluwer Academic, 2002.

Adolphs, R., D. Tranel, and T. W. Buchanan. "Amygdala Damage Impairs Emotional Memory for the Gist but Not Details of Complex Stimuli." *Nature Neuroscience* 8, no. 4 (2005):512–518.

Agar, S. *Omniglot: Writing Systems and Languages of the World*. Retrieved on March 1, 2007 from http://www.omniglot.com/writing/languages.htm.

Alario, F. Xavier, N. O. Schiller, K. Domoto-Reilly, and A. Caramazza. "The Role of Phonological and Orthographic Information in Lexical Selection." *Brain and Language* 84 (2003):372–398.

Albert, M. L., and L. Obler. *The Bilingual Brain: Neuropsychological and Neurolinguistic Aspects of Bilingualism*. New York: Academia Press, 1978.

Alexander, D., G. Kane, and D. Premack. "Language and Systems of Symbols." *Science* 304, no. 5670 (2004):516–518.

Alptekin, C., G. Erçetin, and Y. Bayyurt. "The Effectiveness of a Theme-Based Syllabus for Young L2 Learners." *Journal of Multilingual & Multicultural Development* 28, no. 1 (2007):1–17.

Alvarez, R. P., P. J. Holcomb, and J. Grainge. "Accessing Word Meaning In Two Languages: An Event-Related Brain Potential Study Of Beginning Bilinguals." *Brain & Language* 8, no. 2 (2003):290–304.

Amar, J., and S. Klar. "Human Handedness and Scalp Hair-Whorl Direction Develop From a Common Genetic Mechanism." *Genetics* 165 (September 2003):269–276.

Amaral, D. G., and I. Soltesz. *Definition: Hippocampal Formation. Encyclopedia of Human Biology* (2nd edition, vol. 4). New York: Academic Press, 1997.

American Council on the Teaching of Foreign Languages. *ACTFL Proficiency Guidelines*. Yonkers, NY: ACTFL, 1986.

Amerin, A., and R. A. Peña. "Asymmetry in Dual Language Practice: Assessing Imbalance in a Program Promoting Equality." *Education Policy Analysis* 8 (2000):8.

Anderson, A. K., and E. A. Phelps. "Is the Human Amygdala Critical for the Subjective Experience of Emotion? Evidence of Intact Dispositional Affect in Patients with Amygdala Lesions." *Journal of Cognitive Neuroscience* 14, no. 5 (2002):709–720.

Andrews, L. "Curriculum Development for Multicultural and Multilingual Students." *Multicultural Education* 9, no. 3 (2002):15–18.

Andrews, M. A. "Ask the Brains." *Scientific American Mind* 17, no. 6 (2006):84.

Angelova, M., D. Gunawardena, and D. Volk. "Peer Teaching and Learning: Co-Constructing Language in a Dual Language First Grade." *Language and Learning* 20, no. 3 (2006):173.

Archibald, J., S. Roy, S. Harmel, and K. Jesney. *A Review of the Literature on Second Language*. Alberta, Canada: Minister of Learning, The Language Research Center of the University of Calgary, March 2004. Retrieved on June 1, 2007 from www.ucalgary.ca/lrc/Doc/Reports/litreview.pdf.

Argyris, K., N. C. Stringaris, V. Medford, M. J. Giampietro, M. Brammer, and A. S. David. "Deriving Meaning: Distinct Neural Mechanisms for Metaphoric, Literal, and Non-Meaningful Sentences." *Brain and Language* 100, no. 2 (2007):150–162.

Arnberg, L. *Raising Children Bilingually: The Pre-School Years*. Clevedon, UK: Multilingual Matters, 1987.

Asher, J. *Learning Another Language Through Actions: The Complete Teacher's Guide*. Los Gatos, CA: Sky Oaks Publications, 1977.

Atkins, B. T. S., and K. Varantola. "Language Learners Using Dictionaries: The Final Report of the EURALEX- and AILA-Sponsored Research Project into Dictionary Use." In B. T. S. Atkins and B. T. S. Tübingen, eds., *Using Dictionaries: Studies of Dictionary Use by Language Learners and Translators*. Niemeyer, 1998.

August, D., and K. Hakuta. *Improving Schooling for Language Minority Children*. Washington, D.C.: National Academy Press, 1998.

August, D., and T. Sanan, eds. *Developing Literacy in Second-Language Learners: Report of the National Literacy Panel on Language-Minority Children and Youth*. Mahwah, NJ: Lawrence Erlbaum Associates, 2006.

Bachevalier, J., and L. Málková. "The Amygdala and Development of Social Cognition: Theoretical Comment on Bauman, Toscano, Mason, Lavenex, and Amaral." *Behavioral Neuroscience* 120, no. 4 (2006):989–991.

Bachman, L. F., and A. S. Palmer. *Language Testing in Practice*. Oxford: Oxford University Press, 1996.

Bacon Lee, J. "Racial and Ethic Achievement Gap Trends: Reversing the Progress Towards Equity." *Educational Researchers* 31 (2002):3–12.

Baddeley, A. "Working Memory and Language: An Overview." *Journal of Communication Disorders* 36, no 3 (2003):189–208.

Bader-Rusch, A. "In the Beginning Was the Word: Languages in the Womb." In T. Tokuhama-Espinosa, ed., *The Multilingual Mind: Questions By, For and About People Living with Many Languages*. Westport, CT: Praeger, 2003.

Baetens-Beardsmore, H. *Bilingualism: Basic Principles*. Clevedon, UK: Multilingual Matters, 1982.

———. *European Models of Education*. Clevedon, UK: Multilingual Matters, 1993.

Bailey, N., C. Madden, and S. Krashen. "Is There a 'Natural Sequence' in Adult Second Language Learning?" *Language Learning* 24, (1974):235–243.

Baker, C. *The Care and Education of Young Bilinguals: An Introduction for Professionals*. Clevedon, UK: Multilingual Matters, 2000.

———. *Foundations of Bilingual Education*, 2nd ed. Clevedon, UK: Multilingual Matters, 2006.

Baker, P., and J. Eversley, eds. *Multilingual Capital: The Languages of London's Schoolchildren and their Relevance to Economic, Social and Educational Policies*. London: Battlebridge Publications, 2000.

Balkenius, C., and J. Morén. "Emotional Learning: A Computational Model of the Amygdala." *Cybernetics and Systems* 32, no. 6 (2001):611–636.

Barlow, D. "Tongue-Tied: The Lives of Multilingual Children in Public Education." *Education Digest* 70, no. 4 (2004):77–78.

Barnes, A. "A Passion for Languages: Motivation and Preparation to Teach Modern Foreign Languages in Eight Cohorts of Beginning Teachers." *Research Papers in Education* 20, no. 4 (2005):349–369.

Barnitz, J. G. "Emerging Awareness of Linguistic Diversity for Literacy Instruction." *Reading Teacher* 51, no. 3 (1997):264.

Barrera, R. "A Case for Bilingual Education." *Scholastic Parent and Child* 12, no. 3 (November/December 2004):72–73.

Barriere, I. "The Pioneering Work of Marcé (1856) on the Distinction between Speech and Writing." *Brain and Language* 87, no. 1 (2003):147.

Barron-Hauwaert, S. "Trilingualism: A Study of Children Growing Up with Three Languages." In T. Tokuhama-Espinosa, ed., *The Multilingual Mind: Issues Discussed By, For and About People Living with Many Languages*. Westport, CT: Praeger, 2003.

Baumgartner, T., K. Lutz, C. F. Schmidt, and L. Jancke. "The Emotional Power of Music: How Music Enhances the Feeling of Affective Pictures." *Brain Research* no. 1 (2006):151–164.

Beebe, R. M., and K. S. Leonard. "Second Language Learning in a Social Context." In *Visions and Reality in Foreign Language Teaching: Where We Are, Where We Are Going*. Chicago: National Textbook, 1993.

Bernard, J., and B. Grandcolas. "Apprendre une troisième langue quand on est bilingue: le Français chez un locuteur Anglo-Espagnol." *Aile (Paris)* 14 (2001):111–113.

Berninger, V. W., R. D. Abbott, and J. Jones. "Early Development of Language by Hand: Composing, Reading, Listening, and Speaking Connections; Three Letter-Writing Modes; and Fast Mapping in Spelling." *Developmental Neuropsychology* 29, no. 1 (2006):61–92.

Berninger, V. W., R. D. Abbott, and S. P. Abbott. "Writing and Reading: Connections between Language by Hand and Language by Eye." *Journal of Learning Disabilities* 35, no. 1 (January–February 2002):39–56.

Best, C. T. "The Emergence of Native-Language Phonological Influences in Infants: A Perceptual Assimilation Model." In J. C. Goodman and H. C. Nusbaum, eds., *The Development of Speech Perception: The Transition from Speech Sounds to Spoken Words.* Cambridge, MA: MIT Press, 1994.

Bhatia, T. K., and W. C. Ritchie. *Handbook of Bilingualism.* Oxford: Blackwell Publishing, 2006.

Bialystok, E., ed. *Language Processing in Bilingual Children.* Cambridge, UK: Cambridge University Press, 2000.

Bialystok, E., and K. Hakuta. *In Other Words: The Science and Psychology of Second-language Acquisition.* New York: Basic Books, 1996.

Bialystok, E., F. I. M. Craik, R. Klein, and M. Viswanathan. "Bilingualism, Aging, and Cognitive Control: Evidence from the Simon Task." *Psychology and Aging* 19 (2004):290–303.

Billingsley-Marshall, R. L., P. G. Simos, and A. C. Papanicolaou. "Reliability and Validity of Functional Neuroimaging Techniques for Identifying Language-Critical Areas in Children and Adults." *Developmental Neuropsychology* 26, no. 2 (2004):541–563.

Billington, D. *Seven Characteristics of Highly Effective Adult Learning Environments.* (1997). Retrieved from www.newhorizons.com on January 4, 2005.

Bloomfield, L. *Language.* New York: Holt, Reinhart and Winston, 1933.

Boroditsky, L. "Does Language Shape Thought?: Mandarin and English Speaker's Conceptions of Time." *Cognitive Psychology* 43 (2001):1–22.

Borowsky, R., W. Owen, T. Wile, C. K. Friesen, J. L. Martin, and G. E. Sarty. "Neuroimaging of Language Processes: fMRI of Silent and Overt Lexical Processing and the Promise of Multiple Process Imaging in Single Brain Studies." *Canadian Association of Radiologists Journal* 56, no. 4 (2005):204–213.

Bowers, C. *Elements of a Post-Liberal Theory of Education.* New York: Teachers College Press, 1989.

Bradford, J. D., A. L. Brown, and R. R. Cocking, eds. *How People Learn: Brain, Mind, Experience, and School.* Washington, D.C.: National Academy Press, 2003.

Bragdon, A. D., and D. Gamon. *Brains That Work a Little Bit Differently: Recent Discoveries about Common Mental Diversities*. Cape Cod, MA: The Brainworks Center, 2000.

Bremer, J., and L. McGeehan. "Teaming Foreign Language with Technology: Collaboration for Real-World Application." *Library Media Connection*. Columbus, OH: Linworth Publishing 2006.

Briellmann, R. S., M. M. Saling, A. B. Connell, A. B. Waites, D. F. Abbott, and G. D. Jackson. "A High-Field Functional MRI Study of Quadri-Lingual Subjects." *Brain and Language* 89, no. 3 (2004):531–542.

Brinton, D., M. A. Snow, and M. B. Wesche. *Content-based Second Language Instruction*. Boston: Heinle & Heinle Publishers, 1989.

Brown, B. *New Mind, New Body*. New York: Harper and Row, 1974.

Bruer, J. *Child's Talk: Learning to Use language*. New York: W. W. Norton, 1983.

Buchanan, T. W., D. Tranel, and R. Adolphs. "Cognitive Neuroscience of Emotional Memory." *Brain*. 129, no. 1 (2006):115.

Burck, C. *Multilingual Living: Explorations of Language and Subjectivity*. Hampshire, UK: Palgrave Macmillan, 2005.

Burgdorf, J., and J. Panksepp. "The Neurobiology of Positive Emotions." *Neuroscience and Biobehavioral Reviews* 30, no. 2 (2006):173–187.

Burgess, P. *Executive Functions Group Leader*. Institute of Cognitive Neuroscience, London. Retrieved from http://www.icn.ucl.ac.uk/Research-Groups/Executive-Functions-Group/index.php on May 10, 2007.

Butterworth, B., M. Cappelletti, and M. Kopelman. "Category Specificity in Reading and Writing: The Case of Number Words." *Nature Neuroscience* 4, no. 8 (2001):784.

Byram, M., and J. Leman, eds. *Bicultural and Tricultural Education*. Clevedon, UK: Multilingual Matters, 1990.

Byram, M., and K. Risager. *Language Teachers, Politics and Cultures*. Clevedon, UK: Multilingual Matters, 1999.

Cahill, L., and J. L. McGaugh. "NMDA-Induced Lesions of the Amygdaloid Complex Block the Retention-Enhancing Effect of Post-Training Epinephrine." *Psychobiology* 19, (1991):206–210.

———. "Emotions and Memory." Presentation at the Learning Brain Expo, San Diego, California, January 19, 2000.

Cahill, L., R. Babinsky, H. J. Markowitsch, and J. L. McGaugh. "Memories for Emotional Autobiographical Events Following Unilateral Damage to Medial Temporal Lobe." *Nature* 377, no. 6547 (1995):295.

Cahill, L., B. Prins, M. Weber, and J. McGaugh. "Beta-Adrenergic Activation and Memory or Emotional Events." *Nature* 371, (1994):702–704.

Calderon, M. E., and L. M. Rowe. *Designing and Implementing Two-Way Bilingual Programs.* Thousand Oaks, CA: Corwin Press, 2003.

Californians for Justice. *First Things First: Why We Must Stop Punishing Students and Fix California's Schools. A Report on School Inequality and the Impact of the California High School Exit Exam.* Long Beach, CA: Californians for Justice Education Fund, 2003.

Calvin, W. H. *How Brains Think: Evolving Intelligence, Then and Now.* New York, NY: Basic Books, 1996.

———. "The Emergence of Intelligence." *Scientific American Presents* 9, no. 4 (November 1998):44–51. Retrieved on March 20, 2007 from http://www.williamcalvin.com/1990s/1998SciAmer.htm.

Campbell, L., and T. E. Smith. "A Meta-Analytic Review of Gender Variations in Children's Language Use: Talkativeness, Affiliative Speech, and Assertive Speech." *Developmental Psychology* 40, no. 6 (2004):993–1027.

Canales, J. A., and J. A. Ruiz-Escalante. "A Pedagogical Framework for Bilingual Education Teacher Preparation Programs." Proceedings of the Third National Research Symposium on Limited English Proficient Student Issues: Focus on Middle and High School Issues. Washington, D.C.: United States Department of Education Office of Bilingual Education and Minority Languages Affairs, 1992. Retrieved from http://www.ncela.gwu.edu/pubs/symposia/third/canales.htm on September 14, 2007.

Caramazza, A. Classroom Lecture: The Psychology of Language, Harvard University, class notes, spring 1997.

Caramazza, A., Y. Bi, A. Costa, and M. Miozzo. "What Determines the Speed of Lexical Access: Homophone or Specific-Word Frequency? A Reply to Jescheniak et al. 2003." *Journal of Experimental Psychology / Learning, Memory and Cognition* 30, no. 1 (January 1, 2004):278–282.

Caramazza, A., and B. Z. Mahon. "The Organization of Concept Knowledge in the Brain: The Future's Past and Some Future Directions." *Neuropsychology* 22 (2005):1–25.

Carlson, N. R. *Physiology of Behavior,* 8th ed. Boston: Pearson Education, 2004.

Carroll, J. B., ed., *Language, Thought, and Reality: Selected Writings of Benjamin Lee Whorf.* Cambridge, MA: MIT Press, 1956.

Carroll, J. B., and S. Sapon. *Modern Language Aptitude Test (MLAT): Manual.* San Antonio, TX: The Psychological Corporation. Republished by Second Language Testing, Inc., www.2LTI.com, 1959/2000.

Castro, P., L. Sercu, and M. del Carmen Méndez García. "Integrating Language-and-Culture Teaching: An Investigation of Spanish Teachers'

Perceptions of the Objectives of Foreign Language Education." *International Education* 15, no. 1 (March 2004):91.

Cavanagh, S. "'Math Anxiety' Confuses the Equation for Students." *Education Week* 26, no. 24 (2007):12.

Cazden, C. B. *Effective Instructional Practices in Bilingual Education.* Washington, D.C.: National Institute of Education, 1984.

———. *Language Minority Education in the United States: Implications of the Ramirez Report.* Educational Practice Report 3. Cambridge, MA: Harvard Graduate School of Education, National Center for Research on Cultural Diversity and Second Language Learning, 1991.

Cazden, C. B, and C. E. Snow, eds. "English Plus: Issues in Bilingual Education." *The Annals of the American Academy of Political and Social Sciences* 508 (1990).

Cenoz, J. "Learning a Third Language: Basque, Spanish and English." In A. Roca and B. J. Jensen, eds., *Spanish in Contact: Issues in Bilingualism.* Somerville, MA: Cascadilla, 1996.

———. "The Additive Effect of Bilingualism on Third Language Acquisition: A Review." *International Journal of Bilingualism* 7, no. 1 (2003):18–71.

———. "The Effect of Linguistic Distance, L2 Status and Age on Cross-Linguistic Influence in Third Language Acquisition." In J. Cenoz, B. Hufeisen, and U. Jessner, eds., *Cross-Linguistic Influence In Third Language Acquisition: Psycholinguistic Perspectives*, 8–20. North York, ON: Multilingual Matters, 2003.

Cenoz, J., and F. Genesee, eds. *Beyond Bilingualism. Multilingualism and Multilingual Education.* Clevedon, UK: Multilingual Matters, 1998.

Cenoz, J., and U. Jessner, eds. *English in Europe: The Acquisition of a Third Language.* Clevedon, UK: Multilingual Matters Ltd., 2000.

Cenoz, J., B. Hufeisen, and U. Jessner. "Towards Trilingual Education." *International Journal of Bilingual Education and Bilingualism* 4, no. 1 (2001):1–10.

Cenoz, J., B. Hufeisen, and U. Jessner, eds. *The Multilingual Lexicon.* Dordrecht, Netherlands: Kluwer Academic Publishers, 2003.

Cenoz, J., and D. Lindsay. "Teaching English in Primary School: A Project To Introduce a Third Language to Eight Year Olds." *Language and Education* 8, no. 4 (1994):201–210.

Center for the Brain Basis of Cognition. *The Neurocognition of Second Language Workshop.* Washington, D.C.: Georgetown University, 2006. Retrieved from http://cbbc.georgetown.edu/workshops/2006L2.html.

Chamberlain, S. R., U. Muller, T. W. Robbins, and B. J. Sahakian. "Neuropharmacological Modulation of Cognition." *Current Opinion in Neurology* 19, no. 6 (2006):607–612.

Chang, Y., C. Wu, and H. Yu Ku. "The Introduction of Electronic Portfolios to Teach and Assess English as a Foreign Language in Taiwan." *TechTrends: Linking Research and Practice to Improve Learning* 49, no. 1 (2004):30–35.

Charney, D. S. "Neuroanatomical Circuits Modulating Fear and Anxiety Behaviors." *Acta Psychiatrica Scandinavica Supplementum,* no. 417 (2003):38–50.

Chase, K. "A Second Language before the Second Grade." *Teaching PreK–8* 28, no. 2 (1997):46–48.

Chenhappa, S., S. Bhat, and P. Padakannaya. "Reading and Writing Skills in Multilingual/Multiliterate Aphasics: Two Case Studies." *Reading and Writing: An Interdisciplinary Journal* 17, no. 1–2 (2004):121–135.

Cheuk, D. K. L., V. Wong, and G. M. Leung. "Multilingual Home Environment and Specific Language Impairment: A Case–control Study in Chinese Children." *Paediatric and Perinatal Epidemiology* 19, no. 4 (2005):303–314.

Cheung, M. C., A. S. Chan, and Y. Chan. "Language Lateralization of Chinese-English Bilingual Patients with Temporal Lobe Epilepsy: A Functional MRI Study." *Neuropsychology* 20, no. 5 (2006):589–597.

Childs, M. R. "The Practical Linguist: Make the Most of the Bilingual Advantage." *The Daily Yomiuri* (Japan) (March 2002).

Chiswick, B., Y. L. Lee, and P. W. Miller. "Family Matters: The Role of the Family in Immigrants' Destination Language Acquisition." *Journal of Population Economics* 18, no. 4 (2005):631–647.

Cho, K., K. Ahn, and S. Krashen. "The Effects of Narrow Reading of Authentic Texts on Interest and Reading Ability in English as a Foreign Language." *Reading Improvement* 42, no 1. (2005):58–64.

Cho, K., and H. J. Kim. "Using the Newspaper in an English as a Foreign Language Class." *Knowledge Quest* 34, no. 2 (2005):47–49.

———. "Home Run Search." *Knowledge Quest* 34, no. 2 (November/December 2005).

Chomsky, N. *Syntactic Structures.* The Hague: Mouton, 1957.

———. *Language Minority Education in the United States: Implications of the Ramirez Report.* Educational Practice Report 3. Cambridge: Harvard Graduate School of Education, National Center for Research on Cultural Diversity and Second Language Learning, 1991.

———. *Language and Mind,* 2nd ed. New York: Harcourt Brace Jovanovich, 2000.

Chomsky, N., and W. T. Fitch. "The Faculty of Language: What Is It, Who Has It, And How Did It Evolve?" *Science* 298, no. 5598 (2002):1569–1580.

Chow, P., and J. Cummins. "Valuing Multilingual and Multicultural Approaches to Learning." In S. R. Scheter and J. Cummins, eds., *Multilingual Education in Practice: Using Diversity as a Resource.* Portsmouth, NH: Heinemann, 2003.

Christensen, L. *Reading, Writing and Rising Up: Teaching about Social Justice and the Power of the Written Word.* Milwaukee, WI: Rethinking Schools, 2000.

Christian, D., E. R. Howard, and M. I. Loeb. *Bilingualism for All: Two-Way Immersion Education in the United States: Theory Into Practice.* Columbus, OH: The Ohio State University, 2000.

Christian, D., C. Montone, K. Lindholm, and I. Carranza. *Profiles in Two-Way Immersion Education.* Washington, D.C.: Center for Applied Linguistics, 1997.

Christian, D., I. Pufahl, and N. C. Rhodes. "Fostering Foreign Language Proficiency: What the U.S. Can Learn from Other Countries." *Phi Delta Kappan* (November 2005):226–228.

Chuang, H., and M. H. Rosenbusch. "Use of Digital Video Technology in an Elementary School Foreign Language Methods Course." *British Journal of Educational Technology* 36, no. 5 (2005):869–880.

Clachar, A. "It's Not Just Cognition: The Effect of Emotion on Multiple-Level Discourse Processing in Second-Language Writing." *Language Sciences* 21, no. 1 (1999):360.

Claire, E. "The Brave New World of Bilingual Teaching." *Times Educational Supplement* no. 4418 (1986).

Clark, A. *Being There: Putting Brain, Body, and World Together Again.* Cambridge, MA: MIT Press, 1997.

Clarke, H. A., D. van der Kooy, and D. M. Skinner. "Combined Hippocampal and Amygdala Lesions Block Learning of a Response-Independent Form of Occasion Setting." *Behavioral Neuroscience* 115, no. 2 (2000):341–368.

Cline, T., L. Ganschow, and R. Reason. "Multilingualism and Dyslexia Including the Teaching of Modern Foreign Languages." *Dyslexia* 6, no. 2 (2000):85–86.

Cloud, N., F. Genesee, and E. Hamayan. *Dual Language Instruction: A Handbook for Enriched Education.* Boston: Heinle and Heinle, 2000.

Clyne, M. *Multilingual Australia.* Melbourne: River Seine Publications, 1982.

———. "Some of the Things Trilinguals Do." *The International Journal of Bilingualism* 1, no. 2 (1997):95–116.

Clyne, M., and P. Cassia. "Trilingualism, Immigration and Relatedness of Language." *ITL Review of Applied Linguistics* 123–124 (1999):57–78.

Coggins, P. E., T. J. Kennedy, and T. A. Armstrong. "Bilingual Corpus Callosum Variability." *Brain and Language* 89, no. 1 (2004):69–75.

Cohen, L., S. Lehericy, F. Chochon, C. Lemer, S. Rivaud, and S. Dehaene. "Language-Specific Tuning of Visual Cortex? Functional Properties of the Visual Word Form Area." *Brain: A Journal of Neurology* 125, no. 5 (2002):1054–1069.

Cohen, R. "Meaning, Interpretation and International Negotiation." *Global Society* 14, no. 3 (2000):325.

———. "Language and Conflict Resolution: The Limits of English." *International Studies Association* (2001):26.

Collier, V. P. "A Synthesis of Studies Examining Long-Term Language-Minority Student Data on Academic Achievement." *Bilingual Research Journal* 6 (1992):187–212.

———. "Promising Practices in Public Schools." Paper presented at the Annual Meeting of the Teachers of English to Speakers of Other Languages, Baltimore, MD, 1994.

———. "Acquiring a Second Language for School. Directions in Language and Education." *National Clearinghouse for Bilingual Education* 1, no. 4 (Fall 1995).

———. *Promoting Academic Success for ESL Students: Understanding Second Language Acquisition for School.* Elizabeth, NJ: TESOL-Bilingual Educators, 1995.

Collier, V. P., and W. Thomas. *School Effectiveness for Language Minority Students.* Washington, DC: National Clearinghouse for Bilingual Education, 1997. Retrieved from http://www.ncbe.gwu.edu/ncbepubs/resource/effectiveness/thomas-collier97.pdf on March 22, 2007.

Comeau, S. "Stress, Memory and Social Support." *McGill Reporter* 35, no. 2 (2007). Retrieved from http://www.mcgill.ca/reporter/35/02/lupien/ on March 14, 2007.

Comie, B. *The World's Major Languages.* New York: Oxford University Press, 1990.

Conboy, B. T., and D. L. Mills. "Two Languages, One Developing Brain: Event-Related Potentials to Words in Bilingual Toddlers." *Developmental Science* 9, no. 1 (2006):F1.

Cook, V. "Multi-Competence and the Learning of Many Languages." In M. Bensousannan, I. Kreindler, and E. Aogain, eds., *Multilingualism and Language Learning: Language, Culture and Curriculum.* Clevedon, UK: Multilingual Matters, 1995.

Corder, S. "A Role for the Mother Tongue." In S. Gass and L. Selinker, eds., *Language Transfer in Language Learning.* Rowley, MA: Newbury House, 1983.

Corson, D. *Language Diversity and Education*. Mahwah, NJ: Lawrence Erlbaum Associates, 2001.

Cortazzi, M., and M. Hunter-Carsch. "Multilingualism and Literacy Difficulties: Bridging Home and School." *Literacy* 34, no. 3 (November 3, 2000):140.

Costa, A., and A. Caramazza. "The Cognate Facilitation Effect: Implications for Models of Lexical Access." *Journal of Experimental Psychology/ Learning, Memory and Cognition* 26, no. 5 (September 5, 2000):1283–1297.

———. "The Production of Noun Phrases in English and Spanish: Implications for the Scope of Phonological Encoding in Speech Production." *Journal of Memory and Language* 46 (2002):178–198.

Costa, A., D. Kovacic, J. Franck, and A. Caramazza. "On the Autonomy of the Grammatical Gender Systems of the Two Languages of a Bilingual." *Bilingualism: Language and Cognition* 6 (2003):81–200.

Council of Europe. *The Sociocultural and Intercultural Dimension of Language Learning and Teaching*. Strasbourg: Council of Europe, 1997.

Cowlishaw, G., and R. Dunbar. *Primate Conservation Biology*. Chicago: University of Chicago Press, 2000.

Crago, M., A. Eriks-Brophy, D. Pesco, and L. McAlpine. "Culturally Based Miscommunication in Classroom Interaction." *Language, Speech and Hearing Services in Schools* 28 (1997):245–254.

Crandall, J. "Content-Centered Learning in the United States." *Annual Review of Applied Linguistics* 13 (1992):111–127.

Crawford, J. *Bilingualism in Education: A Forgotten Legacy*. In *Bilingual Education: History, Politics, Theory and Practice*, 1999. Retrieved from http://ourworld.compuserve.com/homepages/JWCRAWFORD/ BECh1.htm on February 17, 2007.

———. *Obituary: The Bilingual Education Act: 1968–2002*. (Spring 2002). Retrieved from http://ourworld.compuserve.com/homepages/ JWCRAWFORD/T7obit.htm on September 14, 2007.

Croft, W. *Typology and Universals*. Cambridge: Cambridge University Press, 1990.

Cromdal, J. "Childhood Bilingualism and Metalinguistic Skills: Analysis and Control in Young Swedish-English Bilinguals." *Applied Psycholinguistics* 20, no. 1 (1999):1–20.

Cruickshank, K. "Literacy in Multilingual Contexts: Change in Teenagers' Reading and Writing." *Language and Education* 18, no. 6 (2004): 459–473.

Crystal, D. *English as a Global Language*. Cambridge: Cambridge University Press, 1997.

Cummins, J. "The Role of Primary Language Development in Promoting Educational Success for Language Minority Students." In California Department of Education, ed., *Schooling and Language Minority Students: A Theoretical Framework*. Los Angeles: UCLA, 1981.

——. "Language Proficiency, Bilingualism, and Academic Achievement." In P. A. Richard-Amoto, and M. A. Snow, eds., *The Multicultural Classroom: Readings for Content-Area Teachers*. Reading, MA: Addison Wesley, 1992.

——. "Bilingualism and Second Language Learning." *Annual Review of Applied Linguistics* 13, (1993):51–70.

——. *Negotiating Identities: Education for Empowerment in a Diverse Society*. Covina, CA: California Association for Bilingual Education, 1996.

——. *Language, Power and Pedagogy; Bilingual Children in the Crossfire*. Clevedon, UK: Multilingual Matters, 2000.

——. *Negotiating Identities: Education for Empowerment in a Diverse Society*. Los Angeles: California Association for Bilingual Education, 2001.

——. "Instructional Conditions for Trilingual Development." *International Journal of Bilingual Education and Bilingualism* 4, no. 1 (2001):61–75.

——. "Language, Power, and Pedagogy: Bilingual Children in the Crossfire." *Bilingual Education and Bilingualism* 23, (April 2001).

Cummins, J., V. Bismilla, P. Chow, S. Cohen, F. Giampapa, L. Leonia, P. Sandhu, and P. Sastri. "Affirming Identity in Multilingual Classrooms." *Educational Leadership* 63, no. 1 (2005):38–43.

Cysouw, M. "Quantitative Methods in Typology." In A. Gabriel, R. Köhler, and R. Piotrowski, eds., *Quantitative Linguistics: An International Handbook*. Berlin: Mouton de Gruyter, 2005.

Dagenais, D., and E. Day. "Classroom Language Experiences of Trilingual Children in French Immersion." *Canadian Modern Language Review* 54, no. 3 (1998):376–393.

——. "Home Language Practices of Trilingual Children in French Immersion." *The Canadian Modern Language Review* 56, no. 1 (1999):99–123.

Dale, R. "Cognitive and Behavioral Approaches to Language Acquisition: Conceptual and Empirical Intersections." *Behavior Analyst Today* 5, no. 4 (2004):336–358.

Daloz, L. *Effective Teaching and Mentoring: Realizing the Transformational Power of Adult Learning Experiences*. San Francisco: Jossey-Bass, 1986.

Damasio, A. *The Feeling of What Happens*. New York: Harcourt, 1999.

———. *Looking for Spinoza: Joy, Sorrow, and the Feeling Brain*. New York: Harcourt, Inc., 2003.

———. *Descartes' Error: Emotion, Reason, and the Human Brain*. New York: Penguin, 2005.

Damico, J. S., M. Smith, and L. Augustine. "Multicultural Populations and Language Disorders." In M. D. Smith and J. S. Damico, eds., *Childhood Language Disorders*. New York: Theme Medical Publishers, 1995.

De Angelis, G., and L. Selinker. "Interlanguage Transfer and Competing Linguistic Systems in the Multilingual Mind." In J. Cenoz, B. Hufeisen, and U. Jessner, eds., *Cross-Linguistic Influence in Third Language Acquisition: Psycholinguistic Perspectives*. Clevedon, UK: Multilingual Matters, 2001.

De Avila, ed. "Assessment of Language Minority Students: Political, Technical, Practical and Moral Imperatives." Proceedings of the First Research Symposium on Limited English Proficient Student Issues. Washington, D.C.: Office of Bilingual Education and Minority Languages Affairs, 1990. Retrieved on September 14, 2007 from http://www.ncbe.gwu.edu/ncbepubs/symposia/first/assessment.htm.

De Bot, K., and J. K. Kroll. "Psycholinguistics." In N. Schmitt, ed., *Applied Linguistics*. London: Oxford University Press: London, 2002.

De Jong, E. *The Bilingual Experience*. Cambridge: Cambridge University Press, 1986.

Dehaene-Lambertz, G., S. Dehaene, and L. Hertz-Pannier. "Functional Neuroimaging of Speech Perception in Infants." *Science* 298, no. 5600 (2002):2013–2015.

Delgado-Gaitan, C. *Literacy for Empowerment: The Role of Parents in Children's Education*. New York: Falmer, 1990.

———. "Involving Parents in the School: A Process for Empowerment." *American Journal of Education* 100, no. 1 (1991):20–46.

Depue, R. A., and P. F. Collins. "Neurobiology of the Structure of Personality: Dopamine, Facilitation of Incentive Motivation, and Extraversion." *The Behavioral and Brain Sciences* 22, no. 3 (1999):491–569.

Dewaele, J. "Second Language Learning in a Social Context." *CAL Digest on Foreign Language Education*. Iowa State University of Science and Technology and Santa Clara University, California. (January 1994).

———. "Activation or Inhibition? The Interaction of L1, L2 and L3 on the Language Mode Continuum." In J. Cenoz, B. Hufeisen, and U. Jessner, eds., *Cross-Linguistic Influence on Third Language Acquisition:*

Psycholinguistic Perspectives. Clevedon, UK: Multilingual Matters, 2001.

———. "Psychological and Sociodemographic Correlates of Communicative Anxiety in L2 and L3 Production." *The International Journal of Bilingualism* 6 (2002):1.

Diamond, A. *Brain Diagram*. Retrieved on July 10, 2007 from www.newhorizons.org/neuro/diamond_aging.htm.

Dickinson, D., A. McCabe, N. Clark-Chiarelli, and A. Wolf. "Cross-Language Transfer of Phonological Awareness in Low-Income Spanish and English Bilingual Preschool Children." *Applied Psycholinguistics* 25 (2004):323–347.

Dominguez de Ramírez, R., and E. Shapiro. "Curriculum-Based Measurement and the Evaluation of Reading Skills of Spanish-Speaking English Language Learners in Bilingual Education Classrooms." *School Psychology Review* 35, no. 3 (2006):356–369.

Donahue, T. S. "American Language Policy and Compensatory Opinion." In J. W. Tollefson, ed., *Power and Inquiry in Language Education*. New York: Cambridge University Press, 1995.

Doniger, W. *Splitting the Difference*. Chicago: University of Chicago Press, 1999.

Donovan, M. S., and C. T. Cross. *Minority Students in Special and Gifted Education*. Washington, D.C.: National Research Council, 2002.

Dörnyei, Z. *The Psychology of the Language Learner: Individual Differences in Second Language Acquisition*. Mahwah, NJ: Lawrence Erlbaum Associates, 2005.

Dorsaint-Pierre, P., N. Watkins, B. Lerch, and R. J. Zatorre. "Asymmetries of the Planum Temporale and Heschl's Gyrus: Relationship to Language Lateralization." *Brain: A Journal of Neurology* 129, no. 5 (2006):1164–1176.

Doughty, C., and Long, M. H. (Eds.). *Handbook of Second Language Acquisition*. New York: Basil Blackwell, 2003.

Early, M. *From Literacy to Multiliteracies: Designing Learning Environments for Knowledge Generation within the New Economy*. Ontario: Social Science and Humanities Research Council of Canada, 2002.

Ecke, P. "Lexical Retrieval in a Third Language: Evidence from Errors and Tip-of-the-Tongue States." In J. Cenoz, B. Hufeisen, and U. Jessner, eds., *Cross-Linguistic Influence on Third Language Acquisition: Psycholinguistic Perspectives*. Clevedon, UK: Multilingual Matters, 2001.

Economist Global Executive, The. "Don't Point: In International Business, a Little Cultural Knowledge Can Go a Long Way." (February 10, 2003). Accessed on September 22, 2006 from http://www.economist.

com/globalExecutive/education/executive/printerFriendly.cfm?story_id=1562688.

Edelsky, C. *With Literacy and Justice For All: Rethinking the Social in Language and Education,* 2nd ed. London: Taylor and Francis, 1994.

Education (UK). "Lack of Languages Could Damage UK Business in the Single Market." *Education (UK),* no. 174 (April 15, 2005).

Edwards, V. *The Tower of Babel: Teaching and Learning in Multilingual Classrooms.* Stoke-on-Trent, England: Trentham Books, 1998.

Eggen, P. D., and D. P. Kauchak. *Strategies for Teachers. Teaching Content and Thinking Skills.* Boston: Allyn and Bacon, 1996.

Ehrman, M., and R. Oxford. "Cognition Plus: Correlates of Language Learning Success." *Modern Language Journal* 79 (1995):67–89.

Eimas, P. D. "Percepción del habla en la primera infancia." *Investigación y Ciencia* (March 1985):4–31.

Einhorn, K. *ESL Activities and Mini-Books for Every Classroom: Terrific Tips, Games, Mini-Books and More to Help New Students from Every Nation Build Basic English Vocabulary and Feel Welcome!* New York: Scholastic, Inc., 2001.

Eisenstein, M., and R. J. Starbuck. "The Effect of Emotional Investment in L2 Production." In *Variation in Second Language Acquisition: Volume II. Psycholinguistic Issues.* Clevedon, UK: Newbury House, 1989.

Ekman, P., and W. V. Friesen. *Facial Action Coding System, Parts 1 and 2.* San Francisco: Human Interaction Laboratory, Department of Psychiatry, University of California San Francisco, 1978.

Elders, L., and P. Richards. "Critical Thinking... and the Art of Substantive Writing, Part III." *Journal of Developmental Education* 30, no. 1 (2006):32–33.

Elias, M. J., J. E. Zins, R. P. Weissberg, K. S. Frey, M. T. Greenberg, N. M. Haynes, R. Kessler, M. E. Schwab-Stone, and T. P. Shriver. *Promoting Social and Emotional Learning: Guidelines for Educators.* Alexandria, VA: Association for Supervisions and Curriculum Development, 1997.

Ellis, A. *Reading, Writing and Dyslexia: A Cognitive Analysis.* Mahwah, NJ: Lawrence Erlbaum Associates, 1994.

Ellis, R. *Reason and Emotion in Psychotherapy.* New York: Birch Lane Press, 1994.

Elmes, S. *The Routes of English.* London: BBC Factual and Learning, 2000.

Elston-Güttler, K. E., S. Paulmann, and S. A. Kotz. "Who's in Control? Proficiency and L1 Influence on L2 Processing." *Journal of Cognitive Neuroscience* 17, no. 10 (2005):1593–1610.

Elwert, W. T. *Das Zweisprachige Individuum: Ein Selbstzeugnis.* Weisbaden: Franz Steiner Verlag, 1959.

Epstein, J. L. "School/Family/Community Partnerships." *Phi Delta Kappan* 42 (1995):701–712.

Epstein, J. L., and M. Sanders. "What We Learn from International Studies of School-Family-Community Partnerships." *Childhood Education* 7 (1998):392–394.

Everatt, J., I. Smythe, D. Ocampo, and E. Gyarmathy. "Issues in the Assessment of Literacy-Related Difficulties across Language Backgrounds: A Cross-Linguistic Comparison." *Journal of Research in Reading* 27, no. 2 (2004):141–151.

Eviatar, Z., R. Ibrahim, and D. Ganayim. "Orthography and the Hemispheres: Visual and Linguistic Aspects of Letter Processing." *Neuropsychology* 18, no. 1 (2004):174–184.

Fabbro, F. "The Bilingual Brain: Cerebral Representation of Languages." *Brain and Language* 79, no. 2 (2001):211–222.

Facione, P. A. *Critical Thinking: What It Is and Why It Counts*. Millbrae, CA: Insight Assessment, 2004.

Fantini, A. E. *Language Acquisition of a Bilingual Child*. Clevedon, UK: Multilingual Matters, 1985.

Faust, M., and N. Mashal. "The Role of the Right Cerebral Hemisphere in Processing Novel Metaphoric Expressions Taken from Poetry: A Divided Visual Field Study." *Neuropsychologia* 45, no. 4 (2006):860–870.

Fiez, A. J. "Sound and Meaning: How Native Language Affects Reading Strategies." *Nature Neuroscience* 3, no. 1 (2000):3.

Fink, L. Dee. *Creating Significant Learning Experiences*. Hoboken, NJ: Jossey-Bass, 2003.

Finkbeiner, M., J. Almeida, N. Janssen, and A. Caramazza. "Lexical Selection in Bilingual Speech Production Does Not Involve Language Suppression." *Journal of Experimental Psychology/Learning, Memory and Cognition* 32, no. 5 (September 2006):1075–1089.

Finkbeiner, M., T. Gollan, and A. Caramazza. "Lexical Access in Bilingual Speakers: What's the (Hard) Problem?" *Bilingualism: Language and Cognition* 9, no. 2 (2006):153–166.

Fishman, J. *Reversing Language Shift: Theoretical and Empirical Foundations of Assistance to Threatened Languages*. Clevedon, UK: Multilingual Matters, 1991.

Fitzgerald, D. A., M. Angstadt, L. M. Jelsone, P. J. Nathan, and K. L. Phan. "Beyond Threat: Amygdala Reactivity Across Multiple Expressions of Facial Affect." *NeuroImage* 30, no. 4 (2006):1441–1448.

Fitzgerald, J. "Multilingual Reading Theory." *Reading Research Quarterly* 38, no. 1 (2003):118–122.

Fledge, J. "A Critical Period For Learning to Pronounce Foreign Languages?" *Applied Linguistics* 8 (1987):162–177.

―――. "The Interlingual Identification of Spanish and English Vowels: Orthographic Evidence. Special Issue: Hearing and Speech." *Quarterly Journal of Experimental Psychology: Human Experimental Psychology* 43 (1991):701–731.

Floel, A., A. Buyx, C. Breitenstein, H. Lohmann, and S. Knecht. "Hemispheric Lateralization of Spatial Attention in Right- and Left-Hemispheric Language Dominance." *Behavioural Brain Research* 158, no. 2 (2005):269–275.

Flores, B., P. Cousin, and E. Diaz. "Transforming Deficit Myths about Learning, Language, and Culture." *Language Arts* 68 (1991):369–377.

Flynn, S., C. Foley, and I. Vinnitskaya. "The Cumulative-Enhancement Model for Language Acquisition: Comparing Adults' and Children's Patterns of Development in First, Second and Third Language Acquisition of Relative Clauses." *The International Journal of Multilingualism* 1, no. 1 (2004):3–16.

Foundas, A. L., C. M. Leonard, and B. Hanna-Pladdy. "Variability in the Anatomy of the Planum Temporale and Posterior Ascending Ramus: Do Right- and Left-Handers Differ?" *Brain and Language* 83, no. 3 (2002):403–424.

Foxton, J. M., J. B. Talcott, C. Witton, and H. Brace. "Reading Skills Are Related to Global, but Not Local, Acoustic Pattern Perception." *Nature Neuroscience* 6, no. 4 (2003):343–347.

Fradd, S. H., and M. J. Weismantel. *Meeting the Needs of Culturally and Linguistically Different Students: A Handbook for Educators.* Boston: College-Hill Press, 1989.

Franceschini, R., D. Zappatore, and C. Nitsch. "Lexicon in the Brain: What Neurobiology Has to Say about Languages." In J. Cenoz, B. Hufeisen, and U. Jessner, eds., *The Multilingual Lexicon.* Dordrecht, Netherlands: Kluwer, Dordrecht, 2004. Retrieved from http://pages.unibas.ch/multilingualbrain/english.html on February 23, 2007.

Franceschini, R., D. Zappatore, G. Lüdi, E. Radü, E. Wattendorf, and C. Nitsch. "Learner Acquisition Strategies (LAS) in the Course of Life: A Language Biographic Approach." In *Interactive CD-ROM L3-Conference, Second International Conference on Third Language Acquisition and Trilingualism.* Ljouwert/Leeuwarden, The Netherlands: Fryske Akademy, 2002.

Francis, N. "Bilingualism, Writing, and Metalinguistic Awareness: Oral-Literate Interactions between First and Second Languages." *Applied Psycholinguistics* 20 (1999):533–561.

Freitas, C. O. A., F. Bortolozzi, and R. Sabourin. "Study of Perceptual Similarity between Different Lexicons." *International Journal of Pat-

tern Recognition and Artificial Intelligence 18, no. 7 (November 7, 2004):1321–1338.

Frey, W. "Multilingual America." *American Demographics* (July/August 2002):20–23.

Friederici, A. D. "The Brain Basis of Language Learning: Insights from Natural and Artificial Grammar Acquisition." *Language Learning Roundtable: The Cognitive Neuroscience of Second Language Acquisition*. September 18, 2003, University of Edinburgh.

———. "Language Processing in Natives and Non-Natives." Presented at the Center for the Brain Basis of Cognition, The Neurocognition of Second Language Workshop, Georgetown University, Washington, DC, 2006. Retrieved from http://cbbc.georgetown.edu/workshops/2006L2.html on June 1, 2007.

Friedrich, M., and A. D. Friederici. "Phonotactic Knowledge and Lexical–Semantic Processing in One-Year-Olds: Brain Responses to Words and Nonsense Words in Picture Contexts." *Journal of Cognitive Neuroscience* 17, no. 11 (2005):1785.

Fry, R. *Hispanic Youth Dropping Out of U.S. Schools: Measuring the Challenges*. Washington, D.C.: Pew Hispanic Center, 2003.

Fuller, J. M. "Between Three Languages: Composite Structure and Interlanguage." *Applied Linguistics* 20, no. 4 (1999):534–561.

Fung, C. Y. *Towards an Interactive View of L3 Acquisition: The Case of the German Vorfeld*. Hong Kong: University of Hong Kong, February 2002.

Gallese, V., and G. Lakoff. "The Brain's Concepts: The Role of the Sensory-Motor System in Conceptual Knowledge." *Cognitive Neuropsychology* 22, nos. 3–4 (2005):455–479.

Ganschow, L., and R. Sparks. "Foreign Language Anxiety Among High School Women." *Modern Language Journal* 80 (1996):199–212.

Garakani, A., S. J. Mathew, and D. S. Charney. "Neurobiology of Anxiety Disorders and Implications for Treatment." *The Mount Sinai Journal of Medicine* 73, no. 7 (2006):941–949.

Garcia, E. E. *Teaching and Learning in Two Languages: Bilingualism and Schooling in the United States*. New York, NY: Teacher's College, Colombia University, 2005.

Garcia, G. *Lessons for Research: What is the Length of Time it Takes Limited English Proficient Students to Acquire English and Succeed in an All-English Classroom?* Washington, DC: National Clearinghouse for Bilingual Education, 2000.

García-Vásquez, E., L. A. Vásquez, I. C. López, and W. Ward. "Language Proficiency and Academic Success: Relationships between Proficiency in Two Languages and Achievement Among Mexican American Students." *Bilingual Research Journal* 21 (1997):334–347.

Gardner, R. C., and W. E. Lambert. *Attitudes and Motivation in Second Language Learning*. Rowley, MA: Newbury House, 1986.

Garland, S. *The Bilingual Spectrum*. Orlando, FL: Guirnalda Publishing, 2007.

Gazzaniga, M. *Conversations in the Neurosciences*. Cambridge, MA: The Massachusetts Institute of Technology Press, 1997.

———. *The Mind's Past*. Berkeley, CA: University of California Press, 1998.

———. "Smarter on Drugs." *Scientific American Mind* 11, (2005):32–37.

Gazzaniga, M., ed. *The Cognitive Neuroscience, III*. Cambridge: MIT Press, 2005.

Gazzaniga, M., R. Ivry, and G. R. Mangun. *Cognitive Neuroscience*. New York: W. W. Norton, 1998.

Genesee, F., and N. Cloud. "Multilingualism Is Basic." *Educational Leadership* 55, no. 6 (1998).

Genesee, F., K. Lindholm-Leary, W. Saunders, and D. Christian. "English Language Learners in U.S. Schools: An Overview of Research Findings." *Journal of Education for Students Placed at Risk* 10, no. 4 (2005):363–386.

Genishi, C. *Young Children's Oral Language Development*. Princeton, NJ: Princeton Child Development Institute, LLC, 2006. Retrieved on April 4, 2007 from http://www.childdevelopmentinfo.com/development/oral_language_development.shtml.

Gernsbacher, M. A., and M. P. Kaschak. "Neuroimaging Studies of Language Production and Comprehension." *Annual Review of Psychology* 54, no. 1 (2003):91.

Geva, E. "Issues in the Assessment of Reading Disabilities in L2 Children—Beliefs and Research Evidence." *Dyslexia* 6 (2000):13–28.

Gillespie, M. K. "Profiles of Adult Learners: Revealing the Multiple Faces of Literacy." *TESOL Quarterly* 27, no. 3 (1993):529–533.

Giordano, P. J. "Teaching and Learning When We Least Expect It: The Role of Critical Moments in Student Development." In B. K. Saville, T. E. Zinn, and V. W. Hevern, eds., *Essays From E-xcellence in Teaching*, 2005. Retrieved on March 2003 from the Society for the Teaching of Psychology Web site: http://teachpsych.org/resources/e-books/eit2004/eit04-04.html.

Gladwell, M. *Blink: The Power of Thinking Without Thinking*. New York: Little Brown, 2005.

Glenn, C. L. "Educating Immigrant Children: School and Language Minorities in Twelve Nations." *Principal* (November/December 2002):28–31.

———. "Two-Way Bilingual Education." *Education Digest* 68, no. 5 (2003):42.

Goldstein, T. *Teaching and Learning in a Multilingual School: Choices, Risks, and Dilemmas.* Mahwah, NJ: Lawrence Erlbaum Associates, 2003.

Goleman, D. *Emotional Intelligence.* New York: Bantam, 1995.

Golestani, N., F. X. Alario, S. Meriaux, D. LeBihan, S. Dehaene, and C. Pallier. "Syntax Production in Bilinguals." *Neuropsychologia* 44, no. 7 (2006):1029–1040.

Gomeztortosa, E., E. M. Martin, M. Gaviria, F. Charbel, and J. I. Ausman. "Selective Deficit of One Language in a Bilingual Patient Following Surgery in the Left Perisylvian Area." *Brain and Language* 48, no. 3 (1995):320–325.

Gonzalez, J. M., and L. Darling-Hammond. *New Concepts for New Challenges: Professional Development for Teachers of Immigrant Youth.* Washington, D.C.: Center for Applied Linguistics, 1997.

Gonzalez, V. *Cognition, Culture and Language in Bilingual Children.* Bethesda, MD: Austin and Winfield, 1996.

Gonzalez, V., R. Brusca-Vega, and T. Yawkey. *Assessment and Instruction of Culturally Linguistically Diverse Student.* Needham Heights, MA: Allyn and Bacon, 1997.

Goodman, Y. M. *Valuing Language Study: Inquiry into Language for Elementary and Middle Schools.* Urbana, IL: National Council of Teachers of English, 2003.

Goral, M., E. S. Levy, L. K. Obler, and E. Cohen. "Cross-Language Lexical Connections in the Mental Lexicon: Evidence from a Case of Trilingual Aphasia." *Brain and Language* 98, no. 2 (2006):235–247.

Gordon, A. I. *Intermarriage.* London: Beacon Press, 1966.

Gottman, J. "Predicting Divorce among Newlyweds from the First Three Minutes of Marital Conflict Discussion." *Family Process* 38, no. 3 (1999):293–301.

Graddol, D. *The Future of English.* London: The British Council, 1997.

———. "The Decline of the Native Speaker." In David Graddol and Ulrike H. Meinhof, eds., *English in a Changing World*, 57–68. *AILA: The AILA Review* 13 (1999):57–68.

———. "The Effect of Linguistic Distance, L2 Status and Age on Cross-Linguistic Influence in Third Language Acquisition." In J. Cenoz, B. Hufeisen, and U. Jessner, eds., *Cross-Linguistic Influence in Third Language Acquisition: Psycholinguistic Perspectives*, 8–20. North York, ON: Multilingual Matters, 2003.

Grant, R. "Forging Multilingual Communities: School-based Strategies." *Multicultural Perspectives* 6, no. 3 (2004):22.

Grant, R., and S. Wong. "Barriers to Literacy for Language-Minority Learners: An Argument for Change in the Literacy Education Profession." *Journal of Adolescent and Adult Literacy* 46 (2003):386–394.

Greenberg, J. H. *Universals of Language*. Cambridge, MA: MIT Press, 1966.

Greene, J. P. "A Meta-Analysis of the Rossell and Baker Review of Bilingual Education Research." *Bilingual Research Journal* 21 (1997): 103–122.

Gregory, E. "Cultural Assumptions and Early Years' Pedagogy: The Effect of Home Culture on Minority Children's Interpretation of Reading in School." *Language, Culture and Curriculum* 7, no. 2 (1994):111–24.

———. "Siblings as Mediators of Literacy in Linguistic Minority Communities." *Language and Education* 12, no. 1 (1998):33–54.

Gregory, G. H., and C. Chapman. *Differentiated Instructional Strategies: One Size Doesn't Fit All*. Thousand Oaks, CA: Corwin Press, 2002.

Griessler, M. "The Effects of Third Language Learning on Second Language Proficiency: An Austrian Example." *International Journal of Bilingual Education and Bilingualism* 4, no. 1 (2001):50–60.

Groshek, F., E. Kerfoot, V. McKenna, A. S. Polackwich, M. Gallagher, and P. C. Holland. "Amygdala Central Nucleus Function Is Necessary for Learning, but Not Expression, of Conditioned Auditory Orienting." *Behavioral Neuroscience* 119, no. 1 (2005):202–212.

Grosjean, F. *Life with Two Languages. An Introduction to Bilingualism*. Cambridge, MA: Harvard University Press, 1982.

———. "A Psycholinguistic Approach to Code-Switching: The Recognition of Guest Words by Bilinguals." In L. Milroy and P. Muysken, eds., *One Speaker, Two Languages: Cross-Disciplinary Perspectives on Code Switching*. Cambridge, UK: Cambridge University Press, 1995.

———. "The Bilingual's Language Modes." In J. Nicol, ed., *One Mind, Two Languages: Bilingual Language Processing*. Oxford, UK: Blackwell, 2001.

Guinness Book of World Records. *Guinness World Records series*. London: Guinness World Records, 2007.

Gullenberg, M., and P. Indefrey, eds. *The Cognitive Neuroscience of Second Language Acquisition*. Malden, MA: Blackwell Publishing, 2006.

Guron, L., and I. Lundberg. "Identifying Dyslexia in Multilingual Students: Can Phonological Awareness Be Assessed in the Majority Language?" *Journal of Research in Reading* 26, no. 1 (2003):69–82.

Guthrie, J. T. "Teaching for Literacy Engagement." *Journal of Literacy Research* 36 (2004):1–30.

Hahne, A., K. Eckstein, and A. Friederici. "Brain Signatures of Syntactic and Semantic Processes during Children's Language Development." *Journal of Cognitive Neuroscience* 16, no. 7 (2004):1302–1318.

Hakuta, K. *Bilingualism and Bilingual Education: A Research Perspective. Occasional Papers in Bilingual Education.* Washington, D.C.: Delta Systems and the Center for Applied Linguistics, 1990.

Hakuta, K., E. Bialystok, and E. Wiley. "Critical Evidence: A Test of the Critical-Period Hypothesis for Second-Language Acquisition." *Psychological Science* 14, no. 1 (2003):31–39.

Hakuta, K.,Y. G. Butler, and D. Witt. *How Long Does it Take English Learners to Attain Proficiency?* Santa Barbara, CA: California University, 2000.

Hakuta, K., and H. Cancino. "Trends in Second Language Acquisition Research." *Harvard Educational Review* 47 (1977):294–316.

Hakuta, K., and D. D'Andrea. "Some Properties of Bilingual Maintenance and Loss in Mexican Background High-School Students." *Applied Linguistics* 13, no. 1 (1992):72–99.

Hall Haley, M., andT. Y. Austin. *Content-Based Second Language Teaching and Learning: An Interactive Approach.* Boston: Allyn and Bacon, 2004.

Halpern, D. F., and M. D. Hakel. *Applying the Science of Learning to University Teaching and Beyond.* San Francisco: Jossey-Bass, 2003.

Hammarberg, B. "Roles of L1 and L2 in L3 Production and Acquisition." In J. Cenoz, B. Hufeisen, and U. Jessner, eds., *Cross-Linguistic Influence on Third Language Acquisition: Psycholinguistic Perspectives* 69–89. Clevedon, UK: Multilingual Matters, 2001.

Haney, M., and J. Hill. "Relationships between Parent-Teaching Activities and Emergent Literacy in Preschool Children." *Early Child Development and Care* 174, no. 3 (2004):215–228.

Hansford, R. "Language Minorities in Britain: A Summary of the Available Statistical Data." In *Statistics in the Teaching and Learning of Modern Foreign Languages in the U.K.: Directory of Sources.* London: Centre for Information on Language Teaching, 1997.

Harding-Esch, E., and P. Riley. *The Bilingual Family: A Handbook for Parents.* Cambridge, UK: Cambridge University Press, 1986.

Harley, B. *Age in Second Language Acquisition.* San Diego: College Hill Press, 1989.

Harley, B., and D. Hart. "The Effects of Early Bilingual Schooling on First Language Skills." *Applied Psycholinguistics* 7, no. 4 (1986): 295–322.

Harris, J. R. *The Nurture Assumption.* New York: The Free Press, 1998.

Hartshorne, J. K., and M. T. Ullman. "Why Girls Say 'Holded' More Than Boys." *Developmental Science* 1 (2006):21–32.

Hauser, M. D., N. Chomsky, and W. T. Fitch. "The Faculty of Language: What Is It, Who Has It, and How Did It Evolve?" *Science* 298, no. 5598 (2002):1569–1580.

Heasley, P. "Reading and Language Arts Worksheets Don't Grow Dendrites: 20 Literacy Strategies That Engage the Brain." *Library Media Connection* 24, no. 6 (2006):87.

Heckathorn, D. D. "Collective Sanctions and Compliance Norms: A Formal Theory of Group-Mediated Social Control." *American Sociological Review* 55 (1990):366–384.

Heitner, R. "Book Review: Language, Brain and Cognitive Development: Essays in Honor of Jacques Mehler." *Minds and Machines* 14, no. 3 (2004):427–431.

Helmuth, L., G. C. Daily, P. R. Ehrlich, T. H. Ricketts, S. Bailey, S. Kark, C. Kremen, and H. Pereira. "Dyslexia: Same Brains, Different Languages." *Science* 291, no. 5511 (2001):2064.

Henry, M. L., P. M. Beeson, A. J. Stark, and S. Z. Rapcsa. "The Role of Left Perisylvian Cortical Regions in Spelling." *Brain and Language* 100, no. 1 (2007):44–52.

Herdade, K. C., C. V. de Andrade Strauss, H. Z. Junior, and V. M. de Barros. "Effects of Medial Amygdala Inactivation on a Panic-Related Behavior." *Behavioural Brain Research* 172, no. 2 (2006):316–323.

Hernandez, A. E., A. Martinez, and K. Kohnert. "In Search of the Language Switch: An fMRI Study of Picture Naming in Spanish–English Bilinguals." *Brain and Language* 73, no. 3 (2000):421–431.

Hernandez, S., J. Camacho-Rosales, A. Nieto, and J. Barroso. "Cerebral Asymmetry and Reading Performance: Effect of Language Lateralization and Hand Preference." *Child Neuropsychology* 3, no. 3 (1997):206–226.

Herod, L. 2002. *Adult Learning from Theory to Practice.* Retrieved March 1, 2007 from http://www.nald.ca/adultlearningcourse/module1/4.htm.

Hickey, T. M. "Children's Language Networks in Minority Language Immersion: What Goes in May Not Come Out." *Language and Learning* 21, no. 1 (2007):46–65.

Hickok, G., and D. Poeppel, eds. "Special Issue: Towards a New Functional Anatomy of Language." *Cognition* 92, nos. 1–2 (2004).

Hillis, A. E., R. J. Wityk, P. B. Barker, and A. Caramazza. "Neural Regions Essential for Writing Verbs." *Nature Neuroscience* 6, no. 1 (January 2003):19.

Hines, M. E. "Foreign Language Curriculum Concerns in Times of Conflict." *Delta Kappa Gamma Bulletin* 70, no. 1 (2003):15–21.

Hiraoka, L. "When Trilingual Isn't Enough." *National Educators Association Today* (January 1, 2006):55.

Hiroshi Review Publishing Committee, The. *Language, Culture, and Communication. Special Issue on Foreign Language Education Research (24).* Tokyo, Japan: Keio University, 2000.

Hirsch, J. "Distinct Cortical Areas Associated with Native and Second Languages." *Nature* 388 (10 July 1997):171.

Hitchcott, P. K., C. M. T. Bonardi, and G. D. Phillips. "Enhanced Stimulus-Reward Learning by Intra-Amygdala Administration of a D_3 Dopamine Receptor Agonist." *Psychopharmacology* 133, no. 3 (1997): 240–249.

Hoffmann, C. "Towards a Description of Trilingual Competence." *The International Journal of Bilingualism* 5 (2001):1–17.

———. "Language Acquisition in Two Trilingual Children." *Journal of Multilingual and Multicultural Development* 6, no. 6 (1985):479–495.

Hohlfeld, A., K. Mierke, and W. Sommer. "Is Word Perception in a Second Language More Vulnerable Than in One's Native Language? Evidence from Brain Potentials in a Dual Task Setting." *Brain and Language* 89, no. 3 (2004):569–579.

Holden, C. "Training the Brain to Read." *Science* 304, no. 5671 (2004):677.

Holland, P. C., Y. Chik, and Q. Zhang. "Inhibitory Learning Tests of Conditioned Stimulus Associability in Rats with Lesions of the Amygdala Central Nucleus." *Behavioral Neuroscience* 115, no. 5 (2001):1154–1158.

Honnert, A., and S. Bozan. "Summary Frames: Language Acquisition for Special Education and ELL Students." *Science Activities* 42, no. 2 (2005):19–29.

House, J. "A Stateless Language That Europe Must Embrace." *The Guardian Weekly*. Brighton UK: IATEFL, 2004.

Howard, E. R., and D. Christian. *Two-Way Immersion 101: Designing and Implementing a Two-Way Immersion Education Program at the Elementary Level*. Santa Cruz, CA: Center for Research on Education, Diversity, and Excellence, University of California-Santa Cruz, 2002.

Hufeisen, B. "A European Perspective: Tertiary Languages with a Focus on German as L3." In J. Rosenthal, ed., *Handbook of Undergraduate Second Language Education* 209–229. Mahwah, NJ: Lawrence Erlbaum Associates, 2000.

Hutchinson, H. B., A. Rose, B. B. Bederson, A. C. Weeks, and A. Druin. "The International Children's Digital Library: A Case Study in Designing for a Multilingual, Multicultural, Multigenerational Audience." *Information Technology and Libraries* 24, no. 1 (2005):4–12.

Illes, J., W. S. Francis, J. E. Desmond, J. D. E. Gabrieli, G. H. Glover, R. Poldrack, R., C. J. Lee, and A. D. Wagner. "Convergent Cortical Representation of Semantic Processing in Bilinguals." *Brain and Language* 70, no. 3 (1999):347–363.

Jacquemot, C., C. Pallier, S. Dehaene, and E. Dupoux. *The Neuroanatomy of Language-Specific Speech Processing: A Cross Linguistic Study*

Using Event Related Functional Magnetic Resonance Imagery. Paris, France: SHFJ, 2003.

James, W. H. *Principles of Psychology.* New York: Holt, 1890. Excerpts retrieved from Classics in the History of Psychology, retrieved on March 13, 2007 from http://psychclassics.yorku.ca/James/Principles/index.htm.

Jansen, A., H. Lohmann, S. Scharfe, C. Sehlmeyer, M. Deppe, and S. Knecht. "The Association between Scalp Hair-Whorl Direction, Handedness and Hemispheric Language Dominance: Is There a Common Genetic Basis of Lateralization?" *NeuroImage* (29 December 2006).

Jenkins, J., and B. Seidlhofer. "Bringing Europe's Lingua Franca into the Classroom." *The Guardian Weekly.* Brighton UK: IATEFL, 2004.

Jenkins, K. "Recognizing the Values of Foreign Language Skills." *Diverse Issues in Higher Education* 22, no. 26 (2006):35.

Jennische, M., and G. Sedin. "Gender Differences in Outcome After Neonatal Intensive Care: Speech and Language Skills Are Less Influenced in Boys Than in Girls at 6.5 Years." *Acta Paediatrica* 92, no. 3 (March 2003):364–375.

Jensen, E. *Teaching With the Brain in Mind.* Alexandria, VA: Association for Supervision and Curriculum Development, 1998.

———. *Brain-Based Learning: The New Science of Teaching and Training*, rev. ed. San Diego, CA: Brain Store Inc., 2000.

Johansson, B. "Cultural and Linguistic Influence on Brain Organization for Language and Possible Consequences for Dyslexia: A Review." *Annals of Dyslexia* 56, no. 1 (2006):13–50.

Johnson, M. "Slippery Lingualism: Are All Bilinguals Really Bilingual (in Bibliography (Sociolinguistics)." *Journal of Communication Disorders* 36 (1991):189–208.

Kacinik, N. A., and C. Chiarello. "Understanding Metaphors: Is the Right Hemisphere Uniquely Involved?" *Brain and Language* 100, no. 2 (2007):188–207.

Kahn-Horwitz, J., J. Shimron, and R. Sparks. "Weak and Strong Novice Readers of English as a Foreign Language: Effects of First Language and Socioeconomic Status." *Annals of Dyslexia* 56, no. 1 (2006):161–185.

Kaiser, A., E. Kuenzli, D. Zappatore, and C. Nitsch. "On Females' Lateral and Males' Bilateral Activation during Language Production: A fMRI Study." *International Journal of Psychophysiology* 63, no. 2 (2007):192–198.

Kalat, J. W. *Biological Psychology,* 8th ed. Belmont, CA: Wadsworth/Thompson Learning, 2004.

Keane, A. M., C. Sanders, M. Diego, M. Fernandez, T. Field, M. Hernandez-Reif, and A. Roca. "Direction of Hand Preference: The Connection with Speech and the Influence of Familian Handedness." *International Journal of Neuroscience* 112, no. 11 (2002):1287–1304.

Kellerman, R. "An Eye For An Eye: Crosslinguistic Constraints on The Development of the L2 Lexicon." In M. Sharwood Smith and E. Kellerman, eds., *Crosslinguistic Influence in Second Language Acquisition.* Oxford, UK: Pergamons Press, 1983.

Kempadoo, M., and M. Abdelrazak. *Directory of Supplementary and Mother-Tongue Classes.* London: Resource Unit, 2001.

Kesner, R. P., and J. M. Williams. "Memory for Magnitude of Reinforcement: Dissociation between the Amygdale and Hippocampus." *Neurobiology of Learning and Memory* 64 (1995):237–244.

Khubchandani, L. "Potentials of Literacy: A Multilingual Perspective." *United Nations Chronicle* 40, no. 2 (2003):42.

King, D. F., and K. Goodman. "Cherishing Learners and Their Language." *Language,* 1990.

Kit-fong Au, T., L. M. Knightly, J. Sun-Ah, and J. S. Oh. "Overhearing a Language during Childhood." *Psychological Science* 13, no. 3 (2002):238–246.

Klein, E. C. "Second Versus Third Language Acquisition: Is There a Difference?" *Language Learning* 45, no. 3, (1995):419–465.

Kleinert, S. "How Does The Brain Handle Bilingualism?" *Lancet* 354, no. 9196 (1999):2140.

Klinger, J., and A. J. Artiles. "English Language Learners Struggling to Learn to Read: Emergent Scholarship on Linguistic Differences and Learning Disabilities." *Journal of Learning Disabilities* 39, no. 5 (2006):386–389.

———. "When Should Bilingual Students Be in Special Education?" *Educational Leadership* (October 2003):66–71.

Knaus, T. A., A. M. Bollich, and D. M. Corey. "Sex-Linked Differences in the Anatomy of the Perisylvian Language Cortex: A Volumetric MRI Study of Gray Matter Volumes." *Neuropsychology* 18, no. 4 (2004): 738–747.

Knecht, S., A. Flöel, B. Dräger, and C. Breitenstein. "Degree of Language Lateralization Determines Susceptibility to Unilateral Brain Lesions." *Nature Neuroscience* 5, no. 7 (2002):695–702.

Knight, M., W. Wang, and J. Luk, J. "Teaching and Learning in a Multilingual School." *Race, Ethnicity and Education* 7, no. 1 (2004):85–90.

Kovas, M. A. "Reporting on Student Learning: Lessons from the Past, Prescriptions for the Future." In T. R. Guskey, ed., *Communicating Student Learning: 1996 Yearbook of the Association for Supervision and Curriculum Development*, 13–24. Alexandria, VA: Association for Supervision and Curriculum Development, 1996. Retrieved on September 15, 2007 from http://course1.winona.edu/lgray/el626/Articlesonline/Guskey_helping.html.

Krashen, S. *The Power of Reading.* Westport, CT: Libraries Unlimited, 2003.

——. "False Claims About Literacy Development." *Educational Leadership* 61, no. 6 (2004):18–21.

Kroll, J. "Reading and Speaking Words in Two Languages: A Problem in Representation and Control." Presented at the Center for the Brain Basis of Cognition, The Neurocognition of Second Language Workshop, Georgetown University, 2006. Retrieved on May 26, 2007 from http://cbbc.georgetown.edu/workshops/2006L2.html.

Kuhl, P. "Early Language Acquisition: Cracking the Speech Code." *Nature Reviews Neuroscience* 5 no. 11 (2004):831–843.

LaBar, K. S., and R. Cabeza. "Amygdala Damage Impairs Emotional Memory for Gist But Not Details of Complex Stimuli." *Nature Reviews. Neuroscience* 7, no. 1 (2006):54.

Laitin, D. D. "What Is a Language Community?" *American Journal of Political Science* 44, no. 1 (2000):142–156.

Lambert, W. E. "The Effects of Bilingualism on the Individual: Cognitive and Socio-Cultural Consequences." In P. Hornby, ed., *Bilingualism. Psychological, Social and Educational Implications*, 15–28. New York: Academic Press, 1977.

Landis, D. "Reading and Writing as Social, Cultural Practices: Implications for Literacy Education." *Reading & Writing Quarterly* 19, no. 3 (2003):281–308.

Langdon, H. W., J. M. Novak, and R. S. Quintanar. "Setting the Teaching-Learning Wheel in Motion in Assessing Language Minority Students." *Multicultural Perspectives* 2, no. 2 (2000):3–9.

Laponce, J. A. "The Multilingual Mind and Multilingual Societies: In Search of Neuropsychological Explanations of the Spatial Behavior of Ethno-Linguistic Groups." *Politics and the Life Sciences* 4, no. 1 (August 1985):3–9.

Lasagabaster, D. "Learning English as an L3." *ITL Review of Applied Linguistics* 121–122 (1998):51–83.

Laumann, E. O., J. H. Gagnon, R. T. Michael, and S. Michaels. *The Social Organization of Sexuality: Sexual Practices in the United States.* Chicago: University of Chicago Press, 1994.

Leaper, C., and T. E. Smith. "A Meta-Analytic Review of Gender Variations in Children's Language Use: Talkativeness, Affiliative Speech, and Assertive Speech." *Developmental Psychology* 40, no. 6 (2004):993–1027.

LeDoux, J. *The Emotional Brain*. New York: Simon and Schuster, 1996.

Lee, J. "Racial and Ethnic Achievement Gap Trends: Reversing the Progress Towards Equity." *Educational Researchers* 31 (2002):3–12.

Lennenberg E. H. *Biological Foundations of Language*. New York: Wiley, 1967.

Lett, J., and F. O'Meara. "Predictors of Success in an Intensive Foreign Language Learning Context: Correlates of Language Learning at the Defense Language Institute Foreign Language Center." In T. Karry and C. Stansfield, eds., *Language Aptitude Reconsidered*, 222–260. Englewood Cliffs, NJ: Prentice Hall, 1999.

Levine, M. *A Mind at a Time*. New York: Simon and Schuster, 2000.

Levis, N. "The Brave New World of Bilingual Teaching." *Times Educational Supplement*, no. 4418 (July–September 2003).

Lieberman, P. "The Evolution of Human Speech: Its Anatomical and Neural Bases." *Current Anthropology* 48, no. 1 (2007):39–66.

Lieven, E. V. M. "Crosslinguistic and Crosscultural Aspects of Language Addressed to Children." In C. Gallaway and B. J. Richards, eds., *Input and Interaction in Language Acquisition*. Cambridge, UK: Cambridge University Press, 1994.

Lindholm Leary, K. J. *Dual-Language Education*. Clevedon, UK: Multilingual Matters, 2001.

Lindsey, K., F. Manis, and C. Bailey. "Prediction of First-Grade Reading in Spanish-Speaking English-Language Learners." *Journal of Educational Psychology* 95 (2003):482–494.

Linse, C., and K. White. "ESL Fourth Graders Teach Monolingual English Speakers about Language Diversity." *Multicultural Perspectives* 3, no. 1 (2001):36–38.

Listerri, J., and D. Pooch. "Influence de la L1 (Catalan) et de la L2 (Castillan) sur l'apprentissage du Système Phonologique d'une Troisième Langue (Français)." In Actas de las IX Jornadas Pedagógicas Sobre la Enseñanza del Francés en España. Barcelona: Institut de Ciències de l'Educació, Universitat Autònoma de Barcelona, Spain, (1986):153–167. Retrieved from http://liceu.uab.es/~joaquim/publicacions/Llisterri_Poch_86/Llisterri_Poch_86.pdf.

Lopez, G. R., J. D. Scribner, and K. Mahitivanichcha. "Redefining Parental Involvement: Lessons from High-Performing Migrant-Impacted Schools." *American Educational Research Journal* 38 (2001): 253–288.

Lopez, M. G., and A. Tashakkori. "Narrowing the Gap: Effects of a Two-Way Bilingual Education Program on the Literacy Development of At-Risk Primary Students." *Journal of Education for Students Placed At Risk* 9, no. 4 (2004):325–326.

Lüdi, G. "Plurilinguisme Précoce - Représentations Sociales et Évidence Neurolinguistique." 4e Conférences Internationales sur l'acquisition Dune 3e Langue et le Plurilinguisme. Basel, Switzerland: University of Basel, 2004.

Luke, A., "Linguistic Stereotype, the Divergent Speaker and the Teaching of Literacy." *Journal of Curriculum Studies* 18 (1986):397–408.

Lynch, E. W., and M. J. Hanson. *Developing Cross-Cultural Competence: A Guide for Working with Young Children and Their Families*. Baltimore, MD: Paul H. Brooks Publishing, 1992.

Macedonia, M. "Games and Foreign Language Teaching." *Support for Learning* 20, no. 3 (2005):135–140.

Mack, W. J., E. Teng, and L. Zheng. "Category Fluency in a Latino Sample: Associations with Age, Education, Gender, and Language." *Journal of Clinical and Experimental Neuropsychology* 27, no. 5 (July 2005):591–598.

MacSwan, J. *The Threshold Hypothesis, Semilingualism, and Other Contributions to a Deficit View of Linguistic Minorities*. London: Sage, 2002.

Mac Whinney, B. "The Emergence of a Second Language." Presented at the Center for the Brain Basis of Cognition, The Neurocognition of Second Language Workshop, Georgetown University, 2006. Retrieved on May 27, 2007 from http://cbbc.georgetown.edu/workshops/2006L2.html.

Mägiste, E. "Selected Issues in Second and Third Language Learning." In J. Vaid, ed., *Language Processing in Bilinguals: Psycholinguistic and Neurolinguistic Perspectives*, 97–122. Hillsdale, NJ: Lawrence Erlbaum Associates, 1986.

Maher, J. "The Practical Linguist: Make the Most of the Bilingual Advantage." *The Daily Yomiuri* (Japan). Reformatted by Tokuhama-Espinosa, 2005.

Mandelbaum, D. G., ed. *Selected Writings of Edward Sapir in Language, Culture, and Personality*. Berkeley, CA: University of California Press, 1963.

Manyak, P. C. "What Did She Say?": Translation in a Primary-grade English Immersion Class." *Multicultural Perspectives* 6, no. 1 (2004): 12–18.

Marcus, G. F., S. Vijayan, S. B. Rao, and P. M. Vishton. "Rule Learning by Seven-Month-Old Infants." *Science* 283, no. 5398 (1999):77–81.

Marian, V., M. Spivey, and J. Hirsch. "Shared and Separate Systems in Bilingual Language Processing: Converging Evidence from Eyetracking and Brain Imaging." *Brain and Language* 86, no. 1 (2003):70–82.

Markram, K., M. A. L. Fernandez, D. N. Abrous, and C. Sandi. "Amygdala Upregulation of NCAM Polysialylation Induced by Auditory Fear Conditioning Is Not Required for Memory Formation, But Plays a Role in Fear Extinction." *Neurobiology of Learning and Memory*, (2007).

Marshall, M. "Lack of Languages Could Damage UK Business in the Single Market." *Education* 174 (April 15, 2005):1.

Martin-Jones, M., and S. Romaine. "Semilingualism: A Half-Baked Theory of Communicative Competence." *Applied Linguistics* 7, no. 1 (1986):26–38.

Marx, G. *Future-Focused Leadership: Preparing Schools, Students, and Communities For Tomorrow's Realities.* Alexandria, VA: Association for Supervision and Curriculum Development, 2006.

Marzano, R. J., D. J. Pickering, and J. E. Pollock. *Classroom Instruction that Works: Research-Based Strategies for Increasing Student Achievement.* Alexandria, VA: Association for Supervision and Curriculum Development, 2001.

Mayberry, R. I., and E. Lock. "Age Constraints on First Versus Second Language Acquisition: Evidence for Linguistic Plasticity and Epigenesis." *Brain and Language* 87, no. 3 (2003):369–384.

McAleer Hamaguchi, P. *Childhood Speech, Language, and Listening Problems: What Every Parent Should Know.* New York: John Wiley and Sons, 1995.

McCleod, B. ed. *Language and Learning: Educating Linguistically Diverse Students.* New York: State University of New York Press, 1994.

McGaugh, J. L. *Memory and Emotions: The Making of Lasting Memories.* New York: Guilford, 2003.

McGrath K., D. Taylor, and R. Kamen. "Storytelling: Enhancing Language Acquisition In Young Children." *Education* 125, no. 1 (2004):3.

McLaughlin, B. *Educational Practice Report Five Myths and Misconceptions about Second Language Learning: What Every Teacher Needs to Unlearn.* Washington, D.C.: National Center for Research on Cultural Diversity and Second Language Learning, 2006. Retrieved on October 10, 2006 from http://www.ncela.gwu.edu/pubs/ncrcdsll/epr5.htm.

McLaughlin, B., A. G. Blanchard, and Y. Osani. "Assessing Language Development in Bilingual Preschool Children." *NCB Program Information Guide,* no. 22 (Summer 1995).

McLaughlin, B., and R. Nation. "Experts and Novices: An Information-Processing Approach to the 'Good Language Learner' Problem." *Applied Psycholinguistics* 7 (1986):41–56.

McLeay, H. "Teaching Mathematics in Multilingual Classrooms." *MT: Mathematics Teaching* (2002).

McManus, C. *Right Hand, Left Hand: The Origins of Asymmetry in Brains, Bodies, Atoms and Cultures.* Cambridge, MA: Harvard University Press, 2004.

McNamara, T. *Language Testing*. Oxford, UK: Oxford University Press, 2000.

Medford, N., M. L. Phillips, B. Brierley, M. Brammer, E. T. Bullmore, and A. S. David. "Emotional Memory: Separating Content and Context." *Psychiatry Research* 138, no. 3 (2005):247–258.

Medgyes, P. *The Non-Native Teacher* 2nd ed., rev. Ismaning, Germany: Hueber Verlang, 1999.

Meier, T. "Why Can't She Remember That? The Importance of Storybook Reading in Multilingual, Multicultural Classrooms." *Reading Teacher* 57, no. 3 (2003):242–252.

Meijers, G. and M. Sanders. "English as L3 in the Elementary School." *Review of Applied Linguistics* 107–8 (1995):59–78.

Meltzoff, A. N. "What Infant Memory Tells Us About Infantile Amnesia: Long-Term Recall and Deferred Imitation." *Journal of Experimental Child Psychology* 59, no. 3 (1995):497–515.

Merriam, S. B. "Andragogy and Self-Directed Learning." In S. B. Merriam ed., *Critical Thinking in Adult Education*, 27–38. Hoboken, NJ: John Wiley and Sons, 2005.

Merriam, S. B., ed. *Critical Thinking in Adult Education*. Hoboken, NJ: John Wiley and Sons, 2005.

Met, M. "Why Language Learning Matters." *Educational Leadership* 59, no. 2 (2001):36–41.

Mezirow, J. *Transformative Dimensions of Adult Learning*. San Francisco: Jossey-Bass, 1991.

Miceli, G., P. Turriziani, C. Caltagirone, R. Capasso, F. Tomaiuolo, and A. Caramazza. "The Neural Correlates of Grammatical Gender: An fMRI Investigation." *Journal of Cognitive Neuroscience* 14 (2002):618–628.

Miller, B. "At Play: Teaching Teenagers Theater." *Library Journal* 131, no. 10 (2006):120.

Mills, D., C. Prat, R. Zangl, C. Stager, H. Neville, and J. Werker. "Language Experience and the Organization of Brain Activity to Phonetically Similar Words: ERP Evidence from 14- and 20-Month-Olds." *Journal of Cognitive Neuroscience* 16, no. 8 (2004):1452–1464.

Miozzo, M., A. Costa, and A. Caramazza. "The Absence of a Gender Congruency Effect in Romance Languages: A Matter of Stimulus Onset Asynchrony?" *Journal of Experimental Psychology: Learning, Memory, and Cognition* 28 (2002):388–391.

Mitchell, D. G., R. A. Richell, A. Leonard, and R. J. Blair. "Emotion at the Expense of Cognition: Psychopathic Individuals Outperform Controls on an Operant Response Task." *Journal of Abnormal Psychology* 115, no. 3 (2006):559–566.

Mohr, C., T. Landis, and H. S. Bracha. "Opposite Turning Behavior in Right-Handers and Non-Right-Handers Suggests a Link between Handedness and Cerebral Dopamine Asymmetries." *Behavioral Neuroscience* 117, no. 6 (2003):1448–1452.

Moje, E. B., J. P. Young, J. E. Readence, and D. W. Moore. "Reinventing Adolescent Literacy for New Times. Perennial and Millennial Issues." *Journal of Adolescent and Adult Literacy* 43 (2000):400–410.

Morris, J. S., A. Öhman, and R. J. Dolan. "Conscious and Unconscious Emotional Learning in the Human Amygdala." *Nature* 393, no. 6684 (1998):467–471.

Murphy, S. *Second Language Transfer during Third Language Acquisition.* New York: Teachers College, Columbia University, 2002.

Mushi, S. L. P. "Acquisition of Multiple Languages among Children of Immigrant Families: Parents' Role in the Home-School Language Pendulum." *Early Child Development and Care* 172, no. 5 (2002): 517–530.

Musso, M., A. Moro, V. Glauche, and M. Rijntjes. "Broca's Area and the Language Instinct." *Nature Neuroscience* 6, no. 7 (2003):774.

Musumeci, D. "Teacher-Learner Negotiation in Content-Based Instruction: Communication at Cross-Purposes." *Applied Linguistics* 17, no. 3 (1996):286–324.

Myers, J., & Boothe, D. (2000) "Multilingual Muppets." *Reading Today* (February/March 2003):44.

Nakamura, Y., and M. Valens. "Teaching and Testing Oral Communication Skills." *Journal of Humanities and Natural Sciences* 111 (2001): 43–53.

National Center for Educational Statistics. *Status and Trends in the Education of Hispanics.* Washington, D.C.: Institute of Educational Sciences, U.S. Department of Education, 2003.

National Educators Association. "Editor's Note." *NEA TODAY Newsletter* (January 2006).

Navarra, J., N. Sebastián-Gallés, and S. Soto-Faraco. "The Perception of Second Language Sounds in Early Bilinguals: New Evidence from an Implicit Measure." *Journal of Experimental Psychology/Human Perception & Performance* 31, no. 5 (2005):912–918.

Nehr, M. "Multilingualism in Educational Institutions." *European Education* 33, no. 3 (2001):74.

Nieto, S. *Affirming Diversity: The Sociopolitical Contexts of Multicultural Education.* White Plains, NY: Longman, 1992.

———. *The Light in Their Eyes: Creating Multicultural Learning Communities.* New York: Teachers College Press, 1999.

Nilipour, R., and H. Ashayeri. "Alternating Antagonism between Two Languages with Successive Recovery of a Third in a Trilingual Aphasic Patient." *Brain and Language* 36, no. 1 (1989):23–48.

Nilsen, A. P., and D. L. F. Nilsen. "Working Under Lucky Stars: Language Lessons for Multilingual Classrooms." *Voices from the Middle* 11, no. 4 (2004):27.

Nissani, H. *Early Childhood Programs for Language-Minority Children. FOCUS Occasional Papers in Bilingual Education.* Washington, D.C.: NCBE, 1990.

Nowak-Fabrykowski, K., and M. Shkandrij. "The Symbolic World of the Bilingual Child: Digressions on Language Acquisition, Culture and the Process of Thinking." *Journal of Instructional Psychology* 31, no. 4 (2004):284–292.

Nuñez, R. *Schools, Parents, and Empowerment: An Ethnographic Study of Mexican-Origin Parents Participation in Their Children's Schools.* Unpublished doctoral dissertation. Claremont, CA: San Diego State University/Claremont Graduate School, 1994.

Odlin, T. *Language Transfer.* Cambridge: Cambridge University Press, 1989.

Ogasawara, N. "Book Discussion Forum on LINGUIST List 15.1440. Review: *Psycholing/Acquisition*: Cenoz, et al. (2003)." (May 6, 2004). Retrieved from http://linguistlist.org/issues.

Ojima, S., H. Nakata, and R. Kakigi. "An ERP Study of Second Language Learning after Childhood: Effects of Proficiency." *Journal of Cognitive Neuroscience* 17, no. 8 (2005):1212.

O'Kearney, R., and M. Dadds. "Developmental and Gender Differences in the Language For Emotions Across the Adolescent Years." *Cognition & Emotion* 18, no. 7, (November 2004):913–938.

Oksaar, E. "On Being Trilingual." In C. Molony, ed., *Deutsch im Kontakt mit andern Sprachen*, 296–306. Kronberg: Scriptor Verlag, 1977.

Olivos, E. M., and C. E. Quintana de Valladolid. "Entre la Espada y la Pared: Critical Educators, Bilingual Education, and Education Reform." *Journals of Latinos and Education* 4, no. 4 (2005):283–293.

Olson, A. C., and A. Caramazza. "Orthographic Structure and Deaf Spelling Errors: Syllables, Letter Frequency, and Speech." *Quarterly Journal of Experimental Psychology* 57, no. 3 (3 April 2004):385–417.

Omaggio, A. *Teaching Language in Context: Proficiency Oriented Instruction.* Boston: Heinle and Heinle, 1986.

Onwuegbuzie, A., P. Bailey, and C. Daley. "Cognitive, Affective, Personality, and Demographic Predictors of Foreign-Language Achievement." *Journal of Educational Research* 94, (2000):3–15.

Organization for Economic Cooperation and Development (OECD). *PISA (Programme for International Student Assessment) 2003 Technical Report*. Paris: OECD, 2003.

Ormrod, J. E. *Learning Theory and the Educational Process*. Boston, MA: Pearson Custom Publishing, 2004.

Ornstein, R. *Psychology: The Study of Human Experience*, 2nd ed. San Diego, CA: Harcourt Brave Jovanovich, 1998.

Ortiz de Urbina, A. *In Praise of Multilingualism*. Paris: UNESCO Courier, 2000.

Otzenberger, H., D. Gounot, and C. Marrer. "Reliability of Individual Functional MRI Brain Mapping of Language." *Neuropsychology* 19, no. 4 (2005):484–493.

Papanicolaou, A. C., P. Pazo-Alvarez, E. M. Castillo, R. L. Billingsley-Marshall, J. I. Breier, P. R. Swank, S. Buchanan, M. McManis, T. Clear, and A. D. Passaro. "Functional Neuroimaging with MEG: Normative Language Profiles." *NeuroImage* 33, no. 1 (2006):326–342.

Paradis, M. "On the Representation of Two Languages in One Brain." *Language Sciences* 7, no. 1 (1985):1–39.

———. "The Bilingual Loch Ness Monster Raises Its Non-Asymmetrical Head Again—Or, Why Bother with Such Cumbersome Notions as Validity and Reliability? Comments on Evans et al. (2002)." *Brain and Languages* 87 (2003):441–448.

———. "Implicit Competence and Explicit Knowledge in Second Language Acquisition and Learning." Paper presented at the Center for the Brain Basis of Cognition, The Neurocognition of Second Language Workshop, Georgetown University, 2006. Retrieved from http://cbbc.georgetown.edu/workshops/2006L2.html on May 28, 2007.

———. "The Implications for Language Therapy of Increasing Multilingualism and Multiculturalism in Europe." Paper presented at the 6th European CPLOL Congress, Berlin, 2006.

Paradis, M., ed. *Readings on Aphasia in Bilinguals and Polyglots*. Cédex, France: Editions Didier, 1983.

Paradis, M., A. Ward, and S. Mathews, eds. *Reading, Writing, Thinking: Proceedings of the 13th European Conference on Reading*. Newark, DE: International Reading Association.

Paulesu, E., E. McCrory, F. Fazio, and L. Menoncello. "A Cultural Effect on Brain Function." *Nature Neuroscience* 3, no. 1 (2000):9.

Pavlenko, A., and S. Jarvis. "Conceptual Transfer: New Perspectives on the Study of Crosslinguistic Influence." In E. Nemth, ed., *Cognition in Language Use: Selected Papers from the 7th International Pragmatics*

Conference, Vol. 1, 288–301. Antwerp, NL: International Pragmatics Association, 2001.

Pearce, J. M. S. "A Note on Aphasia in Bilingual Patients: Pitres' and Ribot's Laws." *European Neurology* 54, no. 3 (2005):127–131.

Pearson, S., and G. Chambers. "A Successful Recipe? Aspects of the Initial Training of Secondary Teachers of Foreign Languages." *Support for Learning* 20, no. 3 (2005):115–122.

Penfield, W., and L. Roberts. *Speech and Brain Mechanisms*. Princeton, NJ: Princeton University Press, 1959.

Pennington, M. "Work Satisfaction and the ESL Profession." *Language, Culture, and Curriculum* 4, no. 1 (1992):59–86.

Perani, D. "The Bilingual Brain as Revealed by Functional Neuroimaging." *Language Learning Roundtable: The Cognitive Neuroscience of Second Language Acquisition*, September 18, 2003. Edinburgh: University of Edinburgh.

Perani, D., E. Paulesu, N. S. Galles, E. Dupoux, S. Dehaene, V. Bettinardi, S. F. Cappa, F. Fazio, and J. Mehler. "The Bilingual Brain. Proficiency and Age of Acquisition of the Second Language." *Brain: A Journal of Neurology* 121, no. 10 (1998):1841–1852.

Peregoy, S. F., and O. F. Boyle. *Reading, Writing and Learning in ESL: A Resource Book for K-12 Teachers*, 4th ed. Boston, MA: Pearson Education, 2005.

Perez, B., and M. E. Torres-Guzman. *Learning in Two Worlds: An Integrated Spanish/English Biliteracy Approach*. Boston: Allyn and Bacon, 2002.

Perlman Lorch, M., and I. Barriere. "The History of Written Language Disorders: Reexamining Pitres' Case (1884) of Pure Agraphia." *Brain and Language* 85, no. 2 (2003):271–279.

Perruchet, P. "Statistical Approaches to Language Acquisition and the Self-Organizing Consciousness: A Reversal of Perspective." *Psychological Research* 69, no. 5/6 (2005):316–329.

Perry, B. D., and R. Pollard. "Homeostasis, Stress, Trauma, and Adaptation. A Neurodevelopmental View of Childhood Trauma." *Child and Adolescent Psychiatric Clinics of North America* 7, no. 1 (1997):33–51.

Persinger, M. A., and G. Chellew-Belanger. "Bilingual Men But Not Women Display Less Left Ear But Not Right Ear Accuracy During Dichotic Listening Compared to Monolinguals." *International Journal of Neuroscience* 112, no. 1 (2002):55–64.

Peterson, T. "The Importance of Being Multilingual." *Business Week Online*, 2002.

Phelps, E. A. "Emotion and Cognition: Insights from Studies of the Human Amygdala." *Annual Review of Psychology* 57 (2006):27.

Philipson, R. "English Yes, But Equal Language Rights First." *The Guardian Weekly*. Brighton UK: IATEFL, 2004.

Phillips, E. M. "Anxiety and Oral Competence: Classroom Dilemma." *French Review* 65 (1991):1–14.

Piaget, J. *La construction du reel chez l'enfant*. Neuchtael: Delachaux et Niestle, 1937.

Pimsleur, P. *Pimsleur Language Aptitude Test*. New York: Harcourt Brace Jovanovich, 1966.

Pinker, S. *The Language Instinct*. New York: Morrow, 1994.

Plutchik, R. "A General Psychoevolutionary Theory of Emotion." In R. Plutchik and H. Kellerman, eds., *Emotion: Theory, Research and Experience*, 3–33. New York: Academic Press, 1980.

———. *The Psychology and Biology of Emotion*. New York: HarperCollins, 1994.

Poncini, G. "Multicultural Business Meetings and the Role of Languages Other Than English." *Journal of Intercultural Studies* 24, no. 1 (2003):17.

Portante, D. "Developing Multilingual Literacy in a Complex Setting: Suggested Principles for Building a Crossnational Research Agenda." *Reading Online* (2004).

Potier, B. "'Two Is Better Than One' Conference Looks at Benefits of Bilingualism." Cambridge, MA: *Harvard University Gazette*, May 6, 2004. Retrieved from http://www.hno.harvard.edu/gazette/2004/05.06/12-bilingual.html.

Poulisse, N., and T. Bongaerts. "First Language Use in Second Language Production." *Applied Linguistics* 15, no. 1 (1994):36–57.

Premack, D. "Is Language the Key to Human Intelligence?" *Science* 303, no. 5656 (2004):318–320.

Pretorius, E., H. Naudé, and U. Pretorius. "Training the Hippocampus and Amygdala of Preschool Children by Means of Priming Tasks: Should Parents Rather Focus On Learning of Facts Than Reading Fairytales?" *Early Child Development and Care* 175, no. 4 (2005): 303–312.

Proctor, C. "Teacher Expectations: A Model for School Improvement." *The Elementary School Journal* (March 1984):469–481.

Pugh, K., R. Sandak, S. Frost, D. Moore, and W. Mencl. "Examining Reading Development and Reading Disability in English Language Learners: Potential Contributions from Functional Neuroimaging." *Learning Disabilities Research and Practice* 20, no. 1 (2005):24–30.

Ramirez, J. D., Yuen, D. R. Ramey, and D. J. Pasta. *Final Report: Longitudinal Study of Structured English Immersion Strategy, Early-Exit and Late-Exit Transitional Bilingual Education Programs for Language Minority Children*. San Mateo, CA: Aguierre International, 1991.

Reyes, L. "Surviving the 'Perfect Storm': Bilingual Education Policymaking in New York City." *Journal of Latinos and Education* 2, no. 1 (2003):23.

Reyes, M. "Unleashing Possibilities: Biliteracy in the Primary Grades." In M. L. Ryes and J. Halcon, eds., *The Best for Our Children: Critical Perspectives on Literacy for Latino Students*, 96–121. New York: Teachers College Press, 2001.

Riccardelli, L. A. "Creativity and Bilingualism." *Journal of Creative Behaviour* 26, no. 4 (1992):242–254.

Richardson, M. P., B. A. Strange, and R. J. Dolan. "The Amygdala and Emotional Memory." *Nature Neuroscience* 7, no. 3 (2004):278.

Risager, K. "Language Teaching and the Process of European Integration." In M. Byram and M. Fleming, eds., *Learning in Intercultural Perspective. Approaches through Drama and Ethnography*, 242–254. Cambridge, UK: Cambridge University Press, 1998.

Rivers, W. "Self-Directed Language Learning and Third Language Learner." Paper presented at the 30th Annual Meeting of the American Council on the Teaching of Foreign Languages, Philadelphia, PA, 22–24, November 1996.

Rodriguez-Fornells, A., A. van der Lugt, M. Rotte, B. Britti, H. Heinze, and T. Münte. "Second Language Interferes with Word Production in Fluent Bilinguals: Brain Potential and Functional Imaging Evidence." *Journal of Cognitive Neuroscience* 17, no. 3 (2005):422–433.

Rodriguez-Fornells, A., M. Rotte, H. Heinze, T. Nösselt, and T. Münte. "Brain Potential and Functional MRI Evidence for How to Handle Two Languages with One Brain." *Nature* 415, no. 6875 (2002): 1026.

Rogan, M. T., K. S. Leon, D. L. Perez, and E. R. Kandel. "Distinct Neural Signatures for Safety and Danger in the Amygdala and Striatum of the Mouse." *Neuron* 46, no. 2 (2005):309–320.

Rogers, C. R., and H. J. Freiberg. *Freedom to Learn*. Columbus, OH: Merrill/Macmillan, 1994.

Rolstad, K. "Effects of Two-Way Immersion on the Ethnic Identification of Third Language Students: An Exploratory Study." *Bilingual Research Journal* 21, no. 1 (1997).

Romaine, S. *Bilingualism*, 2nd ed. Oxford: Blackwell, 1997.

Rosenzweig, M. R., S. M. Breedlove, and N. W. Watson. *Biological Psychology: An Introduction to Behavioral and Cognitive Neuroscience*, 4th ed. Sunderland, MA: Sinauer Associates, 2005.

Rossell, C. "Teaching English through English." *Educational Leadership* 62, no. 4 (2005):32–36.

Rueda, R., and C. B. Chen. "Assessing Motivational Factors in Foreign Language Learning: Cultural Variation in Key Constructs." *Educational Assessment* 10, no. 3 (2005):209–229.

Ruhlen, M. *A Guide to the World's Languages. Vol.1, Classification.* Stanford, CA: Stanford University Press, 1987.

———. Personal communication (ruhlen@stanfordalumni.org_) on April 7, 2007.

Ruskin, D. N., C. D. Liu, E. Kelly, N. G. Bazan, and G. J. LaHoste. "Sleep Deprivation Impairs Hippocampus-Mediated Contextual Learning But Not Amygdala-Mediated Cued Learning in Rats." *European Journal of Neuroscience* 19, no. 11 (2004):3121–3124.

Ruuskanen, D. D. K. "Bilingual and Multilingual Children: Can My New Baby Learn Two or More Languages at Home?" *Ask a Linguist.* Vaasa, Finland: University of Vaasa, 2007.

Sakai, K. L. "Language Acquisition and Brain Development." *Science* 310, no. 5749 (2005):815–819.

Santa Ana, O., ed. *Tongue-Tied: The Lives of Multilingual Children in Public Education.* Lanhan, MD: Rowman and Littlefield Publishers, 2004.

Sanz, C. "Bilingual Education Enhances Third Language Acquisition: Evidence from Catalonia." *Applied Psycholinguistics* 21, no. 1 (2000):23–44.

———. "Novice vs. Experienced Language Learners: Age, Cognitive Capacity and Type of Input." Presented at the Center for Brain Basis of Cognition, The Neurocognition of Second Language Workshop, Georgetown University, 2006. Retrieved on May 20, 2007 from http://cbbc.georgetown.edu/workshops/2006L2.html.

Sass, E. J. "Motivation in the College Classroom: What Students Tell Us." *Teaching Psychology* 16, no. (1989):86–88.

Saunder, W. B. "Hair Characteristics of the Newborn Infant Scalp." *Advanced Neonatal Care* 3, no. 6 (2003):286–296.

Saunders, G. *Bilingual Children: From Birth to Teens.* Clevedon, UK: Multilingual Matters, 1982.

Schechter, S., and R. Bayley. "Language Socialization Practices and Cultural Identity: Contrastive Relevance in Bilingual Maintenance Strategies of Mexican-Descent Families in California and Texas." Paper given at International Symposium on Bilingualism, University of Newcastle upon Tyne, 1997.

Schechter, S., and J. Cummins, eds. *Multilingual Education in Practice: Using Diversity as a Resource.* Portsmouth, NH: Heinemann, 2003.

Schmidt, P. "Three Types of Bilingual Education Equally Effective, E.D. Study Concludes." *Education Week* (February 20, 1991):1–23.

Schoenbaum, G., A. A. Chiba, and M. Gallagher. "Orbitofrontal Cortex and Basolateral Amygdala Encode Expected Outcomes during Learning." *Nature Neuroscience* 1, no. 2 (1998):155–160.

Schumann, J. H. *The Neurobiology of Affect in Language.* Malden, MA: Blackwell Publishers, 1997.

———. "Summing Up: Some Themes in the Cognitive Neuroscience of Second Language Acquisition." *Language Learning* 56, no. 1 (2006):313–319.

Sebastian-Gallés, N., A. Rodríguez-Fornells, R. de Diego-Balaguer, and B. Díaz. "First- and Second-Language Phonological Representations in the Mental Lexicon." *Journal of Cognitive Neuroscience* 18, no. 8 (2006):1277–1291.

Secada, W. G. "Research, Politics, and Bilingual Education." *The Annals of the American Academy of Political and Social Sciences* 508 (1990):81–106.

Selinker, L., and B. Baumgartner-Cohen. "Multiple Language Acquisition: 'Damn It, Why Can't I Keep These Two Languages Apart?'" In M. Bensoussan, I. Kreindler, and E. Aogain, eds., *Multilingualism and Language Learning: Language, Culture and Curriculum*, 115–123. Clevedon, UK: Multilingual Matters, 1995.

Selinker, L., and U. Lakshmanan. "Language Transfer and Fossilization: The 'Multiple Effects Principle'." In S. Gass and L Selinker, eds., *Language Transfer in Language Learning*, 197–216. Philadelphia, PA: John Benjamin's, 1993.

Senechal, M. "Testing the Home Literacy Model: Parent Involvement in Kindergarten Is Differentially Related to Grade 4 Reading Comprehension, Fluency, Spelling, and Reading for Pleasure." *Scientific Studies of Reading* 10 (2006):59–87.

Senechal, M., J. LeFevre, E. Thomas, and K. Daley. "Differential Effects of Home Literacy Experiences on the Development of Oral and Written Language." *Reading Research Quarterly* 32 (1998):96–116.

Sera, M. D., C. Elieff, and J. Forbes. "When Language Affects Cognition and When It Does Not: An Analysis of Grammatical Gender and Classification." *Journal of Experimental Psychology* 131, no. 3 (September 2002):377–397.

Sercu, L. "Implementing Intercultural Foreign Language Education: Belgian, Danish and British Teachers' Professional Self-Concepts and Teaching Practices Compared." *Evaluation and Research in Education* 16, no. 3 (2002):150.

———. "Intercultural Communicative Competence in Foreign Language Education Integrating Theory and Practice." In O. Sjohn, K., E. Harding Esch, and K. Schalkwijk, eds., *New Insights into Foreign Language Learning and Teaching*. Frankfurt, Germany: Peter Lang, 2002.

———. "Foreign Language Teachers and the Implementation of Intercultural Education: A Comparative Investigation of the Professional Self-Concepts and Teaching Practices of Belgian Teachers of English, French, and German." *European Journal of Teacher Education* 28, no. 1 (2005):87–105.

Sergiovanni, T. J. "Organizations or Communities? Changing the Metaphor Changes the Theory." *Educational Administration Quarterly* 30, no. 2 (1994):214–226.

Shapiro, K., and A. Caramazza. "The Representation of Grammatical Categories in the Brain." *Trends in Cognitive Sciences* 7 (2003):201–206.

Sharon, B. "Faulty Language Selection in Polyglots." *Language and Cognitive Processes* 6, no. 4 (1991):339–350.

Shaywitz, S., and B. Shaywitz as cited in Constance Holden. "Training the Brain to Read." *Science* 304, no. 5671 (2004):677.

Shi, R., and J. Werker. "The Basis of Preference for Lexical Words in 6-Month-Old Infants." *Developmental Science* 6, no. 5 (2003):484.

Shohamy, E. "Assessment in Multicultural Societies: Applying Democratic Principles and Practices to Language Testing." In B. Norton and K. Toohey, eds., *Critical Pedagogies and Language Learning*. Cambridge, UK: Cambridge University Press, 2004.

Sikogukira, M. "Influence of Languages Other than the L1 on a Foreign Language: The Case of Transfer from L2 to L3." *Edinburgh Working Papers in Applied Linguistics* 4 (1993):110–132.

Simon, G., C. Bernard, R. Lalonde, and M. Rebaï. "Orthographic Transparency and Grapheme–Phoneme Conversion: An ERP Study in Arabic and French Readers." *Brain Research* 1104, no. 1 (2006): 141–152.

Simonson, S. "What If and Why? Literacy Invitations For Multilingual Classrooms." *Illinois Reading Council Journal* 34, no. 3 (2006):56–57.

Simos, P. G., E. M. Castillo, J. M. Fletcher, D. J. Francis, F. Maestu, J. I. Breier W. W. Maggio, and A. C. Papanicolaou. "Mapping of Receptive Language Cortex in Bilingual Volunteers by Using Magnetic Source Imaging." *Journal of Neurosurgery* 95, no. 1 (2001):76–81.

Simos, P. G., R. Billingsley-Marshall, S. Sarkari, E. Pataraia, and A. Papanicolaou, Andrew C. "Brain Mechanisms Supporting Distinct Languages." *Learning Disabilities Research and Practice* 20, no. 1 (2005):31–38.

Simos, P. G., J. M. Fletcher, B. R. Foorman, D. J. Francis, E. M. Castillo, R. N. Davis, M. Fitzgerald, P. G. Mathes, C. Denton, and A. C. Papanicolaou. "Brain Activation Profiles during the Early Stages of Reading Acquisition." *Journal of Child Neurology* 17, no. 3 (2002):159–163.

Skehan, P. "Theorizing and Updating Aptitude." In P. Robinson, ed., *Individual Differences and Instructed Language Learning*, 69–93. Amsterdam: John Benjamin, 2002.

———. *Individual Differences in Second Language Learning*. London: Arnold, 1989.

Skutnabb-Kangas, T. *Bilingual or Not: The Education of Minorities*, translated by Lars Malmberg and David Crane. Clevedon, UK: Multilingual Matters, 1984.

———. *Teaching Migrant Children's Mother Tongue and Learning the Language of the Host Country in the Context of the Socio-cultural Situations of the Migrant Family*. Tampere, Finland: Tutkimuksia Research Reports, 1976.

Slobin, D. I., ed. *The Crosslinguistic Study of Language Acquisition*, vol. 3. Vol. 1: *The Data* and vol. 2: *Theoretical Issues*. Mahwah, NJ: Lawrence Erlbaum Associates, 1992.

Snow, C. E., W. S. Barnes, J. Chandler, I. F. Goodman, and L. Hemphill. *Unfulfilled Expectations: Home and School Influences on Literacy*. Cambridge, MA: Harvard University Press, 1991.

Snow, C. E., and M. Hoefnagel-Hohle. "The Critical Period for Language Acquisition." *Child Development* 4 (1978):111–128.

Snow, M. A., and A. M. Padilla. "Patterns of Second Language Retention of Graduates of a Spanish Immersion Program." *Applied Linguistics* 9, no. 2 (1988):183–197.

Snow, R. E. "Aptitude-Treatment Interactions as a Framework for Research on Individual Differences in Learning." In P. Ackerman, R. Sternberg, and R. Glaser, eds., *Learning and Individual Differences: Advances in Theory and Research*, 13–59. New York: W. H. Freeman, 1989.

Soifer, D. "NCLB, Accountability, and Bilingual Education." *Education Week* 24, no. 31 (2005):50.

Soto, L. *Language, Culture and Power. Bilingual Families and the Struggle for Quality Education*. Albany: State University of New York Press, 1997.

Sousa, D. *Como Aprende el Cerebro*, 2nd ed. Thousand Oaks, CA: Corwin, 2002.

———. *How the Brain Learns*. Thousand Oaks, CA: Corwin Press, 2000.

Sparks, R. "Is There a 'Disability' for Learning a Foreign Language?" *Journal of Learning Disabilities* 39, no. 6 (November/December 2006): 544–557.

Sparks, R., J. Javorsky, J. Patton, and L. Ganschow. "Principal Components Analysis of a Test Battery to Predict Proficiency in a Foreign Language." *Applied Language Learning* 9 (1998):71–106.

Sparks, R., J. Patton, L. Ganschow, N. Humach, and J. Jovorsky. "Native Language Predictors of Foreign Language Proficiency and Foreign Language Aptitude." *Annals of Dyslexia* 56, no. 1 (2006).

Spolsky, B. "Prognostication and Language Aptitude Testing." *Language Testing* 12 (1995):321–340.

Squire, L. R., and E. R. Kandel. *Memory: From Mind to Molecules.* New York: W. H. Freeman, 2000.

Squire, L. R., and B. J. Knowlton. "The Medial Temporal Lobe, the Hippocampus, and the Memory Systems of the Brain." In M. S. Gazzaniga, ed., *The New Cognitive Neurosciences*, 765–780. Cambridge, MA: MIT Press, 2000.

Stein, D. J., M. Solms, and J. van Honk. "The Cognitive-Affective Neuroscience of the Unconscious." *CNS Spectrum* 11, no. 8 (2006): 580–583.

Sternberg, R. J. *Cognitive Psychology*, 4th ed. Belmont, CA: Thomson Wadsworth, 2006.

Stevens, G. "Commentary: Using Census Data to Test the Critical-Period Hypothesis for Second-Language Acquisition." *Psychological Science* 15, no. 3 (2004):215–216.

Stewart, J. H. "Foreign Language Study in Elementary Schools: Benefits and Implications for Achievement in Reading and Math." *Early Childhood Education Journal* 33, no. 1 (2005):11–16.

Stolpa, J. M. "Math and Writing Anxieties." *Phi Kappa Phi Forum* 84, no. 3 (2004):3–5.

Strid, K., T. Tjus, L. Smith, A. N. Meltzoff, and M. Heimann. "Infant Recall Memory and Communication Predicts Later Cognitive Development." *Infant Behavior and Development* 29, no. 4 (2006):545–553.

Suleiman, Y. "A War of Words: Language and Conflict in the Middle East." *Perspectives: Central European Review of International Affairs* 25, (2004):87–90.

Swain, M., and S. Lapkin. "Heritage Language Children in an English-French Bilingual Program." *Canadian Modern Language Review* 47, no. 4 (1991):635–641.

Swain, Merrill. "The Role of Mother Tongue Literacy in Third Language Learning." *Language, Culture and Curriculum* 3, no. 1 (1990):65–81.

Sylwester, R. *A Celebration of Neurons: An Educator's Guide to the Human Brain.* Alexandria, VA: Association for Supervision and Curriculum Development, 1995.

Taboors, P. O. *One Child, Two Languages: A Guide for Preschool Educators of Children Learning English as a Second Language.* Baltimore, MD: Paul H. Brookes Publishing Co., 1997.

Tainturier, M. J., S. Schiemenz, and E. Leek. "Separate Orthographic Representations for Reading and Spelling? Evidence from a Case of Preserved Lexical Reading and Impaired Lexical Spelling." *Brain and Language* 99, no. 1–2 (2006):31–32.

Tamietto, M., M. Adenzato, G. Geminiani, and B. de Gelder. "Fast Recognition of Social Emotions Takes the Whole Brain: Interhemispheric Cooperation in the Absence of Cerebral Asymmetry." *Neuropsychologia* 45, no. 4 (2007):836–843.

Taylor, A., E. Lazarus, and R. Cole. "Putting Languages on the (Drop Down) Menu: Innovative Writing Frames in Modern Foreign Language Teaching." *Educational Review* 57, no. 4 (2005):435–455.

Taylor, S. G. "Multilingual Societies and Planned Linguistic Change: New Language-in-Education Programs in Estonia and South Africa." *Comparative Education Review* 46, no. 3 (2002):313.

Thilmany, J. "Beating Math Anxiety." *Mechanical Engineering* 126, no. 12 (2004):18.

Thomas, W. P., and V. P. Collier. "Two Languages Are Better Than One." *Educational Leadership* 55, no. 4 (1997/1998):23–26.

———. *School Effectiveness for Language Minority Students.* Alexandria, VA: National Clearinghouse for Bilingual Education, 1998.

———. "Accredited Accelerated Schooling for English Language Learners." *Educational Leadership* 56, no. 7 (1999):46–49.

———. *A National Study of School Effectiveness for Language Minority Students' Long-Term Academic Achievement.* Santa Cruz, CA: Center for Research in Education, Diversity, and Excellence, University of California-Santa Cruz, 2002. Retrieved April 15, 2007 from www.crede.ucsc.edu/research/llaa/a.a_final.html.

———. "The Multiple Benefits of Dual Language." *Educational Leadership* (October 2003):63.

Thomason, S. G. *Language Contact.* Edinburgh: Edinburgh University Press, 2001.

Thompson, P. M., T. D. Cannon, K. L. Narr, T. van Erp, V. Poutanen, M. Huttunen, J. Lönnqvist, C. Standertskjöld-Nordenstam, J. Kaprio, M. Khaledy, R. Dail, C. I. Zoumalan, and A. W. Toga. "Genetic Influences on Brain Structure." *Nature Neuroscience* 4, no. 12 (2001):1253.

Tokuhama-Espinosa, T. *Raising Multilingual Children: Foreign Language Acquisition and Children.* Westport, CT: Greenwood Publishing, 2000.

———. *The Multilingual Mind: Questions By, For and About People Living With Many Languages.* Westport, CT: Praeger Press, 2003.

————. "Myths about Multilingualism." In T. Tokuhama-Espinosa, ed., *The Multilingual Mind: Issues Discussed By, For and About People Living with Many Languages.* Westport, CT: Praeger Publishers, 2003.

Tomlinson, C. A. *The Differentiated Classroom: Responding to the Needs of All Learners.* Alexandria, VA: Association for Supervision and Curriculum Development, 1999.

————. "Deciding to Teach Them All." *Educational Leadership.* (October 2003):6–11.

Tompkins, G. E. "Struggling Readers Are Struggling Writers, Too." *Reading & Writing Quarterly* 18, no. 2 (2002):175–193.

Toohey, K. "Learning English at School: Identity, Social Relations and Classroom Practice." Clevedon, UK: Multilingual Matters, 2000.

Toohey, K., and B. Waterstone. "Negotiating Expertise in an Action Research Community." In B. Norton and K. Toohey, eds., *Critical Pedagogies and Language Learning.* Cambridge, UK: Cambridge University Press, 2004.

Toppo, G. "Is Bilingual Education Report Being Downplayed?" *USA Today. Reading Today Daily.* U.S. Department of Education declines to publish report on literacy education of bilingual children. *Reading Today,* (August 29, 2005). Retrieved from www.reading.org.

Towell, R., and R. Hawkins. "Empirical Evidence and Theories of Representation in Current Research into Second Language Acquisition: Introduction." *Transactions of the Philological Society* 102, no. 2 (2004):131–137.

Tremblay, P. F., and R. C. Garner. "Expanding the Motivation Construct in Language Learning." *The Modern Language Journal* 79 (1995): 505–520.

Tsui, J. M., and M. M. M. Mazzocco. "Effects of Math Anxiety and Perfectionism on Timed Versus Untimed Math Testing in Mathematically Gifted Sixth Graders." *Roeper Review* 29, no. 2 (2007):132–139.

Ullman, E. "Making Foreign Language a Priority." *Curriculum Update,* 2006. Retrieved on April 10, 2007 from www.actif.org.

Ullman, M. T. "A Neurocognitive Perspective on Language: The Declarative/Procedural Model." *Nature Reviews Neuroscience* 2 (2001):717–726.

————. "A Neurocognitive Perspective on Language: The Declarative/ Procedural Model." *Nature Reviews Neuroscience* 2 (2001):717–726.

————. "A Neurocognitive Perspective on Second Language Acquisition and Processing: The Declarative/Procedural Model." Language Learning Roundtable: The Cognitive Neuroscience of Second Language Acquisition, University of Edinburgh (September 18, 2003).

————. "Contributions of Memory Circuits to Language: The Declarative/ Procedural Model." *Cognition* 92 (2004):231–270.

————. "A Cognitive Neuroscience Perspective on Second Language Acquisition: The Declarative/Procedural Model." In C. Sanz, ed., *Mind and Context in Adult Second Language Acquisition: Methods, Theory and Practice*, 141–178. Washington, DC: Georgetown University Press, 2005.

UNESCO. "Multilingualism." *Education Today Newsletter* (July–September 2003).

————. "The Mother-Tongue Dilemma." *Education Today Newsletter* (July–September 2003).

United States Census Bureau Statistics. *National Census.* Washington, DC: U.S. Census Bureau, 2000. Retrieved from www.census.gov on February 14, 2007.

United States Department of Education. *Key Indicators of Hispanic Student Achievement: National Goals and Benchmarks for the Next Decade.* Washington, DC: U.S. Department of Education, June 2003. Retrieved from www.ed.gov/pub/hispanicindicators on March 12, 2007.

University of Minnesota. "Content Based Learning Second Language Instruction. What Is It?" Retrieved from http://www.carla.umn.edu/cobaltt/cbi.html on April 14, 2007.

Usher, J. A., and U. Neisser. "Childhood Amnesia and the Beginnings of Memory for Four Early Life Events." *Journal of Experimental Psychology* 122 (1993):155–165.

Valadez, C., M., J. MacSwan, and C. Martínez. "Toward a New View of Low Achieving Bilinguals: Syntactic Competence in Designated 'Semilinguals.'" Paper presented at the Annual Meeting of the American Educational Research Association (AERA), 1997. Retrieved from http://www.public.asu.edu/~macswan/aera97.pdf on May 2, 2007.

Valencia Garate, J., and J. I. Cenoz. "Bilingualism and Third Language Acquisition." ERIC Database (ED364118), 1993. Retrieved from http://www.eric.ed.gov:80/ERICWebPortal/Home.portal; jsessionid=GtyLpTXz5Dz4GsQlRyVnhnpw7yGNNJ6v84FRQHTK S2PGJly6VvvX!-919636416?_nfpb=true&ERICExtSearch_ SearchValue_0=ED364118&ERICExtSearch_SearchType_0=kw&_ pageLabel=ERICSearchResult&newSearch=true&rnd=1189996747 715&searchtype=keyword on September 14, 2007.

Vales, G. *Con Respeto: Bridging the Distance between Culturally Diverse Families and Schools: An Ethnographic Portrait.* New York: Teachers College Press, 1996.

Van Sluys, K. *What If and Why? Literary Invitations for Multilingual Classrooms.* Portsmouth, NH: Heinemann, 2005.

Viadero, D. "Learning Gap Linked to LEP Instruction." *Education Week* 20, no. 32 (2004):8.

Vianna, M. R., A. S. Coitinho, and I. Izquierdo. "Role of the Hippocampus and Amygdala in the Extinction of Fear: Motivated Learning." *Current Neurovascular Research* 1, no. 1 (2004):55–60.

Vigliocco, G., D. P. Vinson, F. Paganelli, and K. Dworzynski. "Grammatical Gender Effects on Cognition: Implications for Language Learning and Language Use." *Journal of Experimental Psychology/General* 134, no. 4 (November 4, 2005):501–520.

Vikingstad, E. M., Y. Cao, A. J. Thomas, A. F. Johnson, G. M. Malik, and K. M. Welch. "Language Hemispheric Dominance in Patients with Congenital Lesions of Eloquent Brain." *Neurosurgery* 47, no. 3 (2000):562–570.

Violand-Sanchez, E., C. Sutton, and H. Ware. *Fostering Home-School Cooperation: Involving Minority Families as Partners in Education.* Washington, DC: The National Clearinghouse for Bilingual Education. Program Information Series, Summer 1990.

von Tetzchner, S., K. Øvreeide, K. Jørgensen, B. Ormhaug, B. Oxholm, and R. Warme. "Acquisition of Graphic Communication by a Young Girl without Comprehension of Spoken Language." *Disability and Rehabilitation* 26, no. 21/22 (2004):1335–1346.

Vyas, A., S. Jadhav, and S. Chattarji. "Prolonged Behavioral Stress Enhances Synaptic Connectivity in the Basolateral Amygdala." *Neuroscience* 143, no. 2 (2006):387–393.

Walqui, A. *Access and Engagement: Program Design and Instructional Approaches for Immigrant Students in Secondary School.* Washington, DC: Center for Applied Linguistics, 2000.

Walsh, J. "Minority Voices Show Strong Instinct for Survival." *The Guardian Weekly.* Brighton, UK: IATEFL, 2004.

Wang, M., Y. Park, and K. R. Lee. "Korean-English Biliteracy Acquisition: Cross-Language Phonological and Orthographic Transfer." *Journal of Educational Psychology* 98, no. 1 (2006):148–158.

Watkins, K. E., F. Vargha-Khadem, J. Ashburner, R. E. Passingham, A. Connelly, K. J. Friston, R. S. Frackowiak, M. Mishkin, and D. G. Gadian. "MRI Analysis of an Inherited Speech and Language Disorder: Structural Brain Abnormalities." *Brain: A Journal of Neurology* 125, no. 3 (2002):465–478.

Wayne, B. "Conversations with Neil's Brain: The Neural Nature of Thought and Language." *American Journal of Electroneurodiagnostic Technology* 46, no. 1 (2006):71–72.

Weber, B., C. Hoppe, J. Faber, N. Axmacher, K. Fließbach, F. Mormann, S. Weis, J. Ruhlmann, C. E. Elger, and G. Fernández. "Association

Between Scalp Hair-Whorl Direction and Hemispheric Language Dominance." *Neuroimage*, Retrieved from http://www.science direct.com/science?_ob=ArticleURL&_udi=B6WNP4HHWW701& _user=10&_coverDate=04%2F01%2F2006&_rdoc=1&_fmt=&_ orig=search&_sort=d&view=c&_acct=C000050221&_ version=1&_urlVersion=0&_userid=10&md5=ce0ea2162d186975 ec74460c9aac43ec) on November 10, 2005.

Wei, L., N. Miller, and B. Dodd. "Distinguishing Communicative Difference from Language Disorder in Bilingual Children." *The Bilingual Family Newsletter* 14, no. 1 (1997):3–4.

Wei, L. "Dimensions of Bilingualism." In L. Wei, ed., *The Bilingualism Reader*. 3–25. London: Routledge, 2000.

Weissberg, R. *Connecting Speaking and Writing in Second Language Writing Instruction: The Michigan Series on Teaching Multilingual Writers*. Ann Arbor: University of Michigan, 2006.

Werker, J., and R. C. Tees. "Cross-Language Speech Perception: Evidence for Perceptual Reorganization during the First Year of Life." *Infant Behavior and Development* 7 (1984):49–63.

Werker, J., and R. Desjardins. "Listening to Speech in the 1st Year of Life: Experiential Influences on Phoneme Perception." *Current Directions in Psychological Science* 4, no. 3 (1995):76–81.

Wesche, M. B. "Discipline-Based Approaches to Language Study: Research Issues and Outcomes." In M. Krueger and F. Ryan, eds., *Language and Content: Discipline- and Content-Based Approaches to Language Study*, M. Krueger and F. Ryan, eds. Lexington, MA: D. C. Heath, 1993.

Whatley, A., and J. Canalis. "Creating Learning Communities through Literacy." *Language Arts*, 79 (2002):478–487.

Whitaker, H. A., D. Bub, and S. Leventer. "Neurolinguistic Aspects of Language Acquisition and Bilingualism." In H. Winitz, ed., *Native Language and Foreign Language Acquisition*. New York: The New York Academy of Sciences, 1981.

White House Proposes Foreign Language Initiative. "*Diverse: Issues in Higher Education*." (February 9, 2006.)

White Soltero, S. *Dual Language Teaching and Learning in Two Languages*. Boston: Pearson Educational, 2004.

Whitmore, K., and C. Crowell. "Bilingual Education Students Reflect on Their Language Education: Reinventing a Classroom 10 Years Later." *Journal of Adolescent and Adult Literacy* 49, no. 4 (December 2005/January 2006):270–285.

———. *Inventing a Classroom: Life in a Bilingual, Whole Language Learning Community*. York, ME: Sternhouse, 1994.

Widdicombe, S. "Code-Switching, Coining and Interference in Trilingual First Language Acquisition: A Case Study." Unpublished M.Sc. dissertation, 1997.

Wiggins, G., and J. McTighe. *Understanding by Design*. Alexandria, VA: Association for Supervision and Curriculum Development, 1998.

Wiley, E., E. Bialystok, and K. Hakuta. "New Approaches to Using Census Data to Test the Critical-Period Hypothesis for Second-Language Acquisition." *Psychological Science* 16, no. 4 (2005):341–343.

Willems G. M., F. Courtney, E. Aranda, M. Cain, and J. Ritchie, eds. *Towards Intercultural Language Teacher Education*. Nijmegen: HAN Press, 1998.

Williams, A., and E. Gregory. "Siblings Bridging Illiteracies in Multilingual Contexts." *Journal of Research in Reading* 24, no. 3 (2001):248.

Williams, L. "Phonetic Variation as a Function of Second-Language Learning." In G. H. Yeni-Komshian, J. F. Kavanaugh, and C. A. Ferguson, eds., *Child Phonology, Vol.2, Perception*, 185–215. New York: Academic Press, 1980.

Williams, S., and B. Hammarberg. "Language Switches in L3 Production: Implications for a Polyglot Speaking Model." *Applied Linguistics* 19 (1998):295–333.

Winkler, I., T. Kujala, H. Titinen, P. Sivonen, P. Alku, A. Lehtokoski, I. Czigler, V. Csepe, R. J. Lmoniemi, and R. Naathanen. "Brain Responses Reveal the Learning of Foreign Language Phonemes." *Psychophysiology* 36, no. 5 (1999):638–642.

Winter, M. "Brain Science and Language Acquisition." *Human Ecology* 31, no. 1 (2003):8.

Wolfe, P. *Brain Matters: Translating Research into Classroom Practice*. Alexandria, VA: Association for Supervision and Curriculum Development, 2001.

Wolff, E. "Language and Society." In Bernd Heine and Derek Nurse, eds., *African Languages: An Introduction*, 298–347. Cambridge, UK: Cambridge University Press, 2000.

Wong Fillmore, L. "When Learning a Second Language Means Losing the First." *Early Childhood Research Quarterly* 6, no. 3 (1991):323–334.

Wong, S., and S. Teuben-Rowe. "Critical Perspectives on the Language of Family Literacy Research: Use of Native Language with Involved Parents from Diverse Linguistic Backgrounds." *The Journal of Educational Issues of Language Minority Students* 16 (1996):235–261.

Wright, E. "The Language Encounter in the Americas, 1492–1800." *Ethnohistory* 52, no. 1, (2005):237–239.

Wuillemin, D., B. Richardson, and J. Lynch. "Right Hemisphere Involvement in Processing Later-Learned Languages in Multilinguals." *Brain and Language* 46, no. 4 (1994):620–636.

Xue, G., C. Chen, Z. Jin, and Q. Dong. "Cerebral Asymmetry in the Fusiform Areas Predicted the Efficiency of Learning a New Writing System." *Journal of Cognitive Neuroscience* 18, no. 6 (2006):923–931.

Yaden, D. B., and J. M. Tardibuono. "The Emergent Writing Development of Urban Latino Preschoolers: Developmental Perspectives and Instructional Environments for Second-Language Learners." *Reading and Writing Quarterly* 20, no. 1 (2004):29–61.

Yeung, A. S. and E. K. P. Wong. "Domain Specificity of Trilingual Teachers' Verbal Self Concepts." *Journal of Educational Psychology* 96, no. 2 (2004):360–368.

Ytsma, J. "Towards a Typology of Trilingual Primary Education." *International Journal of Bilingual Education and Bilingualism* 4, no. 1 (2001):11–22.

Zehr, M. A. "Study Gives Advantage To Bilingual Education Over Focus on English." *Education Week* 23, no. 21 (2004):10.

———. "Foreign Languages." *Education Week* 25, no. 24 (2006):16.

Zemelman, S., H. Daniels, and A. Hyde. *Best Practice: New Standards for Teaching and Learning in America's Schools.* Portsmouth, NH: Heinemann, 1998.

Zohar, E. "Language Experience and Right Hemisphere Tasks: The Effects of Scanning Habits and Multilingualism." *Brain and Language* 58, no. 1 (1997):157–173.

Index

About the Author

TRACEY TOKUHAMA-ESPINOSA is a teacher, counselor, researcher, project manager, and author. Since 1997 she has conducted workshops for parents, teachers, and educational professionals on language, brain development, learning styles, critical thinking, and teaching methodologies in Argentina, Australia, Belgium, Colombia, Ecuador, France, Germany, Holland, Italy, Norway, Peru, Switzerland, Thailand, and the United Kingdom.

Tokuhama-Espinosa has been acknowledged for her research of various topics, including brain-based teaching methods, motivation and learning, classroom management, the role of emotions in learning, backward curriculum design, the syllabus and planning, learning environments, early childhood education, and creativity.

Tokuhama-Espinosa earned her Master of Education degree from Harvard University in international development, her Bachelor of Arts degree in international relations, and her Bachelor of Science degree in mass communication from Boston University. She is completing her Ph.D. dissertation, "The Scientifically Substantiated Art of Teaching: A Study of the Development of Standards in Neuro-Education," which will be published as a guide for teachers. She is married and raising three multilingual children in English, Spanish, German, and French.